Disaster Recovery Handbook

Disaster Recovery Handbook

Chantico Publishing Company, Inc.

TAB Professional and Reference Books

Division of TAB BOOKS
Blue Ridge Summit, PA

PanValet is a product of Pansophic Systems
Librarian is a product of Ecosoft, Inc.

FIRST EDITION
FIRST PRINTING

© 1991 by **TAB Professional and Reference Books,** an imprint of TAB BOOKS.
TAB BOOKS is a division of McGraw-Hill, Inc.
The TAB Professional and Reference Books logo, consisting of the letters "TPR"
within a large "T," is a registered trademark of TAB BOOKS.

Library of Congress Cataloging-in-Publication Data

Disaster recovery handbook / by Chantico Publishing Company, Inc.
p.   cm.
Includes index.
ISBN 0-8306-7663-5
1. Electronic data processing departments—Security measures-
-Planning—Handbooks, manuals, etc.   2. Disasters—Planning-
-Handbooks, manuals, etc.   3. Risk management—Handbooks, manuals,
etc.   I. Chantico Publishing Co.
HF5548.37.D57   1990
658.4'78—dc20   90-43147
                        CIP

TAB BOOKS offers software for sale. For information and a catalog, please contact TAB
Software Department, Blue Ridge Summit, PA 17294-0850.

Questions regarding the content of this book should be addressed to:

Reader Inquiry Branch
TAB BOOKS
Blue Ridge Summit, PA 17294-0850

Acquisitions Editor: Gerald T. Papke
Book Editor: Eileen P. Baylus
Production: Katherine G. Brown

ABQ4171

Contents

Acknowledgments

Profit Oriented Systems Planning Program

3230 Commander Drive
Carrollton, Texas 75006
1-214-250-3644

Partial List of POSPP Participants

3 M Company
Allstate Insurance Company
American Airlines/Sabre
American Medical Laboratories
AMOCO Corporation
ARCO Oil & Gas Company
ARCO Products
AT&T
AT&T Network Design & Operations Center
Bank of Nova Scotia
Bankers Trust Company
Bantam Doubleday Dell Publishing Group Inc.
Bell Canada
Blue Cross/Blue Shield Association
Blue Cross/Blue Shield of Kentucky
Blue Cross/Blue Shield of Maryland
Blue Cross/Blue Shield of Michigan

Blue Cross/Blue Shield of Minnesota
Blue Cross/Blue Shield of Nebraska
Blue Cross/Blue Shield of New Jersey
Blue Cross/Blue Shield of North Dakota
Blue Cross/Blue Shield of Tennessee
British Columbia Systems
Brooklyn Union Gas
Canadian Imperial Bank of Commerce
Canadian National Railways
Canadian Pacific Forest Products
Canadian Tire Corporation Ltd.
Capital Holding Corp.
Cargill, Inc.
Carter Hawley Stores, Inc.
Chase Manhattan Bank
Chemical Bank
Chemical Network Processing Services
Church of Jesus Christ of Latter-Day Saints
Cominco Ltd.
CONTEL Federal Systems
Cravath, Swaine & Moore
CSX Technology
Digital Equipment Corp.
Dow Chemical USA
Dow Corning Corp.
Equitable
Federal Express Corp.
GATX Corporation
General Signal Corp.
George Weston, Ltd.
Hartford Insurance
HealthNet Corporation
Hewitt Associates
Hughes Aircraft
Hydro-Quebec
ITT Corporation
Integrated Resources
International Finance Corp.
International Paper Co.
Kraft General Foods, Inc.
LTV Aerospace & Defense Co.
Loews Corp.
Manufacturers Hanover Trust
Maxus Energy Corp.

Merrill Lynch & Company
Metpath, Inc.
Metropolitan Life Insurance Co.
Monsanto Company
Mutual Benefit Life Insurance Co.
National Railroad Passengers Corp. (Amtrak)
NYNEX Corporation
Northwest Airlines
Owens Corning Fiberglas
PACS
Pfizer Pharmaceuticals
Philips International B.V.
Phillips Petroleum Company
Public Service Electric & Gas Co.
Royal Bank of Canada
SGI
Salomon Brothers
SaskTel Corporation
Shell Canada Limited
SONY Corporation of America
Temple-Inland Inc.
Texas Instruments Incorporated
TransCanada Pipelines Ltd.
US West Inc.
Union Carbide Corp.
Union Texas Petroleum
Warner Communications
Waste Management, Inc.

For more information, call POSPP at 214-250-3644 or 800-843-4523.

Overview

OVER THE PAST FEW YEARS, NATURAL AND MAN-MADE DISASTERS, which include events such as Hurricane Hugo, the San Francisco Earthquake, and the Hinsdale, Illinois, Bell central office fire, have clearly illustrated the growing dependence of business operations on the information and transaction processing services provided by computer and communications technologies. A vital lesson learned in the aftermath of these disasters was that those companies that have comprehensive, tested business resumption/disaster recovery plans are able to resume business operations faster and more effectively than those that do not have them.

The new buzz words of a modern day era are *disaster recovery plan, contingency plan, business resumption plan, service contingency plan,* and *corporate contingency planning.* People use them with the same connotation. Should they mean the same? Basically, yes. Do they? No. Such plans range from a data center relocation plan to a comprehensive plan for continuing business in the event of damage to a major corporate location. Let's simply call them *business recovery plans.*

Ask yourself, Is the company prepared for disaster? If a disaster does strike, can you implement preplanned, pretested emergency response and recovery procedures to minimize damage and loss?

Companies can overcome the effect of a disaster and continue business functions through business recovery planning. Developing the plan is a proactive function to safeguard company assets and to meet legal or regulatory requirements. Activation of the plan is the reaction to a disaster situation. The plan is directed to the organization's needs as represented by its various critical business processes.

Information services business recovery planning should be a subset of the overall business planning.

1

Planning for informational services continuity

A *DISASTER* CAN BE DEFINED AS ANY ACCIDENTAL OR INTENTIONAL event that causes significant disruption to a company's operation. Each company will be faced with its unique set of threats and corresponding vulnerabilities. These threats and vulnerabilities will depend on the nature of the company's products or services and its geographic location. In the initial *risk analysis*, all possible types of disasters should be reviewed to determine their probability of occurrence as well as their potential for inflicting loss.

Purposes of business recovery planning

The overall purpose of planning is to:

- Resume vital operations within a specified time after the incident occurs.
- Return to normal operations as soon as practical and possible.
- Train personnel and familiarize them with emergency operations.

The plan should consider various types of disasters and varied durations of service interruption. It should detail the actions to be taken based on the level of damage, rather than an individual type of loss. Exceptions to this rule will be regional disasters, such as earthquakes, in which case the plan should detail specific actions.

The methodology used in developing the plan should meet the following goals:

- Provide management with a clear understanding of the risk to business continuance.
- Provide management with a clear understanding of legal and fiduciary responsibilities of corporate officers.
- Provide management with a clear understanding of the scope of the activity.
- Facilitate the development of major portions of the plan by defining the interrelationships and requirements of those activities.
- Provide a structure for developing the plan in four major phases:
  ~ Risk analysis assessment
  ~ Alternatives analysis
  ~ Plan development
  ~ Testing, maintenance, and updating

The methodology involves three major criteria:

- *Planning* Basic decisions must be made by top management. These decisions will lead to the procedures for prevention of and recovery from a disaster.
- *Preparation* Details must be provided of the functions that must be carried out both prior to and following a disaster to minimize the loss and improve the chances of quick recovery.
- *Maintenance and Testing* The disaster recovery plan is a dynamic document that must reflect the continuing changes in the business and in the data processing environment. The following section addresses the maintenance requirements, as well as the need for testing and planning to ensure its continued viability.

The need for a business recovery plan

The automation of daily business activities and the storage of vital records on microfiche, tape, and other magnetic media both have brought about an element of computer dependence. As a result, information processing has become a nerve center of the business enterprise. As dependence on information processing increases, so does the financial risk associated with a loss of processing capability. In some industries such as financial or other services, loss of computing power would bring an organization to a complete halt.

Recognition of computer physical vulnerability has led to the development of business recovery planning procedures for that area. Unfortunately, this solution might offer only partial protection. If the Information Services (I/S) department has a business recovery plan, but the end user does not, damage affecting both the I/S department and other parts of the building could result in the end user being nonoperational while the computer department is operational because they had a plan.

Many of the business recovery planning procedures that were developed for computer departments can be used for the end user and corporate business recovery planning. The comprehensive plan will minimize the effect of a disaster and permit a timely response, a transition of crucial functions and applications to other facilities or to a different mode of operation, and an eventual effective recovery.

Preparation of an overall business recovery plan gives managers an excellent opportunity to alleviate or minimize potential problems that would disrupt company operations or data processing services. The future well-being of company operations will be enhanced if crucial business functions are identified and documented, if a systematic method of emergency response is developed, and if backup operating procedures and recovery planning are accomplished.

Another level of business recovery planning

Companies developing I/S-based applications that are crucial or strategic to the enterprise should incorporate business recovery planning considerations during the design phase. The risk assessment, which normally deals with bringing the application in on time and on budget, should be broadened to include the risks involved in disruptions once it is in place. Consider the potential financial, competitive, and managerial impacts:

- Identify the business objectives.
- Determine the recovery process.
- Assess the risks from an outage. Include potential losses of assets, revenue, market share, opportunity, cash, inventory, programs, and data; disruption of normal daily business operations; and statute and contract violations, litigation fines, and penalties.
- Decide on the acceptability of the risks.
- Provide for business resumption. An important point to remember is that over time, reverting to the old way of doing business will become increasingly difficult as the skills to do so are lost.

In a study, Contingency Planning Research, Inc. cited the exposure by industry, from highest risk to lowest risk, as: financial, manufacturing, service, government, education, utility, transportation, insurance, distribution, and medical. But each has its own set of exposures. Financial institutions must maintain customer confidence, ensuring that customer accounts are safe, as well as providing accurate and timely processing. Medical facilities need to preserve a level of patient care, as well as be concerned with receivables and payables. And most businesses are now dependent on computers and communications for doing order entry, inventory, purchasing, and accounting.

Often the impact on management does not include executive support systems, executive information systems, and decision support systems. Assess how long they can be out without seriously affecting the decision-making and managerial processes of the company.

Part of the results of a recently completed nationwide study by the Center for Research on Information Systems at the University of Texas at Arlington (UTA) shows that:

- As the length of the outage increases, the loss of functionality and integration of functions worsens.
- Reverting to manual methods of backup accomplishes only part of the normal order volume, inventory tracking, and shipping. The backlog increases.
- Coordination of information among the functions and departments is decreased, resulting in errors in order commitment and in loss of sales and profit.
- Computer outages initiate actions that cause the business to incur additional expenses.
- The largest intangible loss is cash-flow interruption.
- Continued loss of customers, competitive edge, and image might prove more damaging than the temporary loss of revenue and additional costs.

Objectives of the business recovery plan

The objectives of the business recovery plan should be to:

- Minimize the extent of disruption and damage and prevent its escalation.
- Establish alternative means of operation.

- Minimize the economic impact.
- Ensure that all legal and regulatory requirements have been observed.

Having a business recovery plan does not guarantee there will be no loss of revenue, but it will reduce the amount of that loss. Insurance can cover *proven loss* of revenue that still occurs. In addition, if correctly arranged, the insurance policy also can cover the extra expenses involved with the operation of the business recovery plan.

The plan complements insurance policies. Together they form an integrated program, providing prudent, effective management of assets.

The need for planning can be seen in a hypothetical scenario. Consider this situation. A fire causes major damage to the main corporate facility. Estimates indicate that it will take at least three months to repair the damage. There are six immediate concerns:

1. *Where* will the company operate for the next three months?
2. *How* will it operate?
3. *Who* will operate it?
4. Do management and employees know *what to do* when disaster strikes? Will they have to deal with the disaster in an ad hoc fashion?
5. What *resources* will be needed to operate for the next three months? Are they readily available?
6. Are duplicate company *records* available or will they have to be recreated?

This simple scenario raises even more serious concerns about business continuity. Will customers and clients accept the situation and the problems associated with it? The company needs them. Insurance might only cover the documented loss of revenue until the building is repaired. What happens when the insurance payments stop? In today's competitive world, customers and clients might not be easy to recapture.

It is difficult to compete under ordinary circumstances, but almost impossible with reduced revenue and increased expenses, such as additional advertising and promotional offers, reduced prices, and so on. Yet a company *must* maintain its customer base to survive.

A business recovery plan covers not only immediate emergency procedures needed to reduce loss of life and damage to property, but also the long-term actions needed to expedite operational recovery. It should address:

- Maintenance of vital functions and operations
- Alternative means of operation
- Training of personnel
- Return to normal operations

Business recovery capability includes standard emergency response items such as emergency organizations and salvage squads. It also encompasses plans for partial operation during the time it will take to accomplish full restoration.

Preparation and procedure objectives

Another set of objectives in planning are that the preparations and procedures for a business recovery plan should:

- Be well understood by all the staff who might be involved, and specify the responsibilities of all participants before, during, and after a disaster event.
- Be integrated with practical security measures and internal controls for routine protection of the computer systems, the applications, the data, and the personnel who are involved.
- Be documented in a manual that is maintained on a current basis and is distributed to and used by all supervisory personnel. Whenever possible, this should be done online.
- Define the basic approach that should be taken in an emergency, state the assumptions and priorities of the plan, and point up areas of particular concern.
- Clearly state all steps that will be taken by the organization at the time of a business interruption event. There will be detailed, step-by-step instructions describing responsibilities and actions to be taken.
- Be workable for activation on short notice in any part of the organization served by the I/S facilities, and dependent on those operations.
- Encompass all phases of the possible migration to, and operations at, the backup sites should that prove necessary.
- Have sections that are practical for use in response to minor emergencies, as well as those for major emergencies.

- Include business interruption recovery procedures and practices that are applicable in the widespread user areas of the organization, considering the many microcomputers involved, with large stores of data and important, if not crucial, user-developed applications.

Procedures to recover from a business interruption normally are written for the most probable serious occurrence of a disaster event. This is often called the *key disaster scenario*. Events of lesser magnitude then can be handled at the appropriate level as a subset of the documented recovery procedures. After the acceptance of the plan by management, it is important to have complete or partial "disaster drills" to activate the procedures and to test the planned backup capabilities.

An overview of the information needed

The detailed information needed to develop a business recovery plan will vary by company. But all plans should include five features:

1. Identification of the *vital or crucial functions* of the company. What company functions, processes, and computer applications must continue if the organization is to survive and fulfill its objectives? This step also will identify crucial interdependencies.

2. Identification of the *minimum resources* needed during recovery. What minimum utilities, equipment, staff, and procedures are needed to perform these functions?

3. Development of an *emergency operation schedule*. Restricted capacity usually involves total loss of some functions and limited access to others. The remaining resources must be efficiently applied.

4. An assessment of the *availability of emergency methods and minimum resources*. What alternate sites, equipment suppliers, raw material sources, off-site storage, and so on are available?

5. An estimation of the *recovery duration*. How long will it take to achieve emergency productivity and how long to fully recover?

The main criterion for judging the expected benefits of a business recovery plan is usually an estimate of the reduction of the dollar loss. However, the financial benefit of a business interruption plan should be only one of several criteria involved when considering its development. Other criteria include public image and credibility, loss of skilled workers, maintenance of services to the public, and legal requirements. All industries are subject to the Foreign Corrupt Practices Act, and some are also regulated by federal, state, and local governments. Compliance with such must be a specific consideration.

Telecommunications considerations

Telecommunications, both voice and data, play an increasingly crucial role in everyday business operations. Telecommunications within many companies are essential to the company's financial and operational health. Competitive and customer strategies are often built around communicating externally or between different locations in the same company. Electronic data interchange (EDI) is a prime example of how important these links have become. Another example is the extensive networks used in the financial and airline industries for transaction processing. These types of telecommunications functionality are integral to the company, having a high degree of impact on the bottom line. As such, and considering the complexities involved, they require special consideration in both the business resumption plan and the I/S recovery plan. This includes the telecommunications link between the recovery site, other company sites, and with customers and/or suppliers linked in to the company.

Network backup solutions include:

- Universal dial backup units
- Alternative site multiplexing
- Software-based remote testing capability
- Satellite communications
- Turnkey backup products to support large-scale T1 networking
- Electronic analog and digital network control consoles
- Value-added services, such as AT&T's ACCUNET Reserve and Switched 56k offerings
- Bypass vendors

Communications links for recovery, except dial-up and switched services, must be in place already. Lead times preclude anything other than activating what is already in place. Telecom circuits cannot be obtained from scratch in one or two weeks, so telecommunications must either be built into the basic network or an on-demand service, such as AT&T's ACCUNET Reserve, must be used.

If a complex network is designed to provide alternate routing and single points of failure are eliminated as part of the design, the cost added by the business recovery plan will be minimized.

Identifying and eliminating single points of failure, dial-up alternatives, and PARADYNE-type channel extenders are essential starting points in the telecommunications recovery plan. Channel extension can provide backup and recovery for line outages, CPU failure, loss of the data center, electronic tape vaulting, and host-to-host database journaling.

Communications traffic in most companies is increasing. The use of central-office digital switches to accommodate its control and routing usually results in concentrating network traffic in central, key network nodes. The effects of an outage in any of these nodes could be severe. Alternative routing products are available to ensure an adequate alternate routing capability.

Local and wide area networking in PC-to-PC networks and PC-to-host networks are becoming a common way to do business. Although a disruption in service will not result in a dangerous situation, except in extraordinary circumstances, there will be a loss of productivity. As more people use the functionality, it will be harder for them to revert to the former way of transacting business. The telecommunications disaster plan has to first identify the importance of the applications on those networks and to provide alternate ways of conducting business until the service is restored. A recent survey by Infonetics Inc, a local area network (LAN) testing and market research firm based in Santa Clara, Ca., reports the loss of an average LAN crash at $25,480 in lost annual revenue.

Networks have become software driven, making it necessary to include the protection of these network software databases in the communications business recovery plan.

Digital microwave and VSAT are two new technologies to consider for providing cost effective alternate routing.

Business recovery planning for communications should make provisions for disruptions resulting from fires and other outages at the providers' facilities. Part of the problem is having to access an outside phone switch that is under control of the vendor. Finding the answers to the right questions and knowing the vendor's capability are the first two steps. The third is negotiating redundancy. As an example, having a backup line that goes through the same central office as does the primary line provides no backup in the event the outage is at the central office. In this case, it is necessary to find out the carrier's capability—first backing up a switch at the central office, and second, the central office itself.

The Hinsdale, Illinois, fire in 1988 is an example of what can happen without a business recovery plan. The unattended Illinois Bell switching station caught fire and went out of service, disrupting telephone service in northern and central Illinois. Although corporations were not severely affected (it was on a Sunday) it suggests the helplessness of a company in this situation and the vulnerability of corporate networks.

You should find out from your telecommunications carrier how long it will take for it to recover from a disruption. The specific information you need is how long will it take for your service to be resumed. This probably will depend on where your company fits in the carrier's order of priority.

Having a multivendor I/S environment and having to support multiple protocols adds complexity. One popular solution to this is to find a vendor or maintenance service that offers multivendor environment support.

The build or buy question also relates to communications. If your company has a straightforward network, a small number of key data centers and a highly skilled technical staff, building might bring about more innovative options. On the other hand, business recovery vendors provide experience, equipment, facilities, and management know-how that would relieve the company from a heavy capital investment and the management burden of planning for, equipping, and operating the alternative facilities.

Where the plan begins

The planning process should begin at the corporate level and be applied in top-down fashion to each division and location to ensure that individual division and location plans fit in with the corporate plan.

Two crucial considerations in the development of a plan are:

- Senior management commitment
- The involvement of key departments

A steering committee also should be appointed to provide overall management of the plan development project. Representatives of key departments and senior management should participate in that committee.

The plan should be comprehensive from a "performance standard" viewpoint. It should not consider loss scenarios on an individual basis. Instead, it should detail the actions to be taken based on the level of damage rather than the individual type of loss. Exceptions to this will be type disasters, such as an earthquake. In these cases, the plan should detail specific actions for the type of loss.

Unfortunately, the ultimate value of the plan will be demonstrated only in the most undesirable situations. This is similar to insurance coverages, loss control systems, and other risk management techniques. There will be no spectacular successes—only spectacular failures.

2

Management and user considerations

INFORMATION SERVICES DISASTER RECOVERY PLANNING IS primarily a management issue, rather than a technical issue. Management and users must consider not only the large, central data centers and networks, but also the many smaller computers distributed through the organization. They must take a realistic look at all facets of the effect of computer loss on the organization. There must be an organizational commitment to fund and support the development and installation of the recovery plan. Such plans are not confined to I/S, but must interface with many existing policies and programs in the organization.

Set up a study and planning group and appoint an I/S security coordinator. It is both helpful and necessary to have the involvement of the Internal Audit department with the planning group.

A number of areas of planning relevant to application system emergencies are briefly discussed here. All application systems cannot be recovered rapidly after a disaster. Cost must be balanced against need, and it is helpful to consider these three levels of security and disaster recovery measures in dividing the application systems:

- Mandatory measures
- Necessary measures
- Desirable measures

These three levels are handled differently in the planning process. An I/S disaster recovery plan can be briefly outlined. The plan should be tailored to the organization. It is preferable to start with a short-term, high-impact plan, then proceed to a full disaster recovery plan. The phases of such a full disaster planning effort are outlined in this book. The effort is large, and a long-term strategy should be developed.

The requirements of a disaster recovery program can be best assessed by interviews with management and users. Helpful checklists and procedures are provided in this book for such an assessment. It is prudent to draw out the priority concerns of management.

The first principle of disaster recovery is to review, examine, and strengthen all basic I/S security controls, standards, and procedures, to limit the chances of a disaster and its effects beforehand. Some basic checklists are included in this chapter to help management ascertain whether they should first strengthen their security practices, then adopt a disaster recovery plan.

Management and user considerations

The purpose of an I/S disaster recovery plan is to prepare in advance to ensure the continuity of flow of business information if all or part of the computer capability is lost. The computer capability is not only in the large, central data centers and the networks, but it is also in the many personal computers and the departmental minicomputers that are scattered throughout the organization. The I/S disaster recovery plan cannot stand alone, but must be a subset of the overall business recovery plan covering disasters.

The recovery plan cannot be an imposed solution from the central data center. It must deal with the realities of people's attitudes, organizational relationships, and special interests. Disaster recovery actions are always a priority, and many normal operations are neglected during an emergency. I/S staff and user management must take the lead, and review the technical considerations and assessments that are presented to them by the recovery plan staff.

All concerned members of management, including user management, must realize that I/S professionals agree that there are no secure computers. This is particularly true in the distributed computing environment of microcomputers. Many data centers and smaller computer operations might have generally accepted measures for security in place, and management can be assured that the proper actions have been taken; but there are always personnel problems, electronics failures, fires, and natural disasters that can suddenly disrupt any part of the operation. It is therefore crucial that management take a realistic look at the following:

- The company's legal obligations
- The maintenance of business operations and cash flow
- The continuity of customer services
- The retention of any competitive advantages obtained through the computer systems
- The way in which production and distribution decisions are made
- The use of computers in operations control and logistics
- The management of purchasing functions and vendor relationships
- The ongoing control of projects
- Communications with branches or agencies
- Shareholder and public relations
- Personnel and union relationships

Management must assess the importance of its computers, computer networks, microcomputers, and other I/S to these facets of business. The staff can then make a reasonable decision about the level and type of effort that should be put into planning the disaster backup of the I/S functions.

The computing function is pervasive in virtually all facets of business. The loss of general productivity for a significant section of the work force in the event of a disaster could become very expensive. The willingness of a company to understand and estimate such productivity losses, then to determine what it could accept, should be the prime consideration in determining the size and scope of its disaster recovery planning effort. Most I/S people understand this, but often at senior management levels, the degree to which their work place relies on computing to achieve the work results they expect is not well understood.

Management can draw on many sources of information, both from the I/S technical staff and from other security and facilities management people in their organization. The insurance specialists, for example, should have recent information available about the possibilities of disasters and the use of insurance as one tool to ameliorate its effect. The engineering and mechanical staff will be familiar with fire prevention and containment. Management should require that personnel who are responsible for security in general, and contingency planning in particular, maintain an awareness of accidents, fires, disasters, and emergencies that have afflicted similar computer systems in other organizations, in order to minimize the possibility of similar events occurring at their own facilities.

One of the more difficult decisions for management and users centers on the cost-benefit considerations in contingency planning and readiness. There is the problem of balancing the adequacy of training and testing against its cost. How much training and testing should be done? Even if contingency plans are well documented, kept up to date, disseminated, and tested, and even if the personnel are well trained, there still might be unanticipated or unfamiliar situations that require an emergency response in a time frame that is difficult to handle. In some situations, personnel will simply not have time to stop and read the procedures they need to follow. Even well-trained personnel who have been active in the periodic testing of the contingency procedures cannot be expected to memorize all of them. Although it is obvious that more frequent testing will improve the employee's familiarity with the plan and their readiness to handle emergency situations, the costs of having a disaster recovery plan can increase quickly.

Organizational commitment

The organizational commitment to developing and maintaining an I/S disaster recovery plan can only come from management and the users. Without their wholehearted support and participation, it is hard to accomplish anything really useful. The organizational commitment must include:

- Funding the development and ongoing maintenance of the plan
- Assigning both technical and user staff for planning and training
- Obtaining the continuing interest of senior and middle management
- Getting cooperation from the user departments
- Involving all related departments, such as security, buildings, purchasing, etc.
- Setting priorities for the planning effort
- Reviewing the development effort of the plan
- Considering the use of consulting support
- Directing periodic testing of the plan
- Integrating the management of the plan into normal business procedures

Interfacing with existing policies and programs

Management must consider how the I/S disaster recovery plan will interface with existing organizational policies and procedures. There already should be a disaster plan for the overall business. Most organizations have plans in place for at least some of the following:

- Fire protection equipment, installation, and maintenance
- Emergency fire alarm procedures
- Security guard training, duties, and procedures
- Relationships with external emergency alarm services
- Relationships with local fire and police departments
- Bomb or mob threat procedures
- Storm emergency information and restoration plans
- Emergency control centers

These procedures are all supportive of I/S recovery, and management must see that the I/S plan fits in with them. These procedures, particularly when the police or fire departments are involved, will always take precedence over any internal I/S disaster plan. In fact, for any serious disaster, I/S personnel usually will find that they are prevented from entering the premises. This problem must be taken into consideration in the plan procedures.

Setting up the study and planning group

Management must consider setting up the disaster recovery study and planning group so that the many facets of an I/S contingency plan can be realized. On the one hand, a great deal of technical work must be done by people such as the systems programming group. Without their work, there will be no operable plan. They are not normally in a position to know the priorities required, however. On the other hand, the users will all feel that they must have high priority and will be dismayed if their systems are low on the list. These forces mean that a strong study team must be set up that can understand both the technical and business aspects. Good people must be chosen to make a "plan for the plan" and indicate the problem areas that will need management attention.

Management must cooperate with the planning group, provide the funding, and open the doors to accomplish the task. One of the first steps is to appoint a competent, experienced person as I/S security coordinator (or administrator or director). This person can coordinate the plan's development, testing, and ongoing maintenance.

The planning process should look first at the organization's disaster recovery objectives, and then determine how to accomplish them. To do so, the planners must have a basic understanding of the areas that should be addressed as part of the disaster recovery program. The following discussion describes the type of problems that disaster recovery must address, and the types of planning that are relevant for those problems.

The two situations to which user and application systems generally are vulnerable are:

- Loss of processing capability
- Damage to data

It follows that the kinds of contingency planning required are:

- What to do if the network or computing system serving the application is down
- What to do if the application databases are corrupted and preclude further use without compounding the damage

In both instances, the urgency of the mission supported and the requirement for system output must be considered. The less delay a mission or system can tolerate, the more extensive the planning must be.

All plans must be carefully and extensively documented, kept current, and disseminated to all personnel who will be affected by them. Personnel must be trained in their assigned tasks, and plans must be tested for feasibility.

The following areas of planning are relevant for application system emergencies:

Identifying crucial functions

The functions in an application system that are crucial to an organization's mission should be identified by performing a risk analysis, which will indicate not only which functions are immediately crucial, but also how quickly other functions also can become crucial.

Finding alternate site operations   Another organization or service that uses the same or compatible equipment, and which, during an emergency, would be able to allot time should be found. Such an arrangement should be effected on a formal basis between the organizations involved, not left as a friendly arrangement between individuals. Planning should extend to ensuring the readiness at the alternate site of up-to-date, tested software and sufficient preprinted forms and any other special supplies to last through one reorder cycle. Forms, for example, can be handled by the use of all-points addressable printing to create forms on the fly, and to minimize the expense of forms storage. In addition, a method must be devised for communicating with the alternate site (telephone lines, messenger, etc.). Adequate transportation facilities might have to be provided and specific personnel must be designated and trained.

Replacing limited processing   It might be possible that processing of some limited crucial functions can revert to preautomation procedures. Certain types of financial data are amenable to manual processing for short periods of time. For others, only a severely streamlined version of the function can be accomplished. When continuity is important, any special equipment required for manual operations must be close at hand. Necessary particulars include working space, availability of timely data, page copies of source data, conversion of data to manual use, special equipment, preprinted forms, communications, transportation, selecting and training personnel, and a process for recording all manual transactions.

Backing up data   The easiest way to ensure against loss of data is to keep backup copies in readily accessible and secure places. Decisions concerning how many copies to keep, where to store them, and how long to keep them will depend on the importance of the application, the vulnerability of the data, the size of the databases, and costs.

Recovering data   Sometimes data that has been either accidentally or intentionally modified will be so altered that further transactions will only compound the damage. Therefore, it is important to maintain a list of key personnel for each database so that they can be summoned without delay when needed. The list would include senior systems programmers and senior applications programmers. Include in the list the security officer or someone else who could authorize the substitution of extraordinary procedures if necessary, such as access to the computer room not ordinarily granted, access to computer resources not ordinarily authorized, and use of unapproved programs on live data. Instruct all personnel who might be involved in such a situation, including the computer operator, in emergency measures in advance. Keep these lists up to date and include names of alternates. Establish a priority, based on experience, for checking the source of the errors and maintain a small database for testing recovery procedures.

Restoring the facility

If a computer facility is destroyed or damaged, there must be plans for continued operations, as well as plans for restoration or relocation of the facility. Recovery from destruction can include locating space or real estate; building or remodeling existing buildings; procuring computer hardware, supplies, office furnishings, and ancillary equipment; and transferring operations from the emergency site to the permanent one. Such plans normally will be the direct responsibility of facility management, but applications systems management might be called on for support, especially in the areas of work-load planning, space requirements, equipment requirements, and moving operations. Advance preparation and periodic updating of the information necessary to these activities will ensure its completeness and timeliness.

Involving internal audit

The Internal Audit department should be involved as an integral part of the I/S disaster recovery planning process at the points where it is deemed most fruitful for them to contribute. Some areas can be:

Deciding on an acceptable level of business degradation   This is a decision that senior management must make, but the analysis can be most readily developed by the Internal Audit.

Checking the ongoing I/S security practices   The audit staff will use the attached checklists, and will go deeper into the analysis of the practices.

Accepting a staff assignment on the team   The Internal Audit staff have a strong part to play in establishing the necessary controls to be installed in the routine backup of files and during a disaster recovery operation. It can be very difficult to maintain audit trails at such times, yet it is imperative that there be no audit control breaks.

Reviewing the vital resources and record requirements This is a fundamental area requiring stringent control.

Reviewing the risk analysis calculations   These calculations might be basic to the justification of the project. If they are not needed, the overriding operational necessity should be reviewed by Internal Audit.

Planning the management of resources   The input of the audit staff will be helpful in this area.

Considering salvage value and handling   The Insurance Group might want the audit staff's evaluation of the salvage process.

Ongoing monitoring and periodic testing   Internal Audit should be in charge of the timing of tests, areas tested, and evaluating the results.

Refereeing the tests of the recovery procedures   Good technical procedures and smooth computer operations do not necessarily indicate a good recovery in a controlled manner. The Audit group can referee the tests analytically.

Considering the levels of disaster recovery measures

A disaster recovery plan is developed to minimize the costs resulting from losses of, or damages to, the resources or the capabilities of an I/S facility and related services. Its success depends on recognizing the potential consequences of undesirable happenings. There are many resources related to I/S operations. Some particular subset of these resources is required to support each function that is provided to others in the organization. These resources include: people, programs, data, computer hardware, communications equipment and systems, electric power, the physical facility and access to it, and even items such as paper forms.

All resources are not equally important, nor are they equally susceptible to harm. The selection of safeguards and the elements of a contingency plan should, therefore, be done with an informed awareness of which system functions are supported by each resource element, and of the susceptibility of each element to harm. The cost-effective recovery of an I/S operation is thus dependent on:

- The importance to the organization of each of the component parts of the I/S functions
- The general probability of something undesirable happening to each of the components
- The likely results and ramifications of various types of disasters that could occur
- Preparations that can be made to minimize the chances of disasters, and the costs, if they do occur

Any part of a disaster recovery plan includes its overhead cost until it becomes necessary to activate it. It is, therefore, necessary to consider the importance of the resources and services and to justify all the parts of security and disaster recovery measures by estimating the losses that could occur through lack of these precautions. The combination of initial expenditures and insurance coverage must be balanced against the necessity of the service and the probability of the need of the recovery procedures.

Some options are mandatory, however, and must be taken, whatever the cost. There are three levels of security and disaster recovery measures that should be considered in balancing cost to need:

- Mandatory measures
- Necessary measures
- Desirable measures

These three levels will be handled differently in the planning process. There is no absolute scale, and these measures will vary as conditions change. Management must review what is mandatory and necessary for the organization, support those efforts first, and then consider the justification analysis of desirable measures. It is important that this analysis be made in the user areas as well as in the central computer facility. These measures are outlined below:

Mandatory measures

Mandatory security and disaster recovery measures are those related to fire control, alarm systems, evacuation procedures, and other emergency precautions necessary to protect the lives and safety of people in the area involved. Mandatory measures also include those needed to protect the books of account of the organization, and to hold its officers free from legal liability based on an assertion of negligence. The assets of the organization must be protected as much as possible.

The cost of these mandatory measures must be included in the cost of doing business. The mandatory disaster recovery measures must be reviewed periodically to assess adequacy and to make sure they are being included in routine operations. These measures also should be reviewed with organizational counsel.

Necessary measures

Necessary security and disaster recovery measures include all reasonable precautions taken to prevent serious disruption of the operations of the organization. They will include selected areas of operation, such as:

- Manufacturing and distribution
- Engineering and planning
- Sales and marketing
- Employee relations

The necessity of the measures must be determined by senior management. Because the necessary measures will be included in the base operating cost of the organization, each selected measure must be reviewed as to both degree and speed of emergency backup required.

Desirable measures

Desirable security and disaster recovery measures include reasonable precautions taken to prevent real inconvenience or disruption to any area of the organization, and to keep the business under smooth control. The cost of some precautions related to personnel is small, but planned action is important to maintain operational efficiency and morale. The cost of other measures, such as arrangements for alternate sites for systems and programming personnel and their terminals, can be large. Estimates and plans must be made, however, to allow reasonable and cost-effective management decisions once the extent of a disaster is understood.

The mandatory measures should be implemented as soon as possible. The necessary measures should be implemented in time-phased, priority order, with a definite plan approved by senior management. The desirable measures should be implemented as circumstances allow. Overhead cost is balanced against perceived need and desirability by both senior and user management.

Products of an I/S disaster recovery planning effort

An I/S disaster recovery planning effort should produce the disaster recovery plan report. This report should outline the following:

- Assumptions and considerations
- Recovery requirements
- Descriptions of all resources reviewed, highlighting the crucial resources
- Strategies considered and recommended strategy
- Detailed recovery procedures
- Emergency plan and backup plan
- Staffing and responsibilities
- Maintenance and testing procedures

Recommendations for management action are actions to be taken by management to put the plan in place and test it regularly.

Disaster recovery procedures should give detailed assignments and locations for actions to be taken at the time of an emergency, until the backup operation is running. This is the emergency plan to be followed if there is a service disruption incident.

Recovery and restoration procedures are the part of the plan that details how and when to return to the original site or another one selected by management.

Documentation and related information should be included as an appendix, which might not be provided with most copies of the plan.

These products of an I/S disaster recovery planning effort are more fully described in chapter 5.

Tailoring the plan to the organization

An I/S disaster recovery plan must be specific to the organization and tailored to its needs. An off-the-shelf plan is of no use whatsoever at the time of a service disruption incident, when individuals need to know exactly what their role is and the steps they must take. The presence of a "paper plan" does not in itself provide a disaster recovery capability. All people in the organization who are involved in a recovery activity also should be involved in the plan preparation, training, and testing.

Starting with a short-term, high-impact plan

The disaster recovery planning process can take many months, a great deal of activity, and many days if the full process is carried out in a monolithic way, including:

- Review of all data sets and data files
- Discussion with all users
- Complete assembly of all documentation
- Full risk identification and risk analysis study
- Detailed review of ongoing security practices

Such an approach could be self-defeating because it would be very costly and time-consuming, and management would lose interest in supporting it. It would also put off the installation of mandatory and necessary security measures that are most vital to the organization.

A better approach for the initial effort is for a small team to gather under the direction of a senior I/S manager and make a short-term, high-impact plan to get sufficient procedures in place that will handle the most pressing needs and have high visibility. The steps they take should include:

- Assemble all readily available operations and systems documentation

- Assemble the reports of any audits or security studies of the I/S functions

- Create lists of the application systems estimating the order of priority, separated by major functional organizations

- Consult with senior management in the financial, administrative, and operational areas for opinions and agreement as to the order of priority of mandatory and necessary applications

- Work with systems programming and operations to see that all such systems are backed up as frequently as given in the plan and stored in a secure site

- Determine the minimum configuration on which these mandatory and necessary systems can run (it may be more than one computer) and arrange for tests

- Determine if these vital systems can be backed up and run off-site in an emergency in the time required

- Keep management informed of the results of the studies and tests, and when the tests are completed ask for a full study to be funded to cover all security factors and all applications

It is important to take a reasonably short time, usually less than six months, to produce a viable backup capability for the vital systems and to do preliminary tests on it. This system should have the visibility and impact needed to get support for a more comprehensive study and capability, in which participation can be delegated and handled at a slower pace.

Full disaster recovery project plan

If it is desired to have a full I/S disaster recovery project, culminating in a comprehensive plan that includes all facets of the I/S operations, then the organization and the "plan-for-the-plan" must be carefully assembled. The disaster recovery study project must be handled as any other systems development project and be broken into phases that have individual plans. The elements of such a project are given in Fig. 2-1, I/S Disaster Recovery Project Plan. This project plan divides the effort into six familiar phases for ready reporting to management and for keeping the study under control:

- Definition phase
- Functional requirements phase
- Design and development phase
- Implementation phase
- Testing and monitoring phase
- Maintenance phase

Fig. 2-1. I/S business recovery project plan.

Definition phase
1. Decide on disaster recovery objectives.
2. Appoint an I/S security coordinator and a planning team.
3. Develop an initial set of assumptions and definitions.
4. Decide on the types of disaster to consider.
5. Select a key disaster scenario.

Functional requirements phase

1. Assemble all existing organizational procedures and standards relative to emergencies.
2. Assemble all documentation relative to the inventory of resources, including hardware, communications, software, forms, facility descriptions, etc.
3. Make an evaluation of what systems are mandatory, necessary, or desirable.
4. Analyze the applications and facilities against the recovery objectives.
5. Decide on long-term strategy or a short-term, high-impact plan.
6. Assess the operational requirements of the crucial resources and applications.
7. Agree on the assumptions and definitions.
8. Determine what is to be covered in the plan.
9. Set priorities and acceptable time frames for recovery.

Design and development phase

1. Decide on the requirements for the important resources and applications.
2. Evaluate alternative recovery strategies.

3. Select one or more specific recovery strategies.
4. Perform a cost/benefit analysis for the management report.
5. Perform a full risk analysis, if appropriate.
6. Decide on the organization for disaster recovery teams.
7. Plan the management of resources during a disaster event.
8. Identify potential vendors and price their services.
9. Select the final design and prepare detailed recovery procedures.
10. Produce the disaster recovery plan report with recommendations.

Implementation phase

1. Acquire any hardware, software, communications lines, etc., that are needed.
2. Negotiate and sign contracts with vendors.
3. Get agreement on final, detailed procedures.
4. Train personnel.
5. Prepare sites.
6. Develop test and monitor plans.
7. Develop a maintenance plan.

Testing and monitoring phase

1. Set up a test plan with internal audit.
2. Schedule tests for individual sections of the plan.
3. Make arrangements to use facilities external to your organization.
4. Test backup systems.
5. Analyze the backup output compared to the normal operations.
6. Correct errors in the plan.
7. Repeat a variety of tests periodically.

Maintenance phase

1. Develop a system to update names, responsibilities, and telephone numbers.
2. See that the system for backup libraries is working smoothly.
3. Standardize documentation and procedures.

Long-term strategy

The long-term I/S strategy for disaster recovery should have as a goal creating an understanding of the need for the plans and procedures on the same level as people understand the need for fire alarm procedures. The long-term strategy should be directed toward creating a full, effective, disaster recovery capability by:

- Assigning full-time personnel to maintain and oversee the plan
- Assigning task groups that report regularly to management on developing areas of the plan
- Obtaining budget funding for a practical, cost-effective capability
- Involving all organizational groups, such as security, facilities, insurance, engineering, etc.
- Developing a full disaster recovery capability covering all areas of I/S
- Having regular training of all staff in the actions and requirements of the plan
- Testing the plan realistically and regularly in cooperation with the internal audit group

Name specific individuals, locations, and actions

When tailoring the plan to the organization, a key necessity is to name specific individuals with their responsibilities, locations where tasks will be accomplished, and actions to take in priority sequence. It is possible to name positions rather than people if there is a handy directory available, but it is not as effective. Positions do not have home telephone numbers, but people do. Individuals should be quite familiar with whom they are calling in a telephone tree, and be able to call them even if they have misplaced their emergency lists. Key people should have their copies of their plans at home to have them available nights and weekends.

Assessing disaster recovery program requirements

A disaster recovery review, the development of a plan, and the maintenance of the contingency plan with appropriate backup of systems and facilities can be time-consuming and expensive. In addition, some senior managers might have little feeling for the need for a disaster recovery plan. A general macro-assessment of the importance to the organization of such a plan should, therefore, be made by means of interviews with as many senior managers as possible. The purpose of these interviews would be:

- To alert the senior managers to the probable need for a disaster recovery plan

- To determine senior management attitudes about the importance and priorities of the data processing programs
- To understand business constraints and the impact of business service interruption
- To determine what records are considered vital, and how their safety and continuity is presently handled
- To find if there are any legal responsibilities involved that are the particular concern of individual managers
- To expedite the appointment of a liaison person from the operating unit who will be routinely involved in further disaster recovery planning

The purpose of such an initial macro-assessment of the need for a disaster recovery plan is to make all managers aware of the activity and to open lines of communication for further work on the plan. After it is completed, and a disaster recovery planning team is established to analyze the situation and create an actual plan, then the team can perform a micro-assessment. This is an in-depth assessment of the individual disaster recovery procedures, such as those described later in this book.

Management can make a general assessment as to the degree of risk they face. Based on that degree of risk, they can decide:

- How extensive the macro-assessment of the situation should be for developing a disaster recovery plan
- How the planning will be handled relative to their own user groups

The macro-assessment, or managerial review, is a risk-oriented review. It does not look at specific aspects of the disaster recovery program, but rather determines the concerns that management has about the adequacy of the arrangements.

How to conduct managerial assessment interviews

A managerial review for a disaster recovery plan normally will consist of arranged interviews between individual senior managers and one or two key people on the disaster recovery planning team. Such a review is best handled with a prepared list of questions, which can be delivered in advance. The first interview should not be too lengthy, because the manager might not be prepared and should not be cornered for decisions until appropriate staff has been consulted. At some point, however, the manager should be expected to sit down for an interview in which all questions on the checklists are answered and discussed.

The results of such an interview should be positive for the manager. It should be made obvious that any deficiencies will be corrected cooperatively, with both the study team and appropriate members of the operating staff. It is crucial to get future cooperation from the manager at this time, with the expectation that a positive, adequate plan will result from mutual action.

The managerial self-assessment requires each manager to look at the organization's business risk, as a result of possible computer disaster, in the following three areas:

- Financial loss
- Business service interruption
- Legal responsibilities

For each of these three areas of business concern, ten predictors have been identified. The responses to these predictors can be used to indicate the degree of business risk faced in that particular area. These are not technical questions, but are indicative of management concern and should help direct further study to concentrate on those areas where management will be interested and helpful.

The self-assessment checklists that can be used in these interviews are:

- Checklist 2-1, Financial Loss
- Checklist 2-2, Business Service Interruption
- Checklist 2-3, Legal Responsibilities

The best approach to handling these checklists is in an interview format in which there is no demand for immediate answers. The responses might not be simply "yes" or "no," but may be modified by other considerations. Such modifications are important to note. Some questions are obviously judgmental, but it might be possible to indicate whether the intent is more "yes" or "no." All answers will be the perception of the manager at that time. This means that there is no problem if the original answer is erroneous, and that answers can be modified at a later time by the manager's staff.

Remember the purpose of the interviews is to alert managers to possible problems and to gain their interest and cooperation. Their responses should give the direction of further study, but should not generally be considered as the final word on the subject.

If possible, the interviews should include the following personnel:

- President
- Administrative or executive vice president
- Controller or chief financial officer
- Vice presidents of user departments or groups
- Key administrative managers
- Chief information officer
- Director of information services

Checklist 2-1. Financial loss.

Key Computer Applications Being Considered

1. Would repetitive or extended periods of computer downtime add significantly to the cost of data processing?

2. Would repetitive or extended periods of computer downtime add significantly to operational costs in areas dependent upon data processing?

3. Would a computer outage reduce cash flow in a crucial manner?

4. Could the financial transactions being processed at the time of a computer failure be lost by the system?

5. Could financial transactions be added or deleted out of control while the automated controls are not operating?

6. Could necessary copies of an automated file be destroyed in a computer disaster?

7. Can controls be transferred and maintained on alternative processing methods?

8. Could the audit trail be reconstructed if the automated files were destroyed?

9. Is the master documentation supporting the adequacy of computer systems controls stored in more than one safe place?

10. Is the organization liable for any fines or penalties in the event the disaster recovery controls are inadequate or fail to recover the system on a timely basis?

Checklist 2-2. Business service interruption.

Company Security

1. Are there written procedures that explain the company security system and define the responsibilities of all personnel?
2. Is there publication, education, and enforcement of company security rules and emergency procedures?
3. Does the company have much pilfering of supplies or other material?
4. Have steps been implemented to reduce causes of fire, theft, and other losses through:
   - Education?
   - Supervision?
   - Housekeeping?
   - Maintenance?
5. Is there a company policy of separation of duties in all systems involving assets?
6. Is the company located in a:
   - High-risk area?
   - Moderate-risk area?
   - Low-risk area?
7. Are entrances to building supervised?
8. Does the company have a security force that receives professional training?

Physical Security

9. Are all working and storage areas of the company protected by sprinkler systems?
10. Are safes and vaults provided for important documents and files?
11. Is there an individual designated as responsible for security:
    - For the company?
    - For the data processing installation?
12. Is there a comprehensive plan for disaster recovery that allows:
    - Quick decision on action to take?
    - Delegation of authority?
    - Vital records protection?

Vital Records

13. Is the information protected relating to:
    - Assets of the corporation?

- Stockholders?
- Employee records?
- Tax records?
- Other vital records?

14. Is there a document that specifies:
    - What information is required?
    - What data processing records contain this information?
    - How they are created?

Fire and Safety Procedures

15. Is there a written emergency procedure that covers the following:
    - Equipment and air conditioning power cutoff?
    - Fire-fighting procedures?
    - Procedures to request police, medical, and fire assistance?
    - Procedures for securing data files and programs?
    - Evacuation procedures and routines?

16. Has an individual been assigned the responsibility for supervising the performance of emergency procedures?

17. Is all or part of the emergency procedures posted in the computer center?

18. Has a test of these procedures been held in the past six months?

19. Has a test of fire detection and extinguishing equipment been held in the past six months?

20. Has the local fire department been called in to provide advice and to familiarize themselves with the computer center and its unique problems?

21. Is a fire survey made regularly by either insurance or fire department personnel?

22. Is there a controlled-access system of admittance to the computer area by positive identification?

Checklist 2-3. Legal responsibilities.

Key Computer Applications Being Considered

1. Would financial assets controlled by the computer systems be adequately protected to the extent required by law in the event of a disaster?

2. Are copies of official business records, which are maintained on electronic media, also kept in a safe storage?

Checklist 2-3. Continued.

3. Is the legal department satisfied with the I/S handling of vital documents and important papers?

4. Have the retention periods of all data processing files and documents been reviewed to ensure that they are in compliance with legal requirements?

5. Is the record retention of your key application systems in compliance with your insurance requirements, and would it be unaffected by a local disaster?

6. Are there personnel requirements that payments to employees be made in a specific time frame?

7. Is employee information covered by various privacy laws adequately protected in the event of a disaster?

8. Are employees subject to unconsidered danger in a disaster situation?

9. Is the master documentation supporting the adequacy of computer system controls stored in the data processing area?

10. Is there an inventory, maintained in a safe place, of all vital records and valuable documents to comply with legal requirements and to facilitate recovery?

How to handle the results of the interviews

The results of the interviews need not be tabulated by question, because each manager is coming from a different perspective, and the computer knowledge involved in the answers will vary widely. The results should simply be used to identify where to expend the most review time and effort, and what questions to return to at a later date. The more detailed review process undertaken later by the study team should be aware of the management objectives and concerns, and direct their investigation of the more sensitive areas.

A good method of displaying the results of the series of management interviews is given in Fig. 2-2, Business Perspective of Information Service Disaster Problems. On the left of this worksheet, the managers interviewed and the names of their departments are listed. Notes of key points are put in corresponding columns or a numbering system giving the range of importance could be used. This system could be:

- 5—Very serious concern
- 4—Serious concern

Person Interviewed	Business Priorities	Critical Areas of Business	Tolerable Duration of Outage	Financial Control Problems	Alternative Processing Possibilities	Possible Legal Problems	Possible Personnel Problems	Vital Records Involved

Fig. 2-2. Business perspective of information services disaster problems.

- 3—Concern
- 2—Minor concern
- 1—No concern

A more extensive range of gradations between priorities of concern do not add to their meaning. The purpose of such a matrix display is simply to pinpoint and highlight those areas of most concern, and to identify the organizations that have the concern.

When the study team moves to its more detailed analysis, working with the staffs of the managers involved, they should use this information as managerial direction regarding emphasis. They should structure the technical program toward the business objectives that were expressed. This should orient the review more toward the principal areas of management concern. It also should sustain the interest of the operational management group as the study and preparations progress.

Priority concerns of management in the event of a disaster

The original interviews with senior management will deal with business concerns and responsibilities. In subsequent interviews with managers and their staffs, it is necessary to draw out what their priority concerns will be in the actual handling of a service disruption incident.

A principal area of concern in disaster recovery operations for most organizations is the safety and well-being of the personnel involved. This concern should remain paramount. The principal business concern usually is the maintenance of accounting records. Other concerns can center on minimizing the disruption to customer services. The business interruption loss must be kept as low as possible, and the required cash flow must be maintained. Legal and reporting requirements must be maintained.

An additional fundamental concern is the protection of facilities, equipment, programs, and supplies. Some of these concerns, of course, might be adequately covered by insurance and need not have as rapid attention as those involving people.

Checklist 2-4, Priority Concerns of Management, covers the kinds of information that should be brought out in discussions as study proceeds. This information should not be pushed upon management in the first interview. This checklist can be used to survey the fundamental, minimum requirements that are in place.

Checklist 2-4. Priority concerns of management.

Staff Protection and Actions

1. Have all staff been trained in fire alarm, bomb threat, and other emergency procedures?
2. Do all staff understand that when the alarm sounds they:
   • Immediately vacate the building?
   • Do not return to pick up items from desks?
   • Report to supervisors at designated points?
3. Do all staff know who to call in times of emergency or where the emergency telephone list is located?
4. Do the disaster recovery planning teams understand that the protection and safety of people in the area is paramount?
5. Have good management notification procedures been developed for any emergency of any size?

Maintenance of Customer Services and Cash Flow

1. Has management set priorities about the most necessary services to be maintained in an emergency?
2. Have all user groups involved in customer services and cash handling worked with the planning teams?
3. Can alternate operations be brought up within the necessary established time period for on-line customer services?
4. Are most cash deposits sent directly to banks and not vulnerable to a disaster in the computer area?
5. Does the organization have plans for controlled public press releases in times of disaster?

Maintenance of Vital Documents

1. Have the vital documents and records of the organization been thoroughly analyzed and have control procedures been set up?
2. Does the organization use a remote, safe document storage vault?
3. Is there adequate use of microfiche, microfilm, CD-ROM, or similar technology to copy vital documents, and are the copies stored in a safe vault?
4. Are application and operations documentation of programs handling vital information backed up in a safe storage?
5. Is the legal department satisfied with the I/S and user handling of vital documents?

Checklist 2-4. Continued.

Protection of Facilities, Equipment, Programs, and Supplies

1. Are the organization's fire, safety, and engineering people working closely with I/S?

2. Have the fire and safety systems in the I/S facility area been reviewed by an independent person?

3. Have discussions been held with all equipment and supplies vendors as to their response to an emergency situation?

4. Has there been a recent review as to the documentation level of programs and the existence of updated backup copies of the programs and the documentation?

5. Is there a complete listing of all supplies and copies of all forms available in a second site, and are emergency backups of important forms held in a second site?

Assessing I/S security preparations

The basis of any good disaster recovery plan is a comprehensive set of security safeguards that are actively used and routinely managed. Proper and sufficient security preparations can greatly lower the possibility of a security incident or disaster occurring. Therefore, one of the first steps to be taken by concerned management or the disaster recovery team should be to review the I/S security preparations that have been made. In most instances, some other group will be responsible for security preparations and will have produced a report on what has been accomplished or what has been determined by a review. There might be an audit report on the subject.

It is a management responsibility to be assured that the I/S security preparations are adequate. It is axiomatic that the best plan for disaster recovery is to prevent the occurrence of disasters in the first place. The cost of prevention is far less than the cost of cure. It generally is agreed by experts in the field, however, that there are no completely secure computers. An astute manager will, therefore, balance the cost of installing as many security precautions as are possible, offset by creating a full disaster recovery plan that can handle nearly all foreseen occurrences.

The first principle of disaster recovery is:

Review, examine, and strengthen all basic I/S security controls, standards, and procedures.

This activity can be done before, during, or after the installation and implementation of the first high-impact, short-term plan. Clearly, it should be done on a continuing basis periodically. Ongoing I/S security practices are the foundation on which disaster recovery can reasonably be expected to be effective and to be only occasionally used.

I/S security preparations checklists

Following are six checklists that can be used for rapid consideration of your present I/S security status. They will aid in determining whether there is sufficient security foundation in place on which to build a disaster recovery activity, and the disaster recovery measures that are most appropriate for your operations. These checklists and the areas of concern they address are:

- Checklist 2-5, Management Security Considerations
  - ~ Company security
  - ~ Physical security
  - ~ Vital records
  - ~ Fire and safety procedures
- Checklist 2-6, Physical Security Considerations
  - ~ Fire detection and action
  - ~ Environmental controls
  - ~ Building structure
- Checklist 2-7, Personnel Security Considerations
- Checklist 2-8, Software Security Considerations
  - ~ Controls
  - ~ Programming
  - ~ File security
  - ~ Documentation and forms
  - ~ Audit
- Checklist 2-9, Data Security Considerations
- Checklist 2-10, Operations Security Considerations
- Checklist 2-11, Data Communications Security Considerations
  - ~ General security
  - ~ Terminal and PC security
  - ~ Data security
  - ~ Communications backup

Checklist 2-5. Management security considerations.

No.	Item	Response
		Yes No N/A Comments

Company Security

1. Are there written procedures which explain the company security system and define the responsibilities of the personnel?

2. Is there publication, education, and enforcement of company security rules and emergency procedures?

3. Does the company have much pilfering of supplies or other material?

4. Have steps been implemented to reduce causes of fire, theft, and other losses through:

   a. Education?

   b. Supervision?

   c. Housekeeping?

   d. Maintenance?

5. Is there a company policy of separation of duties in all systems involving assets?

6. Is the company located in a:

   a. High-risk area?

   b. Moderate-risk area?

   c. Low-risk area?

7. Does the company have a security force that receives professional training?

Physical Security

8. Are all working and storage areas of the company protected by sprinkler systems?

9. Are safes and vaults provided for important documents and files?

10. Is there an individual designated as responsible for security:

    a. For the company?

    b. For the data processing installation?

11. Is there a comprehensive plan for disaster recovery which allows:

    a. Quick decision on action to take?

    b. Delegation of authority?

c. Vital records protection?

Vital Records

12. Is the information protected relating to:
    a. Assets of the corporation?
    b. Stockholders?
    c. Employee records?
    d. Tax records?
    e. Other vital records?

13. Is there a document that specifies:
    a. What information is required?
    b. What data processing records contain this information?
    c. How they are created?

Fire and Safety Procedures:

14. Is there a written emergency procedure that covers the following:
    a. Equipment and air conditioning power cutoff?
    b. Fire-fighting procedures?
    c. Procedures to request police, medical, and fire assistance?
    d. Procedures for securing data files and programs?
    e. Evacuation procedures and routes?

15. Has an individual been assigned the responsibility for supervising the performance of emergency procedures?

16. Is all or part of the emergency procedure posted in the computer center?

17. Has a test of these procedures been held in the past six months?

18. Has a test of fire detection and extinguishing equipment been held in the past six months?

19. Has the local fire department been called in to provide advice and to familiarize themselves with the computer center and its unique problems?

20. Is a fire survey made regularly by either insurance or fire department personnel?

21. Is there a controlled-access system of admittance to the computer area by positive identification?

Checklist 2-6. Physical security considerations.

Fire Detection and Action

1. Are the on-site personnel trained and equipped to take immediate action against incipient and relatively insignificant fires?

2. Have the operating personnel been trained in fire reporting and fire-fighting procedures?

3. Have the operating personnel been assigned individual responsibilities in case of fire?

4. Are there fire detectors located in:
   - The computer room?
   - The tape library?
   - The input control area?

5. Are portable fire extinguishers spread strategically around the computer center with location markers clearly visible over computer equipment?

6. If a central CO2 or Halon system is used, is it linked to an audible alarm?

7. Are there smoke detectors installed:
   - In the ceiling?
   - Under the raised floors?
   - In air return ducts?

8. Are there smoke detectors in both the computer room and the tape storage areas?

9. Do smoke detectors receive power from an independent power source?

Environmental Controls

10. Is there an alarm system connected to:
    - The building air conditioning system?
    - The computer room air conditioning system that sounds when the air conditioning is turned off?

11. Are any of the duct linings of the air systems combustible?

12. Is there a recording device that measures:
    - Temperature?
    - Humidity?

13. Is there an audible or visual alarm when temperature and humidity limits are exceeded?

14. Has emergency lighting been provided for the computer center that operates after the main power has been cut off?

15. Can the air conditioning system for the computer center (whether separate from or part of the central system) be shut off quickly and easily from within the computer center?

16. Do safes and vaults carry the Safe Manufacturers National Association (SMNA) or the Underwriters Laboratories (UL) seal?

Building Structure

17. Have all floors, including floor above and floor below (especially in a multiple tenant building) been checked to ensure adequate:
    • Fireproofing?
    • Waterproofing?
    • Noncollapsible support?

18. Are those doors that are necessary only as fire exits protected with exit alarms?

19. Are all exterior doors of sufficient strength to deter impulse intrusion (i.e., pushing)?

20. Does a solid wall surround the computer area?

21. Are there fire doors at the entrance to the computer room?

22. Is there a water sprinkler or Halon system installed?
    • In the stock room?
    • In the tape library?
    • In the computer room?

23. Is there a problem of water seepage:
    • Under the floor?
    • From condensation or leaks from overhead pipes?

24. Are there high-pressure steam lines or water lines adjacent to the computer room?

Checklist 2-7. Personnel security considerations.

1. Does the organization maintain good employee relations with motivation and loyalty?

2. Is there a known career path for employees?

3. Has any attempt been made to create and sustain employee interest in the prevention of fire and theft?

4. Have specific people been assigned duties in case of an emergency?

5. Have alternates been assigned to all jobs in case of absence of primary handler?

Checklist 2-7. Continued.

6. Are assignment records kept up-to-date?

7. Are programmers and operators transferred at reasonable intervals to handle different programs or to work on different shifts?

8. Are personnel trained to cover more than one function?

9. Are personnel given a debriefing before they leave?

10. Do personnel who have been terminated with cause leave immediately?

11. Are ID badges issued to company employees?

12. Is an employee's ID badge collected before he or she leaves the company?

13. Have any lectures been provided to the employees on the subject of fire and theft?

14. Is security education continuing?

15. Are programmers trained in backup procedures and recovery procedures?

16. Are operations personnel trained in security procedures for normal work flow?

Checklist 2-8. Software security considerations.

Controls

1. Does the system analysis and programming function have written guidelines for the development of procedures and programmed controls necessary for the detection and correction of errors?

2. Do users compare output from the computer center to their own control totals and initiate corrective measures?

3. Does the control group review console logs, error listings, or other error detection evidence to ensure that all detectable errors are reported, corrected, and reprocessed?

4. Has the system designer designated those files that are crucial for reconstruction, and backed them up?

5. Are source documents secured by the control function after data entry?

6. Has protection been standardized to protect crucial files against:
   - Programming errors?
   - Operator errors?
   - System errors?

7. Are batch programs run on a production schedule that is predetermined?

8. Do all cash receipts and disbursement applications, and other applications that process vital or confidential records, have the following controls:
   - Total dollar controls?
   - Counts of documents?
   - Matching and sequence checks?
   - Batch controls?
   - Total run controls?
   - Hash total controls?

Programming

9. Is the system flow of all programs documented before programming starts?

10. Are there programming rules for file handling?

11. Is a final program listing:
    - Created at the time of program?
    - Held in secure storage?
    - Periodically checked against the operating program?

12. Are all program changes made at the source level, then recompiled and tested?

13. Are changes to programs checked and approved by I/S audit and data processing managerial personnel before entry into the program library?

14. Are the changes approved and signed off by user personnel?

15. Is there audit trail information printed out in all financial systems?

16. Are adjustments printed out in detail with the audit trail?

17. Are lists of paid vendors printed out with the audit trail?

18. Are checks of unusual size listed in the audit trail?

19. Have the programs been tested with data with known output results?

20. Is all documentation current, and does it reflect the latest changes in systems and programs?

File Security

21. Does the organization have large, important databases?

22. Are the most important records maintained on magnetic files?

23. Are hard copy files maintained for all vital magnetic files?

Checklist 2-8. Continued.

24. Have files been classified as to importance, such as crucial, important, useful, or non-essential?

25. Are backup copies for all important files maintained off site:
    - Outside the computer center building?
    - Accessible with travel time of less than one hour round trip?
    - Served by a different municipal fire department unit?
    - Provided with assurance that only authorized personnel are allowed to enter the room where backup files are stored?
    - Security control entry procedure rehearsed at least twice a year to assure that authorized persons, and only authorized persons, are allowed to enter the restricted access room?

26. Are sufficient current generations of all important data files maintained?

27. Is the library (i.e., the data files and program storage facilities) segregated from the remainder of the computer center in a backup or secondary storage site?

28. Is access to the library restricted to designated librarians?

Documentation and Forms

29. Is there routine, formal approval of all system, program, and procedures documentation?

30. Are there run manuals for all operating programs containing:
    - Problem definition?
    - System description?
    - Program description?
    - Operating instructions?
    - Listing of controls?
    - Acceptance record?

31. Are duplicate master run manuals kept in a secure location?

32. Is there systematic program change control?

33. Are revised programs and revised documentation signed off by the user with details kept in a secure file?

34. Is documentation for the programs kept on tape?

35. Are manual procedures and data entry information included in the documentation?

36. Are blank checks secured in a locked facility and accessed only by authorized personnel?

37. Is there a forms control program with management support?

Audit

38. Does the I/S audit group formally approve each new cash receipts or disbursements system which is programmed (plus other applications where potential for theft or embezzlement exists) for sufficiency of controls, division of responsibilities, control totals, and other internal control features?

39. Are special audit programs occasionally used to verify the results of these programs (e.g., process payroll data through audit programs to check out the totals produced by the standard payroll programs)?

40. Audit trails:
    - Are there detailed audit trails prepared by these programs that record every transaction and enable reconstruction?
    - If cryptographic protection is available, does the I/S audit group specify and review all applications of cryptographic software and hardware?
    - Do all such applications automatically produce access journal (AJ) records?
    - Are the AJ records generated independently of system accounting data (e.g., in 370 Systems, SMF records, and accounting programs that utilize them)?

41. Have the internal or external auditors recently reviewed the procedures of the users and the control group to determine their adequacy?

Checklist 2-9. Data security considerations.

---

1. Have the values of the various data files been classified into the NFPA classes (i.e., vital important, useful, and nonessential), including:
   - Input records?
   - Source documents?
   - Control documents?
   - Magnetic tape/disk file records?
   - Programs?
   - Output data?

2. Is there understanding of and compliance with legal record retention regulations for:
   - Internal Revenue Service?
   - Insurance?

Checklist 2-9. Continued.

- Legal considerations?
- Customer/product history information?

3. Have the possible types of threats and vulnerabilities that your records/files might be exposed to been evaluated for:
   - Data entry errors?
   - Data transmission errors?
   - Mechanical malfunctions?
   - Program errors?
   - Updating of wrong file?
   - Computer operator errors?
   - Lost files?
   - Defective magnetic media?
   - Theft of records?
   - Criminal activity?
   - Loss by natural disaster?

4. Are duplicate copies of all vital records maintained?

5. Is a list of vital files maintained?

6. Is reconstruction capability maintained for magnetic files? (Possibly in the third-generation, son-father-grandfather, approach.)

7. Are daily file dumps and transaction files maintained for reconstruction purposes?

8. When magnetic files are copied for off-site storage, are the copies checked for:
   - Readability?
   - Accuracy?

9. Are the on-site and off-site magnetic media storage cabinets:
   - Fire resistant?
   - Smoke resistant?
   - Water resistant?
   - Movable so that they can be relocated quickly in the event of disaster?
   - Secure?
   - Fitted with casters for easy evacuation?

10. Are important records microfilmed as an additional means of providing backup?

11. Is there a procedure for evacuating the crucial files in case of emergency?

12. Is a paper shredder or an incinerator used for the disposal of:
   • Computer and typewriter carbon paper?
   • Old classified documents?
   • Program listings and test data?
   • Old reports?
   • Worn-out magnetic diskettes?
   • Microfilm?
13. Is access to information on PC databases controlled?
14. Are detailed transaction records kept for a "safe" period of time? (If a micro user is low on diskettes/cassettes, needed files are sometimes erased accidentally.)
15. Are there ways of ensuring that the correct version of the database file is being used?
16. Are outdated files controlled so they are not processed accidentally?
17. Does the software provide for internal label checking?
18. Have these magnetic media storage controls been considered?
   • Dust-free environment?
   • Fire rated, smoke and water resistant?
   • Lockable, if necessary?
   • Controlled access?
   • Off-site backups: extra copies of software, data files?
   • On-site backups: extra copies of software, data files?
   • Primary copies: handled and stored correctly while in use?
   • Sensitive information files kept separate and controlled?
   • Working files kept separate from scratch files?
   • Proper labeling?
   • Periodic inventory of media taken control?
   • Environmental controls safe temperature and humidity levels?
   • Media stored away from window ledges, magnetic devices?

Checklist 2-10. Operations security considerations.

1. Are operator instructions clear and complete, whether automated or not?

2. Do the operators have ready access to the complete Run manuals?

3. Are personnel prevented from examining or making changes in production state data or programs from system consoles?

4. Have computer center personnel been trained concerning the protection of confidential data?

5. Is a computerized job accounting system used as part of the operating system?

6. Are summary breakdowns of computer use routinely compared to detect deviations from normal patterns?

7. Is there an automated job production schedule?

8. Is the operations monitored for compliance with the schedule?

9. Are meter hours routinely correlated with utilization hours (elapsed time)?

10. Are all periods of downtime verified?

11. Are unexplained gaps in the recorded meter readings checked?

12. Is a detailed schedule of a shift prepared by authorized personnel?

13. Is shift performance checked against the schedule to detect deviations?

14. Is there a formalized procedure to assure that periodic checks are made to determine that:
    - Specific jobs were actually run by checking the outputs?
    - Individual run times conform to the schedule?
    - Frequency of runs of specific programs conforms to the schedule?
    - Total time charged to a specific program over a given time period is reasonable?
    - An unusual number of runs or amount of time has been charged to reruns?

15. Have the causes of reruns been analyzed and determine to be:
    - Program errors?
    - Input errors?
    - Hardware errors?
    - Operator errors?
    - Unclear instructions?

16. If there has been a large amount of rerun time, has corrective action been taken?

17. Is there tight physical and auditable control of checks, purchase orders, and other sensitive forms?

18. Is there an updated distribution list with control of all reports sent out?

Checklist 2-11. Data communications security considerations.

General Security

1. Is there a configuration chart showing:
   - Location of all terminals and connected microcomputer?
   - Number of lines?
   - Types of lines?
   - Location of modems?
   - Types of modems (by manufacturer/model)?
   - Distances of lines?
   - Branches off the main lines?
   - Cryptographic transformation facilities, if available?
   - Locally developed security software?
   - Software that has been crypto protected?
2. Is there a written procedure for what to do in case of an emergency affecting:
   - The data communication lines?
   - The modems?
   - The terminals and microcomputers?
3. Are the personnel who are trained in emergency procedures located in a centralized location as well as remote locations?
4. Are the data communication lines switchable in case one or more of them are down?
5. Are the lines switchable automatically under central control?
6. Did an auditor participate in the network systems design?
7. Has the scattering and loss of source documents been discussed with the auditors, and do programs give audit trails?
8. Is control and audit information supplied from both input transaction data and subsequent adjustments at distributed locations?
9. Are the telecommunications systems important enough to warrant the use of multiprocessor environment?

Checklist 2-11. Continued.
Terminal and PC Security

10. Are specific terminals and PCs designated "security" terminals and PCs?

11. At any time, do any of the "security" terminals and PCs operate in the unattended mode?

12. Is secure teleprocessed information transmitted on leased or dedicated lines?

13. If secure teleprocessed information is on dial-up lines, are checks made on access to it?

14. Are identification codes, passwords, or key words used, including terminal ID and operator ID?

15. Are these codes changed frequently?

16. Is there documented control of these codes or other security features in the teleprocessing system?

17. Is this documented control separate from the programming and operations group?

18. Is access to the system restricted to certain levels of employees?

19. Are there locks on the terminals or PCs when not in use?

20. If a series of errors, regardless of type, continue to be caused by an operator, what happens?

Data Security

21. Can master files only be updated from selected terminals or PCs?

22. Is paper tape, cards, magnetic tape, disk, etc., created first and then transmitted?

23. Are there programmed checks on the remote operators?

24. Are there programmed checks on the computer room operators?

25. Is sufficient audit trail material retained?

26. Is sufficient material retained to assure that nothing is lost during outages?

27. Can individual records be reconstructed if they are accidentally lost?

28. Is vital master information duplicated (e.g., routing lists, etc.)?

29. When all received messages are placed on file (tape disk), does the reference data contain:
    - The identification of the transmitting station (terminal)?
    - A message number of other means of identifying a message?

30. Are all data communication cables and transmission wires in weather-tight conduit?

31. Are all security lines within buildings secured by conduit?

32. Are all lines tested periodically to ascertain that they are good?

Communications Backup

33. Are there written backup procedures at all remote sites?

34. Are the backup procedures periodically tested?

35. Has a priority listing been established on all the teleprocessing work?

36. In case of disaster, would it be possible to transmit priority work via another communications system?

37. Is point-to-point vehicle pickup and delivery possible in case of emergency?

38. If the lines and/or terminals are down, is it possible to use the mails?

39. Has consideration been given to teleprocessing on a backup machine if the data center goes down?

40. Are there programs available that will handle teleprocessing jobs in batch mode on-site?

41. Have these programs been tested on both the primary and backup computer?

42. Have backup processing methods at the terminal ends been considered?

43. Is there routine logging of all transactions in a form that can be rapidly traced?

44. Are there checkpoints in large programs where the information is recorded on tape?

3

Personnel participation in the plan

A USEFUL DISASTER RECOVERY PLAN NEEDS COMMITMENT FROM senior management and the participation of the user departments in the planning. All organizational groups that might be affected or needed in any way should be brought into the planning phase of the project. This chapter covers some of the assignments and responsibilities of different groups in the organization. The types of information that must be requested by the study team also are listed.

The recovery operations should be planned and handled by teams with specific responsibilities. It is important to appoint an I/S disaster recovery coordinator. This person should chair the planning team meetings, and have the ongoing responsibility of assuring that the plan is periodically tested and updated. A position description for this person is supplied in this chapter. The coordinator works with the leaders of all the teams to develop the described plan for developing the disaster recovery plan.

The key team in a disaster is the initial response management team. This team is the first to review the service disruption incident and make the needed decisions regarding the level of response required.

Senior management commitment to the plan

There are good reasons for any organization to have an information services disaster recovery plan, and most of these reasons affect senior management directly. Some have already been discussed in chapter 2. They include:

- Preventing a disruption of the cash flow in the organization
- Protecting the vital records that are legally required to be kept safe and continuous
- Maintaining customer service, particularly to important customers
- Meeting the legal requirements of the Foreign Corrupt Practices Act of 1977
- Being free from customer suit because of the disruption of the operations
- Protecting the employees

Because of the sensitivity of the subject, senior management probably should not be approached for support until I/S management has a good idea of how strong its security is and what might be involved in a disaster recovery program. On the other hand, disaster recovery planning is a management, rather than a technical, issue. It deals with the realities of people, politics, and special interests. It cannot be accomplished properly without senior management support, and senior management must be approached as early as possible after the I/S management feels comfortable with the issues involved.

In most organizations, there are many groups who will have a direct interest in the I/S disaster planning, including:

- All user departments
- Security
- Medical
- Finance
- Legal
- Audit

- Labor relations
- Transportation
- Personnel
- Buildings
- Engineering
- Pubic relations

There is no way these groups can be made to work in concert without strong senior management commitment and an approved formal plan or action.

The I/S disaster recovery coordinator

Before starting to prepare a serious and detailed analysis of an I/S recovery plan, it is helpful to appoint a specific individual as the I/S Disaster Recovery Coordinator, or similar title. This can be a part-time job or a full-time job, but it focuses the effort and assigns responsibility. Figure 3-1, Disaster Recovery Coordinator Position Description, is an appropriate description of the job for a large organization. Smaller organizations can use a modified version of this description.

Fig. 3-1. Disaster recovery coordinator—position description.

Position Title:	Information Service Disaster Recovery Coordinator; or Disaster Recovery Planning Administrator, or Information Services Security Coordinator
Area:	Information Services Department
Reports to:	Senior Management of Information Services
Major functions:	Directs the planning, coordinating, implementing, testing, and training for all phases of the disaster recovery plan and its maintenance, and provides leadership for monitoring the status of the planning and testing process.

Position scope:

- Manages 1 to 6 exempt personnel; 1 to 3 nonexempt
- Coordinates with, and directs personnel from, all sections of Information Services and involved user groups.
- Responsible for the plan that can affect the entire Information Services operations, activities, and budget.

Special duties:

1. Directs the planning, development, and maintenance of an Information Services disaster recovery plan.
2. Follows up on the preplanning preparations required to implement the disaster recovery plan.

Fig. 3-1. Continued.

3. Chairs the planning meetings, and assures that each Team Leader accomplishes the agreed preplanning tasks.

4. Reviews the disaster recovery planning status, requirements, and relationships with other interested groups, such as administrative services, purchasing and supplies, transportation, insurance, and the local police, fire, and emergency services.

5. Inspects personally all physical installations and personnel arrangements related to the disaster plan, both in the data centers and the backup facilities, and discusses the plans and their implications with the responsible affected managers.

6. Maintains the plan on an ongoing basis, keeping the documentation updated and, in particular, corrected names, addresses, and telephone numbers of those with responsibility in the event of a disaster.

7. Assembles information on information services disaster recovery, and keeps files on vendors and equipment related to the activities.

8. Works closely with internal audit to test security measures and disaster recovery activities, and reports on the results to management.

9. Investigates other I/S security and recovery problems that cross departmental lines.

10. Checks periodically with outside groups, such as mutual aid groups and vendors, to reaffirm disaster aid arrangements.

11. Assembles and distributes literature on security and disaster recovery, and attends occasional meetings on the subject to keep abreast of the latest advances and concepts.

Experience and skills required:

General experience in computer operations, systems analysis, and programming.

Ability to communicate both the operational and technical meanings of data processing activities and problems to all levels of Information Services management and user management.

Awareness of potential environmental problems in the Information Services area, such as can occur in utility systems, building control and maintenance, and general security considerations.

The title given to the position depends on organizational policies and the size of the group to be formed. In small I/S facilities, it might be an extra job for an existing position. The position is required, however, to give visibility, continuity, and funding for the work to be done, particularly on an ongoing basis. The appointment is best made at the time of the initial task force studies, so the person can become familiar with all aspects of the plan and the reasons for the various decisions.

Some of the key duties of an I/S disaster recovery coordinator are:

- Take responsibility for following up on the preplanning required to create the disaster recovery plan

- Assemble information on I/S disaster recovery, and keep files on vendors

- Work closely with internal audit to test security measures and disaster recovery plans, and report on the results to management

- Maintain the plan on an ongoing basis, keeping the documentation updated, and, particularly, correcting names, addresses, and telephone numbers

- Investigate other I/S security problems that cross departmental lines

- Check periodically with outside groups, such as mutual aid groups and vendors, to reaffirm disaster aid arrangements

- Assemble and distribute literature on security and disaster recovery, and attend occasional meetings on the subject to keep abreast of the latest advances and thinking

The I/S disaster recovery coordinator position is primarily a staff job that is management related, but it requires a broad knowledge of computer technical considerations to understand what systems programming, operations, and other departments are doing. A supervisor in any of the I/S departments could be the coordinator. The position will have high visibility for the individual. It will entail detailed work more closely related to audit than I/S operations.

The coordination part of the job will be called for most particularly during the planning phase, when the person must do the following:

- Chair the planning meetings to see that everyone is headed in the same direction.

- Follow up with each team leader to see that the agreed preplanning tasks are accomplished.

- Obtain lists of all necessary staff addresses and home telephone numbers, and enter the information in the telephone lists directories. This might be a sensitive area because many people do not wish to release their home telephone numbers. The key people must do it.

- Check on whether schedules for testing sections of the plan have been developed and are being followed.
- Confirm the emergency recovery procedures with each participant, and modify as necessary.
- See that sufficient copies of the emergency recovery procedures are prepared and put into bright colored binders. Distribute these binders and request that team leaders take their copies home to be available in the event of an emergency situation.
- Have important elements of the emergency recovery procedures put up on the automated documentation system, if one is used, so that it is available at terminals.

The I/S disaster recovery planning team

For creation of the plan to develop the disaster recovery plan (The Plan for the Plan), the planning team will be a small group. They will have initial conversations with a number of managers to determine management intent for the plan and the possibilities that first appear to be open to the organization. They will develop a detailed project plan in the normal manner for planning projects in their organization.

Detailed project plan

The detailed project plan will be developed by the planning team to divide the effort into several phases, for ready reporting to management, and for keeping the study under control. These phases could include the following:

- Definition phase (objectives and assumptions)
- Functional requirements phase (fact gathering and decisions)
- Design and development phase (evaluation of alternatives)
- Implementation phase (creating the plan)
- Testing and monitoring phase (postdevelopment review)
- Maintenance phase (updating the plan)

More detail on these phases is given in Fig. 2-1, I/S Disaster Recovery Project Plan.

Commitment to the plan

After the project plan has been created, time and cost estimates must be made for its implementation. The planning team will have to go to management to determine if there is sufficient commitment to develop an adequate plan. If the commitment is forthcoming, the request can be made for full-time and part-time assignments for personnel from all parts of the organization. Some personnel might just be required to give interviews, others to make brief studies, and others to do detailed analyses. There will be sufficient effort involved for getting senior management approval at the start. Doors will be opened as needed.

The planning team might need only one of their members as a full-time participant, preferably the I/S disaster recovery coordinator. The others can discuss the problems or produce analyses as necessary or assign staff members to do the work.

A good plan will cost considerable money to develop and test. It should not be thought of as a quick-and-easy project.

Initial request for information

One of the first jobs of the I/S disaster recovery planning team is to gather as much existing documentation as possible and request ideas and comments from the users and the various I/S groups. The team should find that it has very little raw information gathering to do. Most of the information that the team requires should already exist as documentation somewhere in the I/S department. The team should, therefore, rapidly make out lists of requests for information tailored to each I/S group and distribute them to the appropriate supervisors. When the time comes to interview these group supervisors and discuss the plan with them, the supervisors might not have prepared all the material, but they will have at least started gathering it, and they will know generally what will be needed.

The types of information to be requested will vary greatly between different organizations. It will depend on the computers involved, the number of sites, and the work that has been done already on the backup storage. The information is simply basic data on what is involved so the team can grasp the size of the problem, the relationships involved, and a few of the facts. Figure 3-2, Requests for Information, illustrates typical lists for these early requests. These sample lists include:

- Computer operations documentation
- Application systems documentation
- User departments documention
- Technical support documentation
- Database administration documentation
- Office services documentation

Fig. 3-2. Requests for information.

REQUESTS FOR INFORMATION
Computer Operations Documentation

1. Computer facility layouts for all locations, including site plans, floor plans, and utility lines
2. Organizational chart, including a complete list of supervisors' names, addresses, and telephone numbers
3. Hardware configurations
4. List of hardware vendors and vendor contacts, including for data entry and other miscellaneous equipment
5. Emergency warning systems, emergency controls, emergency communications system in the organization
6. Assigned responsibilities for fire, safety, or other emergencies in both the organization and the I/S departments
7. Emergency and first aid equipment
8. Description of disc and tape files, including documentation of what is duplicated and off-site
9. Operating manuals and written procedures including powering down, emergency shutdown, safety rules, etc.
10. Inventory of paper and other supplies stored and their approximate weekly use

Application Systems Documentation

1. List of applications systems with:
   - Contact responsibility in I/S departments and user departments
   - Processing requirements and schedules
   - Number of PCs and terminals used
   - Program and data files
   - Checklist of documentation: list of programs; control of documentation
2. List of development, maintenance, and test work
   - Personnel
   - Computer requirements
3. List of software vendors and vendors contacts, including purchased or leased systems
4. Organizational chart, including a complete list of supervisors' names, addresses, and telephone numbers

User Departments Documentation

1. Statements concerning users' operational need for specific application systems

2. Requests for priorities for specific application systems at the time of disaster

3. Documentation regarding all systems that should be considered in disaster recovery planning, including:
   • Minicomputer centers and related equipment
   • Personal computers and other microcomputer equipment, such as plotters, etc.
   • LANs and connection to other communications networks
   • Related telephone equipment and services

4. User departments initial review of emergency possibilities, such as:
   • Operating with backup equipment at other specific sites
   • Moving operations to recovery sites or vendor sites
   • Using PCs in the employees' homes, etc.

5. List of vendors and vendor contacts for their systems

6. Organizational Chart, including a complete list of supervisors' names, addresses, and telephone numbers

Technical Support Documentation

1. Documentation of systems software for all computers, including a checklist of documentation and backups required

2. Priority list of applications to be run on backup computer

3. Teleprocessing plan between sites, including various alternatives such as possible reconfigurations of the communications network

4. Review emergency possibilities of:
   Moving some applications to timesharing services
   Moving some applications batch to other computers
   Using other similar computers in the geographic area

5. Backup plan for personal computers, word processing equipment, and other departmental equipment

6. Disaster coordination with a database group, including their plans for reestablishment of required databases

7. List of system vendors and vendor contracts

8. Organizational chart, including a complete list of supervisors' names, addresses, and telephone numbers.

Fig. 3-2. Continued.

Database Administration Documentation

1. General documentation of the priority databases:
   • Document both test and production databases

   • Identify applications on databases

   • Document current and projected size of databases
2. User department databases
3. Documentation of database software
4. List of database software vendors and vendor contracts
5. Organizational chart, including a complete list of supervisors' names, addresses, and telephone numbers.

Office Services Documentation

1. Organization policy statements and positions on the following:
   • Emergencies

   • Security

   • Civil preparedness
2. Organization emergency communications plans
3. Organization plans for protection of vital records and documents
4. Organization medical and first aid facilities
5. Industry or local area mutual aid arrangements
6. Available repair and restoration groups
7. Supplies storage facilities
8. Documentation of:
   • Office equipment required

   • Supplies and forms (estimate)
9. Organizational chart, including a complete list of supervisors names, addresses, and telephone numbers.

Staffing assignments and responsibilities
User department participation

User departments must accept a full role in the development of an I/S disaster recovery plan and be prepared to cooperate with staff at various levels as the planning for it proceeds. Most user departments have a number of smaller computers of their own. I/S facilities generally provide a service to one or more of the functional areas of their organization.

Occasionally, I/S facilities provide data processing support to several organizations. Recognition that the I/S shop is a support organization, not an end in itself, is essential to the generation of realistic, cost-efficient contingency plans.

Because the central I/S facility provides data, computing, and communications services, some of which are vital to the organizations, senior user management should realize the crucial nature of the dependence on contingency plans. Such plans serve to keep within tolerable limits the consequences of loss or damage to computer resources. Economic feasibility of contingency plans requires careful analysis of decisions as to what user functions are deferable, and for how long. The costs of these deferrals should be established by the users.

It is impossible for such decisions to be reached entirely within the I/S organization. I/S management usually is not in a position to accurately access the relative importance of all the work done for the supported areas. Further, the costs of the continued support of each, in the face of adversity, can vary widely. For these reasons, it is appropriate and important that senior user management provide direction and support for disaster recovery planning to provide essential functions following any disruption of the computer facilities. They also must assign knowledgeable individuals to work on details with the team throughout the planning and testing process.

Internal audit staff involvement

Internal audit staff have a crucial role to play in disaster recovery planning. They must be involved directly throughout the process, through to the final testing and maintenance.

Normally, internal audit will not be in charge of producing the plan because their prime function is to review it and comment on its adequacy. They should be involved at the earliest stages, however, to inform the team as to what administrative and accounting controls must be installed to give adequate internal control during a service disruption incident.

It must be recognized that adequate controls are more important during a disaster than at any other time. During normal operations, there is generally sufficient backup information available. If an application needs to be rerun, the data probably is still in existence, and the audit trail can be retracted and kept intact. During a disaster, however, data might have been lost, and it could even be unclear as to exactly when the event occurred during the process.

Audit trail programs and backup and recovery operations must take this problem into consideration. A disaster even could be caused by an employee to cover serious error, losses, or a defalcation. This should be kept in mind and guarded against.

Among the recognized management objectives for which internal control participation is relevant are:

- Maximizing profitability and minimizing cost
- Ensuring that management's policies and procedures are properly followed
- Ensuring that employees function within their scope of authority
- Ensuring the timely preparation of reports, reconciliations, reviews, and other procedures
- Providing for proper documentation procedures to help fix accountability and to substantiate transaction processing
- Ensuring reliability and consistency of accounting records
- Ensuring the prevention, detection, and correction of errors and irregularities
- Providing adequate security over assets including vital information
- Discharging statutory and regulatory agency responsibilities

Discussions should be held with the internal audit personnel regarding what part they should best play in the planning, when their input is appropriate, and when they should review the plan.

Involvement of other organizational departments

An I/S disaster recovery plan should be reviewed with nearly all other departments in the organization because they will either have a direct interest in the outcome (the user departments) or they have been assigned responsibilities that will include aspects of the plan. Such departments are:

User departments   They "own" the systems and have many computers themselves.

Security department   They normally will have security and disaster recovery plans for the organization as a whole, which should be tied in carefully to the I/S plans. Any fire alarm response plans, for example, normally will take precedence over all other plans because of the concern for safety of the employees.

Finance departments   They probably will be one of the largest users of I/S service and, hence, will be well represented in the planning.

Legal department   They should be asked what the legal aspects of handling a disaster are, including moves to other sites. They also should be asked to give management an opinion as to the applicability of the Foreign Corrupt Practices Act of 1977 and other appropriate legislation.

Audit departments   The necessary involvement of Internal Audit has already been covered. They also should be asked at what stage the external auditors should be brought in for discussion.

Medical departments   It should be made clear that personnel safety is paramount during a disaster. The medical department might want to discuss the effects of Halon and carbon dioxide, and the possible dangers from electricity in the computer facility. They should be asked how to handle medical problems at the backup sites.

Public relations department   No one should discuss any computer disasters with outsiders or the press without first consulting the public relations people. They will be responsible for any release of information outside the organization.

Labor relations department   In union situations, there might be a number of restrictions on how the emergency backup operations can be handled and the number of staff that is required at the various sites. Rushing between installations, and changing people's commute patterns, can affect them profoundly. Even in non-union situations, the disaster plan should be discussed with Labor Relations.

Transportation department   They will be a key factor in moving people and equipment, setting up deliveries of supplies in new patterns, and providing shuttle-bus service between the sites.

Personnel department   All aspects of the duties in the plan should be discussed with them. Eager planners can easily over extend their authority in the handling and assigning of people. Personnel will be interested in what types of calling-tree lists will be drawn up and readily available for people to peruse. There might be restrictions on what can be printed.

Engineering department   They normally will have had a part in the design of the facilities, the environmental controls, and the fire protection system. Much free advice is available to information service people on computing facility design, but it should be cleared with the engineering department. They also might be the best source of information as to available backup sites and how they could be prepared.

Buildings department   It is normally their responsibility to keep the buildings operating smoothly and to provide a number of services to this end. Because they work with the whole organization, I/S should discuss the plans with the buildings department to see if there are any unavailable services or actions being taken that could affect other departments harmfully.

Use of consultants or staff

Disaster recovery planning is no different from the many other technology-intense projects that confront I/S management. There always is a question as to whether to speed up the process by using consultants, or to train in-house personnel, go through the learning curve, and, hopefully, benefit from the knowledge retained in house. The advantages of using expert consultants are as follows:

- Past experience
- Rapid start
- Comparison with other installations
- Previously prepared plan details
- Objective viewpoint

The advantages of using in-house personnel are as follows:

- Rapid training and development in the area
- Retention of knowledge in the organization
- Intimate knowledge of many details
- The coordinator knows all aspects of the plan

The decision will be individual with each organization. Many organizations prefer a combination approach, using internal staff, but getting some consultant advice.

Organization for initial response to a disaster

The organization and procedures for the initial response to a disaster should be separate and distinct from the organization and activities of the disaster recovery teams. The initial response procedures should be in the front of the disaster recovery procedures, and they should:

- Be simple
- Be clearly understood by all staff
- Include a list of key management people to call
- Include the actions they will take

When the night watchman, a security guard, a computer operator, or anyone else, detects an apparent disastrous service disruption incident, they should know which management personnel to call, and in which order. They probably will refer to a posted list to do this.

Initial response management team

The initial response management team should not necessarily consist of all senior I/S management, although those people also will be called. It is most advantageous to gather a team consisting of managers in at least the following areas:

- Data center operations
- Systems programming
- Applications systems (covering the most crucial systems)

The disaster recovery procedures should include the home telephone numbers of the managers, plus the telephone numbers of alternatives in case the managers are not available at the time they are called. If a manager gets called, he or she should try to affirm that the others also have been called. The managers should proceed to the site of the disaster as rapidly as possible.

The purpose of the initial response management team is to make an evaluation of which part of the disaster recovery procedures to put into action, confirm their findings with management, and start any necessary actions.

Disaster recovery evaluation

The initial response management team will have a very broad understanding of all the I/S operations and procedures. They will be able to make an accurate technical estimation of the extent of the damages and the backup requirements immediately needed. They will know what responses to the event will be most advantageous.

Having agreed among themselves as to the best technical course of action, the initial response management team will report to senior I/S management, inform them of what has happened, and give them the agreed recommendations. In all likelihood, senior I/S management will have arrived on the scene by this time. Most disasters occur at night or on weekends because there are fewer people around to observe and handle incipient incidents than there are during the day. A small waste basket fire that could be doused with a pot of coffee in the morning working hours could get out of hand and destroy part of a building at night. Thus, this disaster recovery evaluation will likely take place during nonworking hours.

If the senior I/S management agrees with the initial response team's evaluation, management will give the signal to activate the recovery plans. If it is a small disaster, they might take action immediately. If it is a larger disaster, and the results will affect other departments, management probably will not take major actions until they have called and consulted with some senior officers of the organization. This will, of course, depend on circumstances. If it is a large fire, most other managers in the organization already will have been alerted. If the event is confined to the computer area, however, there might not be general knowledge of the fire in the first hours, even though it has the potential for affecting all business operations.

Activation of I/S disaster recovery teams

As soon as the initial response team's recommendations have been accepted or modified, and management has received necessary clearances and started the recovery plan in operation, the phone trees will start to activate all the I/S disaster recovery teams.

It is likely that members of the initial response team also will be leaders of specific disaster recovery teams, so little time should be lost in getting action started. If it is on a weekend or late at night, it could be that many people are unavailable on the first calls. It is general experience, however, that if sufficient people start the action plan, they can arrive quickly. Organizations with beeper systems, who can put out an automatic general alarm message to all beepers, can get a very rapid response.

Once the I/S disaster recovery teams are activated and informed of the course of action to take, they will be operating independently in parallel. A great deal of work will be accomplished in a short time if most people know their assigned tasks. Of course, they all will be routinely reporting to I/S senior management, who will coordinate the planned actions.

One useful concept is that of a disaster recovery control center where I/S management will be located to issue orders and take reports. It is better located in a conference room near the original site rather than near the backup site. The reason is that it will be simpler near the original site to keep in contact with all other departments in the organization. In addition, I/S staff members who had not heard of the disaster or orders probably would come by that way first.

If such a control center is planned and used, the greatest need is for several telephones. These should be located close together so that all management participants are informed of what the others are saying and doing. It is easier to have a conversation overheard than it is to repeat it. A number of telephone lines should be connected to the control center area early in the preparations.

I/S disaster recovery teams: organization and responsibilities
Considerations: Size of organization

The number of disaster recovery teams to be planned and given assignments naturally will depend on the size of the organization and the complexity of the operations. Figure 3-3, Information Services Disaster Recovery Teams, gives examples of how teams can be organized for different sized companies. Clearly, the organization of the teams must be selected by the classical approach of a reasonable "span of control." No one should have more than five people

Fig. 3-3. Information services disaster recovery teams.

Large Organization	Medium Organization	Small Organization
Facility Preparation		
Computer Operations		
	Data center	
Data input		
Data control		
Microcomputer systems		
		Data processing
New hardware selection		
Systems software		
Communications	Technical support	
Standards and procedures		
Training		
	Representative User Groups	
Application systems		
Database administration	Systems and programming	
New system development		
Administrative services		systems
Purchasing and supplies		
Transportation	Administration	
Insurance and salvage		
Internal audit		

reporting to him or her. A normal management pyramid structure can go to many levels. In an emergency, however, the fewer levels, the better to get the message across rapidly, and the span of control can be greatly increased.

Figure 3-4 shows an example of one way of planning the people required in a medium-sized I/S organization. This example is given to show the form of planning only. There is no description attached as to how this fits into any particular organization or grouping of teams. This type of worksheet will be specific to each organization.

Fig. 3-4. Typical staffing for information services.

	Day Shift	Evening Shift	Night Shift	Total
I/S management	2	1	-	3
Computer operations	9	6	6	21
Technical support	5	2	1	8
User representative	6	4	-	10
Systems and programming	6	2	2	10
Administrative & secretary	4	1	-	5
Total	32	16	9	57

Organization and responsibilities

The responsibilities, leadership, team members, management liaison requirements, disaster recovery functions, and the necessary pre-planning must be stated clearly for all teams so that the tasks and the boundaries are understood. The planning will be across department lines, but the activities to be handled for disaster recovery must be strictly defined. Figures 3-5 through 3-23 give nineteen examples that fit the large organization of Fig. 3-3. For an organization, these will be developed to name specific individuals, specific locations, and functions unique to that group. These examples can be used as a base to start the planning.

Fig. 3-5. Facility preparation team.

1. Responsibilities:
   - Arrange for final selection of equipment and services at the backup site.
   - Prepare the backup site for operation.
   - Participate in the occupation of the backup site.
   - Administer the reconstruction of the original site for recovery and re-occupation.
2. Team leader:
   - Manager in either data center operations or engineering staff
3. Team members:
   - Operations supervisors
   - Communications supervisors
   - Engineering staff
   - Real estate and buildings staff
4. Management liaison:
   - Real estate manager
   - Engineering manager
5. Disaster recovery functions:
   - Obtain final decision on site selection from I/S management.
   - Plan required power, heating, air conditioning, and telephone lines; install as many lines and services as possible.
   - Work with communications team to have lines ready for rapid activation.
   - At time of disaster, activate the electrical, heating, communications, telephone, and environmental services.
   - As soon as backup site is occupied, work with salvage team to clean up original site. Determine requirements.
   - Work with engineering and other services to prepare the original site for reoccupation and recovery.
6. Preplanning required:
   - Obtain space, power, communications, and utility requirements for a site.
   - Reduce list of backup sites for reasonable selection.
   - Draw up floor plans with operations people.
   - Establish minimum requirements for office space, furniture, supplies, and ancillary equipment.
   - Work with purchasing and supplies to see that they prepare a list of emergency suppliers of the items needed.

Fig. 3-6. Computer operations team.

1. Responsibilities:
   - Work with facility preparation team to assemble the necessary computer hardware at the new sites.
   - Bring up and operate the new computers, communications, and data input facilities to meet the minimum processing requirements.
2. Team leaders:
   - Data center operations manager
3. Team members:
   - Buildings and facilities
   - Communications, data input, and data control managers
   - Operations supervisors
4. Management liaison:
   - Communications manager
   - Engineering manager
5. Disaster recovery functions:
   - Get sites ready for hardware, communications, data handling, and personnel.
   - Order necessary computer equipment and data preparation equipment from emergency vendor contacts.
   - Notify staff to report to new sites.
   - Establish processing schedule and inform user contacts.
   - Work with CEs to bring up and test computers and communications.
   - Arrange for necessary supplies.
   - Bring up systems in priority sequence.
   - Supervise operation of equipment.
6. Preplanning required:
   - Work with facility preparation team to check backup sites for power, communications, and environmental requirements.
   - Draw up tentative floor plans and disaster office arrangements.
   - Keep list current and handy of all supplier contacts and emergency numbers.
   - Keep a current list of staff who might be required in an emergency, including home telephone numbers.
   - Define computer supplies requirements and notify purchasing and supplies.

Fig. 3-7. Data input team.

1. Responsibilities:
   - Reestablish data input and preparation services to meet the processing requirements.
2. Team leader:
   - Data input manager
3. Team members:
   - Data input supervisors
   - Key entry operators
   - User groups that are handling their own data entry
4. Management liaison:
   - Data center operations manager
   - Crucial user group managers
5. Disaster recovery functions:
   - Determine the availability of resources.
   - Arrange for data input where it can be handled, possibly at vendor locations, other cooperating companies, or emergency sites.
   - Notify staff where they will report for work, arranging for transportation through the transportation team.
   - Obtain backup program tapes and keying instructions at the new sites.
   - Prepare revised production schedules.
   - Ensure that user liaison know how their input will be handled.
   - Supervise data preparation with the new arrangements, probably at more than one site.
6. Preplanning required:
   - Check with vendors to see if they have identical data input equipment available at other locations at times of emergency.
   - Discuss, with other users of the same data input equipment, whether mutual arrangement can be made to use each other's equipment at times of emergency, probably at off-shift hours.
   - Keep a current list of equipment configurations and documentation of programs.
   - Keep a current list of staff who might be required in an emergency, with home telephone numbers.
   - Keep a current list of vendor contacts and compatible installation contacts.
   - Ensure that there is safe off-site storage of backup program tapes and keying instructions.

Fig. 3-8. Data control team.

1. Responsibilities:
   • Reestablish the data control function for all necessary systems at the backup sites.
2. Team leader:
   • Data control manager
3. Team members:
   • Data input supervisor
   • Scheduling supervisor
   • Data control staff
4. Management liaison:
   • Crucial user group managers
   • Data center operations manager
5. Disaster recovery functions:
   • Notify staff to report to backup sites.
   • Obtain backup documentation and establish center at backup site.
   • Notify users how their input will be handled.
   • Reestablish input and output control functions.
6. Preplanning required:
   • Define forms usage and determine that backup supplies will be available.
   • Ensure that documentation is stored off-site.
   • Keep a current list of staff who might be required in an emergency, with home telephone numbers.
   • Keep a current list of user contacts and their telephone numbers.

Fig. 3-9. Microcomputer systems team.

1. Responsibilities:
   • Reestablish required minicomputer and microcomputer operations either at the backup site or with new equipment brought in to a number of sites.
2. Team leader:
   • Microcomputer coordinator
3. Team members:
   • Data center operations manager
   • Key user supervisors

4. Management liaison:
   - Crucial user group managers
5. Disaster recovery functions:
   - Determine the variety and extent of damages to the various minicomputer operations.
   - Arrange with administrative services for the necessary backup locations.
   - Arrange with vendors for delivery of replacement equipment.
   - Bring up and test the various minicomputer operations needed.
6. Preplanning required:
   - Keep a current list of all required minicomputer and microcomputer operations with details of the equipment installed.
   - Keep a current list of vital minicomputer and microcomputer user contacts with their home telephone numbers.
   - Keep a current list of all vendor emergency contacts.
   - Ensure that equipment information and program documentation is stored off site.

Fig. 3-10. New hardware selection team.

---

1. Responsibilities:
   - Obtain the required new hardware, in the planned configurations, to meet the necessary processing requirements. This may entail more than one site, and it may entail some use of salvaged hardware.
2. Team leader:
   - Technical support manager
3. Team members:
   - Data center operations manager
   - Planning manager
   - Administrative services manager
4. Management liaison:
   - Finance department
   - Administration
5. Disaster recovery functions:
   - Locate the new hardware needed to meet the required processing needs.
   - Arrange with vendor contacts to ship the new hardware as it is being ordered. This will include computers, communications

Fig. 3-10. Continued.

equipment, and ancillary equipment, such as photocopies, microfilming, paper handling, etc.

- Arrange with the Transportation and Facilities Teams to handle the new equipment and set it up at backup sites.
- Supervise the hardware installation, testing, and turnover.

6. Preplanning required:
   - Ensure that the minimum configurations needed are defined.
   - Ensure that the systems programmer knows the configurations for preparation.
   - Establish contact with vendors, brokers, and dealers, and keep a current list of their emergency numbers.
   - Keep a current list of operations supervisors and other I/S personnel home telephone numbers that might be required in an emergency.

Fig. 3-11. Systems software team.

---

1. Responsibilities:
   - Supply working versions of the required operating systems, JCL's, and other control systems at the backup sites.
2. Team leaders:
   - Systems software manager
3. Team members:
   - Database administration manager
   - Vendor's software CEs
   - Systems software staff
4. Management liaison:
   - Data center operations manager
   - Technical support manager
   - Applications systems manager
5. Disaster recovery functions:
   - Generate the required systems and restore the functions in priority order at the backup sites.
   - Gather all operating systems program listings on microfiche or other media at the backup site.
   - Strip out information from backup tapes as required.
   - Supervise systems generation to accommodate new configurations and the restoration of systems at whatever sites are required.

- Supervise the rerunning of previous runs for testing and debugging.

6. Preplanning required:
    - Establish the expected emergency configurations for hardware and communications at the backup sites.
    - Confirm the priority list of systems to run during emergency operations.
    - Do as much planning and preprogramming as possible for the emergency configurations.
    - Ensure that all current systems information is backed up off site.
    - Keep a current list of staff who might be required in an emergency with home telephone numbers.
    - Keep a current list of vendor software contacts who might be needed.

Fig. 3-12. Communications team.

---

1. Responsibilities:
    - Arrange for new communications facilities and a communications network.
2. Team leader:
    - Communications manager
3. Team members:
    - Technical support manager
    - Data center operations manager
    - Company communications manager
    - Systems software manager
4. Management liaison:
    - Company communications department
    - Buildings and engineering departments
5. Disaster recovery functions:
    - Evaluate the extent of damage to the communications network and discuss alternate communications arrangements with the telephone company and internal communications supervisors.
    - Develop immediate network changes to bring up the required operations.
    - Supervise the line and equipment installation for the new network.

Fig. 3-12. Continued.

- Order the telecommunications lines and equipment as required.

6. Preplanning required:
  - Establish the expected emergency configurations for hardware and communications lines.
  - Prepare a communications plan for a number of disaster scenarios and keep the plan current.
  - Establish minimum equipment needs and telephone requirements.
  - Preinstall as many telephone lines as possible in conformance with the plan at the backup sites.
  - Keep a current list of other contacts for calling in an emergency, including the telephone company.

Fig. 3-13. Standards and procedures team.

---

1. Responsibilities:
   - See that all documentation for standards, procedures, systems, programs, forms, etc., are reassembled as required at the backup sites.

2. Team leader:
   - Standards and procedures supervisor

3. Team members:
   - Librarian
   - Forms supervisor
   - Training supervisor

4. Management liaison:
   - Data entry operations manager
   - Technical support manager
   - Systems and programming manager
   - Purchasing and supplies manager

5. Disaster recovery functions:
   - Assemble from backup storage the necessary documentation for all involved departments.
   - Work with purchasing and supplies to assure that all necessary forms are taken to the backup site or ordered from vendors.
   - Set up documentation library and forms control facilities as soon as it is convenient, without interfacing with higher priority operations.

6. Preplanning required:
   - Maintain lists and backup copies of all required standards procedures, systems, programs, forms, training material, etc.
   - Determine what materials might be required in the event of an emergency.
   - Periodically review the stored backup material to see that it is current.
   - Keep a current list of telephone numbers of staff contacts and vendor contacts.

Fig. 3-14. Training team.

---

1. Responsibilities:
   - Arrange for continued training at off-site facilities or vendor locations.
2. Team leader:
   - Training supervisor
3. Team members:
   - Standards and procedures supervisor
4. Management liaison:
   - Managers with personnel in training.
5. Disaster recovery functions:
   - Assemble from backup storage or arrange with vendors for the necessary training materials for immediate requirements.
   - Set up a training room, if required, and obtain necessary equipment.
6. Preplanning required:
   - Maintain lists, and backup copies if possible, of all required training materials, and keep off site.
   - Keep a current list of telephone numbers of staff contacts and vendor contacts.

Fig. 3-15. Teams from representative user groups.

---

1. Responsibilities:
   - To represent the requirements of the user departments that are involved, and to put forward the concerns and priorities of those departments.
   - To assure that the plans and preparations for Information Services disaster recovery are conveyed to their department management, and that some action is taken in the department involved.

2. Team leader:
   - Selected by the management of the department involved, after discussion with Information Services representatives.

3. Team members:
   - Selected by the management of the department involved, after the requirements have been described to them.

4. Management liaison:
   - Both their own management and Information Services management.

5. Disaster recovery functions:
   - To represent their department in all disaster recovery planning discussions.
   - To emphasize the operational need of specific application systems considered important by their department, and to work for their priority consideration by the planning group.
   - To consider the implications of an Information Services disaster on all the programs and systems in their department.
   - To supervise the testing and resumption of critical operation for programs in their department.

6. Preplanning required:
   - Assure the adequate coordination of the Information Services disaster recovery plan with their departments.
   - Assure that there has been adequate documentation of all of their department's programs, systems, equipment, and communications systems.
   - Review the file backup and retention arrangements for each of their department's systems.
   - Review the emergency arrangements with their departmental managers and users.
   - Keep a current list of departmental staff who may be required in an emergency, with their home addresses and telephone numbers.
   - Keep a current list of vendor contacts for hardware systems and packaged programs, with emergency telephone numbers.

Fig. 3-16. Application systems team.

1. Responsibilities:
   - Support operable versions of all applications systems needed to satisfy the minimum operating requirements.
2. Team leader:
   - Systems and Programming Manager of the critical systems.
3. Team members:
   - Database administrations manager
   - Other systems and programming managers
   - Systems programmer
   - Technical support analyst
   - Internal audit manager
4. Management liaison:
   - User managers of the crucial systems.
5. Disaster recovery functions:
   - Obtain backup programs, files, and listings from off-site storage, and transfer them to the backup sites.
   - Work with systems programming in reestablishing software and procedure librarians, and restoring user packs and tapes.
   - Supervise the testing and resumption of important processing.
6. Preplanning required:
   - Ensure program, file, and documentation off-site backup arrangements.
   - Review each system's file backup and retention arrangements.
   - Review application JCL to reduce device dependency.
   - Review emergency arrangements with systems programming.
   - Keep current list of staff who might be required in an emergency with their home telephone numbers.
   - Keep current list of vendor contacts for package programs with emergency telephone numbers.

Fig. 3-17. Database administration team.

1. Responsibilities:
   - Bring up, test, and support an operable version of the database required at the backup site to meet the minimum operating requirements.
2. Team leader:
   - Database administration manager

Fig. 3-17. Continued.

3. Team members:
   - Systems and programming managers
   - Systems programmer
   - Internal audit manager

4. Management liaison:
   - User managers of the crucial systems.

5. Disaster recovery functions:
   - Obtain backup database and documentation and transfer them to the backup sites.
   - Bring up an operable version of the database, and test it against a previous run.
   - Work with systems programming in reestablishing the operations.
   - Supervise the testing and the resumption of the use of the database.

6. Preplanning required:
   - Ensure current database and documentation for off-site backup arrangements.
   - Review the requirements for emergency operation with systems programming.
   - Keep a current list of staff and vendor contacts who might be required in an emergency with their telephone numbers.
   - Plan for a variety of scenarios and contingencies.

Fig. 3-18. New system development team.

---

1. Responsibilities:
   - Restart the development of new systems as soon as possible after the disaster event. This might include waiting for space on the backup computers using service bureaus or timesharing.

2. Team leader:
   - Systems and programming manager of development

3. Team members:
   - Other systems and programming managers
   - Systems programmer
   - Technical support analyst

4. Management liaison:
   - User managers of the systems being developed.

5. Disaster recovery functions:
   - Contact and move staff into office as assigned.
   - Support the emergency recovery procedures as required.
   - Contact other sites or other sources for computer use.
   - Arrange to transfer the files and documentation, and possibly people, to the available sites.
   - Supervise as much recovery of system development as is possible.
6. Preplanning required:
   - Ensure program, file, and documentation of off-site backup arrangements.
   - Review the file backup and retention arrangements of each system under development.
   - Review application development JCL to reduce device dependency.
   - Review emergency arrangements with systems programming.
   - Keep a current list of staff who might be required in an emergency, with their home telephone numbers.
   - Keep a current list of vendor contacts for package programs with emergency telephone numbers.

Fig. 3-19. Administrative services team.

---

1. Responsibilities:
   - Arrange for all necessary office support services, and supply administrative support to other teams.
2. Team leader:
   - Administrative services manager
3. Team members:
   - Managers of office support functions.
4. Management liaison:
   - All information services managers
   - Company administrative services manager
5. Disaster recovery functions:
   - Provide administrative support functions as required.
   - Provide secretarial support at the various sites.
   - Contact all secretaries and clerical personnel involved, and arrange for their office locations and transportation to those locations.

Fig. 3-19. Continued.

- Contact vendors of office equipment and services to arrange bursting, collating, envelope stuffing, mailing, photocopying, printing, reproducing, etc., as might be required at off-site locations.
- Notify post office of new delivery address.
- Set up required internal mail and delivery systems.
- Expedite authorization of expenditures by other teams.
- Record emergency extraordinary costs and expenditures.

6. Preplanning required:
   - Prepare and maintain a list of vendors and service suppliers who can provide the necessary office support services on an emergency basis.
   - Prepare a list of contacts in other organizations who could help in an emergency by supplying off-shift use of word processing equipment, for example.
   - Maintain a detailed list of all office supply materials that might be required.
   - Keep a current list of staff who might be required in an emergency with home telephone numbers.

Fig. 3-20. Purchasing and supplies team.

---

1. Responsibilities:
   - Provide all needed office space and operating supplies at the backup sites.
   - Supply or purchase desks, fixtures, and other equipment that might be needed.
   - Supply emergency food services and housing as required.

2. Team leaders:
   - Purchasing and supplies manager

3. Team members:
   - Purchasing and supplies staff

4. Management liaison:
   - Other information services manager
   - Corporate building and supplies personnel

5. Disaster recovery functions:
   - Contact the local management at all sites to be used and arrange for the bringing in of equipment, communications lines, personnel, and supplies.

- Obtain all needed operating supplies, furniture, and other equipment, and arrange for transportation and installation at the emergency sites.
- Salvage available stores, and set up new stores delivery systems.
- Arrange for the supply of emergency food services and any housing that might be required.

6. Preplanning required:
   - Prepare a list of contacts for supplying rental or used office furniture and supplies.
   - Prepare list of supplies consumed each week by I/S departments.
   - Set up an off-site emergency stockpile of consumables to cover the lead time taken to reorder and deliver.
   - Prepare a list of contacts for supplying emergency food services and housing.
   - Keep a current list of staff who might be required in an emergency with home telephone numbers.

Fig. 3-21. Transportation team.

---

1. Responsibilities:
   - Provide transportation for people between the old and new sites.
   - Provide transportation for equipment and supplies as required.
   - Set up a car and van system for staff commuting between the new and old sites.
2. Team leader:
   - Transportation manager
3. Team members:
   - Purchasing and supplies manager
   - Administrative service manager
4. Management liaison:
   - Other information service managers
   - Corporate transportation personnel
5. Disaster recovery functions:
   - Arrange transportation for materials, salvaged hardware, personnel, and computer media.
   - Arrange a car and van system for staff, equipment, supplies, and computer media moving between different locations in the organization.

Fig. 3-21. Continued.

- Arrange a scheduled van system for staff who do not have their own cars or can only conveniently commute to the old site.
6. Preplanning required:
  - Prepare a list of contacts for supplying rental trucks, vans, cars, and any other vehicles which may be needed.
  - Prepare a list of contacts for supplying drivers in an emergency.
  - Keep a current list of staff who may be required in an emergency, with home telephone numbers.

Fig. 3-22. Insurance and salvage team.

---

1. Responsibilities:
  - Appraise the damage, minimize further losses, and salvage what can be saved.
  - Make a detailed accounting of the damage to aid in insurance claims.
2. Team leader:
  - Administrative service manager
3. Team members:
  - Other I/S managers
  - Administrative services staff
  - Company insurance staff
  - Engineering and buildings staff
4. Management liaison:
  - V. P. administration
  - Company insurance manager
5. Disaster recovery functions:
  - Identify materials and hardware to be salvaged.
  - Help prevent further damage.
  - Supply information for initiating insurance claims.
  - Meet for discussions with loss adjusters.
  - See that insurance is arranged for the new site and equipment.
6. Preplanning required:
  - Review insurance coverage with the insurance department and become familiar with the important details.
  - Prepare a list of contacts for handling the salvage work in an emergency. (The most important salvage will be vendor equipment, which will be handled by vendor personnel.)

Fig. 3-23. Internal audit team.

---

1. Responsibilities:
   - Ensure that the conversion to the backup operation is under sufficient audit control to provide reliability and consistency to the accounting records.
   - Ensure that the necessary supervision and controls are in place during the backup operation.
2. Team leader:
   - Internal audit manger
3. Team members:
   - Internal audit staff
4. Management liaison:
   - Finance management
   - External auditors
5. Disaster recovery functions:
   - See that the necessary controls have been embedded in the system for preparing routine backup media.
   - Determine which areas have had destruction of data input, computer media, and recent output files.
   - Run audit tests on the first backup runs shortly after they have been produced.
   - Perform a detailed audit review of the important accounting files after the first backup cycle has been completed.
6. Preplanning required:
   - Establish a strong control environment in the I/S activities.
   - Work with systems analysis and programming to identify control points in the business systems and to design and document the controls.
   - Arrange for sufficient routine collection of control information so that there is a clear trail to the point of disaster and comparable information gathered on the backup systems.

4

Requirements and necessary strategy decisions

THIS CHAPTER COVERS THE TECHNICAL AND ECONOMIC ANALYSIS required for developing a disaster recovery plan. It describes many of the steps required of the I/S disaster recovery planning team and those analysts who work on specific sections of the plan. It discusses many of the important, strategy decision steps that need to be made in the process and gives methods to handle them.

Assembly of the Planning Team gives an overview of organizing a disaster recovery study, and a summary of the requirements and decisions that will be discussed in this chapter.

Development of the Project Plan emphasizes the need for planning, control, and management approval of this major planning effort.

Objectives of the Disaster Recovery Plan covers this first, and most important step in the definition phase of planning for disaster recovery.

Disaster Recovery Plan Assumptions is another basic step that must be reviewed by the analysts with management before too much detailed planning is done.

Types of Disaster to Consider reviews the more commonly expected types of disaster, points out how to decide the most probable disaster occurrences, and gives general material from the Civil Defense Preparedness Agency on disasters.

Selecting the Key Disaster Scenario points out the advantage of agreeing on such a scenario as a base assumption for the creation of a recovery plan, and as a point of comparison for the initial response team.

Assessment of the Resource Requirements briefly outlines the extensive analyses that must be made by technical staff in determining the priorities and requirements for all systems, equipment, and other resources. Several checklists are provided.

Assembling the planning team

The first steps in developing an information service disaster recovery plan are to:

- Obtain management understanding and commitment (chapter 2)
- Decide on organization and responsibilities (chapter 3)

Management commitment usually comes from a feasibility study by an initial planning group. A general evaluation of needs is made. The adaptability of existing policies and programs is reviewed. The probable level of necessary disaster recovery measures is estimated. Managers are interviewed regarding their concerns and priorities.

This initial analysis, and preparation for a project to be planned, usually is conducted by line management in I/S, possibly with the help of internal audit. If it is politically expedient, consultants can be brought in to bridge the differences of opinion that will exist. The initial plan is not a detailed technical analysis (as will be discussed later in this chapter), but is a management appraisal of the need for a disaster recovery plan, and the probable time and costs involved.

Organization of the planning results from the management commitment. An I/S disaster recovery coordinator usually is appointed, an I/S disaster recovery planning team established, and the detailed analytical work commences.

The first step is to create a detailed project plan for the disaster recovery planning effort. Further management commitments are obtained. Initial requests for information are distributed. The involvement of other organizational departments is agreed upon, and the lengthy, detailed, technical planning work is then assigned, as detailed in chapter 3.

This chapter is concerned with that detailed, technical planning work that is fundamental to an operable plan. It principally covers Phase 2, Functional Requirements Definition, and Phase 3, Design and Development of the I/S Disaster Recovery Project Plan, as outlined in chapter 2. Part of the work of the experts, however, is to create that project plan initially. It is not enough to start analyzing the difficult and complex data processing problems that must be faced. To be effective, the analysis must be done according to a systematic and balanced project plan.

Figure 4-1 outlines the technical analysis work that must be accomplished by the planning team, and the strategic decisions that must be made, based upon the analysis that is done. This figure also is an outline of the subject matter in this chapter.

Fig. 4-1. Analysis of requirements and strategy decisions.

1. Assemble the I/S disaster recovery planning team.
2. Develop an I/S disaster recovery project plan:
   * Outline the proposed scope of the plan.
   * Estimate the time and cost of preparation.
   * Get management approvals for the planning process.

Plan phase I—definition

3. Establish the objectives of the information services disaster recovery plan (chapter 1).
4. State the preliminary assumptions and definitions regarding the plan.
5. Determine the types of disaster to consider.
6. Decide on the most probable disaster occurrences.
7. Develop a key disaster scenario.

Plan phase 2—determination of functional requirements

8. Access the resource requirements for the crucial applications.
   * **Application system requirements:**
     ~ Analyze each crucial application system.
     ~ Determine the service availability requirements of the systems.
     ~ Develop a priority list of the systems.
     ~ Decide on the audit control requirements of the systems.
   * **Data and software requirements:**
     ~ Document the data file requirements of the crucial systems.
     ~ Document the database requirements.
     ~ Document the current status of off-site file backup.
     ~ Document the current status of the program library.
     ~ Document the flow of the crucial systems.
     ~ Obtain agreements with the users and owners of purchased software.

Fig. 4-1. Continued.

- **Vital records requirements:**
  ~ Develop a control list of all vital records.

  ~ Develop a records retention analysis for the crucial systems.
- **Hardware and communications requirements:**
  ~ Document the hardware requirements for the existing operation.

  ~ Determine the off-site hardware requirements.

  ~ Determine the microcomputer, mini-computer, and terminal requirements.

  ~ Determine the communication network requirements.

  ~ Determine the above requirements in each user department.
- **Other resource requirements for disaster recovery backup operation.**

9. Analyze the Established Requirements and Facilities Against the Plan Objectives (Step 3 above):
   - Set resource preparation priorities.
   - Establish a time frame for disaster recovery according to importance of application.

Plan phase 3—design and development

10. Select appropriate recovery strategies:
    - Evaluation of alternative recovery strategies
    - Service degradation strategies
    - Internal recovery strategies
    - Commercial recovery strategies
    - Cooperative recovery strategies
    - Combination of recovery strategies

11. Prepare a cost analysis for disaster recovery operation:
    - Cost of possible losses
    - Probability of occurrence of loss
    - Probable economic loss
    - Cost of planned measures for disaster recovery
    - Potential vendors and the cost of their services

12. Develop a risk management and insurance coverage analysis:
    - Possible losses and necessary controls
    - Insurance portfolio
    - Actions to be taken after a loss occurs

13. Perform a risk analysis, if appropriate.

Developing the project plan

The first task of the I/S disaster recovery planning team is to develop a project plan for the disaster recovery plan. The necessary ingredients of such a plan were outlined in Fig. 2-1, I/S Disaster Recovery Project Plan. The organization to handle such a plan was described in chapter 3, I/S Disaster Recovery Planning Team.

A subset of such an approach can be taken if the purpose is simply to develop a short-term, high-impact plan, rather than a full disaster recovery plan. The project plan should concentrate on the scope of the planning effort, the time and cost of the plan preparation, and the steps that will require management approval.

The outline of the proposed scope of the plan should state all departments and organizational groups that will be affected by the plan, and who must cooperate with it for it to be a success. It should state clearly the data processing resources and the operating applications that must be considered in the planning.

The estimate of time and cost of the plan preparation should not be too conservative, but should consider the efforts of all persons who might be asked to participate in the planning. The bulk of the work might be handled by technical support personnel and senior systems analysts who are not part of the planning team.

The desired *sign-offs*, or points of management approval, should be clearly stated up front. The planning process would not have started if senior management had not become interested in the problem. While the interest is still warm, the concerned managers should be asked to give their approval to the types of activities that are necessary to create an adequate plan. This approval should be made known to the people it affects, who will be asked for support later. A plan is useless if it is created in a vacuum by a small team, and is never laid on the table in front of those who will be affected by it, and must participate in it.

The best time for high visibility for the disaster recovery planning team is usually during the development of the project plan. They should make the most of their opportunity, and get promises of support and cooperation in the various stages of the planning process. In many installations, an effective plan will take several weeks of analysis and discussion. Interest will lag as the process unfolds. Commitment must be established at the beginning, and it can be referred to later, as help is needed.

Objectives of the disaster recovery plan

It was pointed out previously that "the objectives of Information Service Disaster Recovery Plan are to make sufficient agreed-upon preparation, and to design and implement a sufficient set of agreed-upon procedures, for responding to a disaster of any size in the Information Services area of responsibility." The purpose of these procedures is to minimize the effect of a disaster on the operations of the organization. The emphasis should be on safeguarding the vital assets of the particular organization, however, these general objects must be stated specifically, referring to the realities that are facing the planning team.

This is the first step in the Definition Phase for developing an I/S disaster recovery plan (see Fig. 4-1).

There are many decisions to be made as the planning process starts. Some questions that arise are:

- What types of disaster are we talking about?
- What are, realistically, the crucial resources and applications?
- What types of strategies are available to us?
- What are the possible costs and losses for different recovery measures?

The planning team must develop initial answers to such questions rapidly so that management will understand the worth of the project and how much effort to put into it. The team's study and analysis will lead to more accurate statements and more refined estimates. Management will be able to make decisions regarding further funding for the project. It is most difficult to guess what will be needed without going through a detailed analysis.

Objectives of the planning will vary with each organization. Some organizations will have exceedingly crucial applications that must be kept running to avoid severe penalties and losses to the company. Others will have useful applications with little time demands, and these organizations might rely more on insurance and a reasonable recovery process. The planning team cannot depend on its own experience and values to determine the objectives. They must develop the objectives based ·on knowledge gained during management interviews.

Study team members might come from a technical computer background, and might be surprised at the more important concerns and priorities of management. Frequently, the safety and preservation of the complex systems analysis and development programming work is far down on the list of priorities. Managers will be interested primarily only in the necessary plan to maintain the profitability of the organization, and to keep themselves free from legal suit in the event of a disaster.

The first step in the preparation of the plan is to make an initial statement of the objective of the planning process. These objectives must come directly as a result of the management interviews. The objectives are preliminary statements of the reason for the planning work, and can be modified at a later date, after much of the planning has been accomplished and the managers have become much more aware of the factors involved.

The objectives can be stated in a variety of ways, depending on the organization. Some examples of the types of objectives that can be used are:

- To maintain customer service at an acceptable level
- To keep operations running smoothly with less than an "x" hour break in computer services
- To meet all legal requirements for continuity of service
- To assure management that the Foreign Corrupt Practices Act requirements have been met adequately
- To handle an interruption and change of computers with a satisfactory audit trail
- To keep any disaster loss below "x" dollars

The objectives are statements of management intent for the smooth operation and profitability of the organization. The objectives and the assumptions that are decided on should be approved by management before the planning work proceeds.

Disaster recovery plan assumptions

Most planning groups will find themselves faced with a great many operational application systems, complex data processing and communications operations, and many departments competing for their interest. There will be a wide array of disaster possibilities and recovery plans to consider. The planning effort can appear to be more formidable than anticipated, and impossible to accomplish in the allotted time. To cut the problem down to size, therefore, preliminary assumptions should be developed by the team and offered for management approval. This is the second step in the Definition Phase in developing an I/S disaster recovery plan (see Fig. 4-1).

The assumptions should include any guidelines that management has given the team to start the project, and any initial boundaries for the project that the team deems appropriate. They can include such statements as:

- The disaster recovery procedures will include all aspects of I/S operations, including purchasing and stores, mail room and distribution, and all on-line terminal areas.

- In the event of a disaster, the intent will be (for example) to restore the key financial production applications within 24 hours, a selected group of applications within 7 days, and a large percentage of the applications within 20 days. (These requirements will be examined in detail in the study.)

- The industry is considered as low-risk, and the operation is in an average-risk area. Special considerations for floods, earthquakes, and riots are not required.

- The costs of any disaster recovery preparations will be funded as required by management and will not be part of the normal operating budget of I/S.

- The recovery procedures will be complementary to existing fire, bomb threat, or other emergency procedures, and will be of lower priority.

- Full risk analysis calculations are only required for a selected list of crucial applications; the requirements of these applications will supply adequate justification for the entire project.

- It is obvious that a disaster could occur and could have extremely damaging consequences, therefore, a disaster recovery plan must be developed and tested expeditiously.

- The disaster recovery plan will deal only with those applications deemed mandatory and necessary by management. Other applications will be covered by degraded or delayed operation, and losses will be handled by insurance.

The list of assumptions always will be drawn from the initial management interviews. If the team feels that there are assumptions that have been overlooked, these should be surfaced in additional interviews. The final list will be discussed with management for approval as soon as possible. The need for a disaster recovery plan might be so obvious that the assumptions can be simply and explicitly stated the first day of the study.

The purpose of the assumptions is to both direct management's attention to a number of required decisions that are made during the preliminary discussions of the team, and to set limitations on the planning effort. The acceptance of the assumptions can be crucial to the efficiency of the planning effort.

Definitions   Clear and simple definitions of some of concepts involved are a necessary part of the preliminary management document. The concepts of I/S disaster recovery are not always familiar to management. Some managers prefer the more positive word, "contingency." The whole process is called I/S contingency planning, although nothing in the process changes.

The first definition is always what the planning group is talking about when it refers to a disaster. This was defined in chapter 1 as "any service disruption incident that can cause significant disruption in the I/S capabilities for a period of time that affects the operations of the organization." It can mean any situation that leaves the computer facility in a nonproductive state.

Other definitions of systems, concepts, risk management, and resource types can be drawn from the discussion in this book if they are considered to be helpful.

Planning Decision Steps   Once the objectives and the assumptions have been clearly stated, and approved by responsible management, the planning team can proceed through the project plan. They will face a number of decision steps that were outlined in Fig. 4-1 and that will now be discussed further in this section. These decision steps are:

- Types of disaster to consider
- Key disaster scenario
- Assessing other resource requirements

Because these decision steps can be discussed with management at different times and with different degrees of urgency, the following sections are relatively independent. Some can be omitted, and some can be given precedence.

Types of disaster to consider

No reasonable recovery planning can be done without first reaching an agreement within the organization as to what types of disaster could realistically affect the operation, and what are the most probable disaster occurrences to expect. This decision will establish the first major assumption to be made in creating the plan. It also will be fundamental to deciding the types of security measures that should be installed. It will be the starting point in estimating the losses to be expected from disaster occurrences and the costs of measures to protect against those losses. Disaster recovery planning is only effective when it is done with specific types of disaster occurrences in mind.

Types of disaster

The various types of disaster to consider include:

Natural disasters:

- Floods
- Winter storms
- Forest fires
- Earthquakes
- Hurricanes
- Tornadoes

Man-made disasters:

- Building fires
- Transportation accidents
- Chemical accidents
- Sabotage or willful destruction
- Bomb threats
- Burst pipes
- Building collapse

Political disasters:

- Riots, strikes, and civil disturbances
- War and nuclear attack

Information on disaster possibilities and emergency management is available from a number of sources. Local government, including your local fire and police departments can be consulted. National or regional information is available from the Weather Service, trade associations, and the Federal Emergency Management Agency.

Each individual plant, bank, office building, institution, or other large facility must be evaluated individually in terms of the most likely disaster to occur, the effects the disaster would have, and the capability of reacting to, and minimizing those effects. In the analysis of the vulnerability of the facilities, you must consider environmental, indigenous, and economic factors. These will be the basis for:

- Estimating the likelihood of indirect damage
- Preparing the disaster recovery measures to minimize both the damage and the operational effect

For disaster recovery planning, the study group must assume that most disasters probably will occur rapidly with little warning, and will have the potential for substantial destruction. Figure 4-2, Possible Disaster Occurrences, reviews some of the possibilities for consideration. Much of the material in this figure was extracted from *Disaster Planning Guide for Business and Industry*, now out of print. It was published by a predecessor of the Federal Emergency Management Agency (FEMA), which has similar information. For a more detailed analysis of this subject, useful information is available in the FEMA publication, TD-8, *Industrial Protection Guide, 1981*. Updated information in different form is available from FEMA.

This list of the types of disasters to consider first should be reviewed by the study team, using all available historical and technical data, plus some common sense about what the real problems might be. The list should be considered by the management involved, along with the study team's recommendations. The necessary response to realistic problems should be agreed upon.

The types of disaster to consider will depend upon the area of operation of the organization, the location of the computer equipment, and the location of the information needs. If the organization's entire operations are located in a limited geographic area, its disaster response requirements will be different than those with a countrywide operation. A regional disaster could realistically wipe out the need for computer operations if it affected all of the organization's customers, as well as the organization's operations in a limited area. For example, some groups will have more concern with earthquakes or hurricanes than will others, but they also might find that rapid recovery is not necessary until after the event has subsided. Very few I/S groups should be concerned with the effects of a nuclear attack, because such an occurrence would wipe out the need for their efforts.

Disasters, such as major building fires or hurricanes, must be planned for, if applicable, by I/S staff people. However, the principal actions that will be taken will be the responsibility of other groups in the organization, because the actions will be too extensive for

Fig. 4-2. Possible disaster occurrences.

Natural disasters
Floods

Except in the case of flash flooding, the onset of most floods is a relatively slow process with adequate warning. The buildup usually takes several days. Progressive situation reports are available from NOAA (the National Oceanic and Atmospheric Administration), through its weather services, river forecast centers, and river district offices.

Flash flood warnings are the most urgent type of flood warnings issued. These are transmitted to the public over radio and television. They also should be transmitted through local warning systems, by means of sirens, horns, or whistles; through telephone alerts; or by means of police cars using loudspeakers.

If your community has a history of recurring floods, the community's minimum requirement is to establish continuing communication with the National Weather Service. For example, flood forecasts and warnings should be telephoned to the local police headquarters, or some other centralized facility, at designated periods. During the flood-control planning phase communities should coordinate closely with the nearest office of the U.S. Army Corps of Engineers, according to established state procedures. Also, the Corps of Engineers can provide preventive assistance for flood control as authorized under Public Law 99.

Winter storms

Winter storms vary in size and intensity. A winter storm can be a minor ice storm or a full-blown blizzard.

Prestorm Season Preparations:

- Organize mobile emergency rescue and medical teams, if these would be useful in your area.
- Contact your local government or the National Weather Service and learn winter storm warnings that pertain to your area.
- Publish winter storm safety rules in the plant newspaper.
- Contact local civil agencies, military installations, and private organizations to determine their capability to assist under varying winter storm situations.
- Designate snow emergency routes and place identifying signs within the yard areas of the buildings.
- Establish a system for employee-stay-home announcements. Determine if any I/S tasks can be done at home by employees during such a period.

Forest fires

Any small fire in a wooded area, if not quickly detected and suppressed, can get out of control. An uncontrolled fire is one of the most destructive forces caused by nature or by man. It is a multiple killer of people, livestock, fish, and wildlife. It can destroy property that is in proximity to a wooded area.

Responsibility for fire protection on federal lands is centered primarily in the Department of Agriculture, the Department of Interior, and to a lesser degree in such agencies as the Department of Defense and the Tennessee Valley Authority. The states have recognized their responsibilities on state and private forest lands through passage of numerous laws, and have set up state forest agencies to protect these resources. Often, private interests have established their own fire control organizations.

Besides training and equipping their own fire department personnel for brush and forest fire fighting, organizations near forest areas should consider such activities as fire prevention programs, obtaining fire weather forecasts from the National Weather Service, and development of mutual-aid compacts with other plants, adjacent communities, and private agencies. Employees can be trained and equipped to fight forest fires without much cost in time and money. Plant fire departments can provide the nucleus of a force that can prevent, detect, or suppress forest fires before they reach the disaster stage.

Earthquakes

Earthquakes are unpredictable and strike without warning. They can range in intensity from slight tremors to great shocks, and can last from a few seconds to as much as five minutes. They could come in a series over a period of several days. The actual movement of the ground in a earthquake is seldom the direct cause of injury or death. Most casualties result from falling materials or subsequent fires or explosions. Quakes can disrupt power and telephone lines, and gas, sewer, or water mains. They also can trigger landslides and generate tidal waves.

During the shaking, employees should be warned to:

- Stay indoors.
- Take cover under sturdy furniture, such as work tables.
- Stay near the center of the building.
- Stay away from glass windows and doors.
- Not run through or near buildings where there is danger of falling debris.

Fig. 4-2. Continued.

- Stay in the open, when outdoors, away from buildings and utility wires.

  After the shaking stops:

- Employees should stay out of damaged buildings; the after shock can shake down the building.
- Officials should check utilities. If water pipes are damaged or electrical wires are shorted, they should be turned off at the primary control point.
- If gas leakage is detected, the main valve should be shut off, windows opened, and the building cleared until utility officials say it is safe.

Hurricanes

The National Weather Service is responsible for issuing warnings when hurricanes appear to be a threat to the U.S. mainland.

As soon as there are definite indications that a hurricane is forming, even though it is a thousand miles or more from the mainland, the storm is given a name and the National Weather Service begins issuing hurricane advisories. The advisories are issued frequently throughout the day and night and tell where the storm is, the intensity of its winds, and speed and direction of its movement.

If a hurricane moves toward the mainland, hurricane watch notices are included. A hurricane watch does not indicate that hurricane conditions are imminent, but rather indicates that the hurricane is close, and that everyone in the area covered by the watch should listen for further advisories and be ready to take precautionary actions.

As soon as the forecaster determines that a particular section of the coast will feel the full effects of a hurricane, he issues a hurricane warning. Hurricane warnings specify coastal areas where winds of 74 MPH or higher are expected. When the warning is issued, all precautions should be taken immediately against the full force of the storm.

Tornadoes

Tornadoes are violent local storms with whirling winds of tremendous speed that can reach 200 to 400 MPH. The individual tornado appears as a rotating, funnel-shaped cloud that extends toward the ground from the base of a thundercloud. It varies from gray to black in color. The tornado spins like a top, and can sound like the roaring of an airplane or locomotive. These small, short-lived storms are the most violent atmospheric phenomena, and over a small area, are the most destructive.

The width of a tornado path generally ranges from 200 yards to one mile. They travel 5 to 50 miles along the ground, at speeds of 30 to 75 MPH. Tornadoes sometimes double back or move in circles, and some have remained motionless for a while before moving on. They have struck in every state, but the principal areas of frequency are the Middle Plains and Southeastern States.

Because tornadoes are highly localized and recurring in some areas, it is recommended that plants in areas prone to tornadoes participate in a Tornado Watch System build around a local emergency service (usually the local police department).

The National Weather Service is responsible for issuing weather warnings to the public. Severe weather warnings are issued, using the following terms:

Severe Thunderstorm indicates the possibility of frequent lightning and/or damaging winds of greater than 50 MPH, hail 3/4-inch or more in diameter (about the size of a nickel), and heavy rain.

Severe Thunderstorm Watch indicates the possibility of tornadoes, thunderstorms, frequent lightning, hail and winds of greater than 75 MPH.

Tornado Watch means that tornadoes are expected to develop.

Tornado Warning means that a tornado actually has been sighted in the area, or is indicated by radar.

Manmade disasters
Building fires

The most important aspect of plans for coping with major building fires is development of mutual assistance agreements with local governments and other organizations. Fire control methods and techniques vary widely in different parts of the country, as well as between the various fire protection agencies. It is difficult to prescribe standard procedures. International fire organizations generally develop plans and procedures over the years to meet various fire hazards.

Small companies usually cannot afford to maintain the standing forces required to meet a major fire situation, so they rely on local government services and mutual aid. To be effective in cases of large fires, industrial explosions, and forest fires, mutual aid requires good communications, accessibility to the fire scene, prearrangement for use of apparatus and manpower, and centralized command.

The biggest single need usually is not manpower and equipment. Most often it is the ability to respond quickly and to confine the fire to manageable limits before it reaches the disaster stage. This calls for a prefire plan of action for mutual aid response by existing local fire organizations. Where such plans exist at the time of a large fire, the emergency usually is manageable, with life and property loss held to a minimum.

Fig. 4-2. Continued.

Transportation accidents

Most buildings are exposed daily to the possibility of air, automobile, railroad, or shipping accidents in or near its boundaries. Management should be prepared to handle the type of problems they will have to face if there is a major transportation accident close by.

Because not all buildings have the same exposure nor the same resources to handle such emergencies, each should develop its own plan of action. Local plans should include listings of the type of equipment or services, and the person or point of contact to give or obtain immediate response to an emergency request.

Major transportation accidents often cause chemical spills, fires, explosions, and other results, which call for special operations, such as rescue and evacuation. Usually, transportation accidents affect only relatively small areas and involve only a few people.

An airplane crash can create the need for fire fighting and other operations in the area of impact.

An automobile crash involving busses or carriers of hazardous cargoes can involve substantial rescue, fire fighting, and evacuation operations.

A railroad accident can produce hazardous situations when it occurs in or near buildings, particularly if the cargo is flammable or explosive. This also can involve substantial rescue, fire fighting, and evacuation operations.

Despite the type of transportation accident, the first consideration should be to save lives. This can be accomplished through quick response and coordination of the plant emergency services and local police, fire, and medical services.

Chemical accidents

Several thousand chemicals in daily use can cause an emergency that would affect a substantial number of employees and others in the neighborhood. These effects could include massive contamination of a community, explosions, and fires. The U.S. Department of Transportation is responsible for regulating the movement of hazardous chemicals, and hazardous chemicals being transported interstate must be labeled with appropriate words of identification and caution.

Emergency coordinators and safety personnel should be familiar with the following sources of technical information on chemical hazards:

National Fire Protection Association
60 Batterymarch Street
Boston MA 02110

Publications:

- No. 49-*Hazardous Chemicals Data*
- No. 325-*Properties of Flammable Liquids, Gases and Volatile Solids*
- No. 491-*Manual of Hazardous Chemical Reactions*
- No. 704M-*Fire Hazards of Materials*
  Manufacturing Chemists Association
  1825 Connecticut Avenue, N. W.
  Washington DC 20009

Chemical Safety Data Sheets

National Agriculture Chemists Association
1155-15 Street, NW
Washington DC 20005
   (Members of this Association have a network of more than 40 safety teams nationwide prepared for prompt cleanup and decontamination of poison pesticides involved in a major accident.)

Association of American Railroads
Bureau of Explosives
1920 L Street, NW
Washington DC 20036
Publications:

- B. E. Pamphlet No. 8A, *Dangerous Articles Emergency Guide*
- B. E. Pamphlet No. 22, *Handling Collisions and Derailments Involving Explosives, Gasoline, and other Dangerous Articles*
- B. E. Pamphlet No. 29, *Procedures for Handling Special Atomic Energy Commission Shipments*

Sabotage or willful destruction

No organization is immune to sabotage. However, the types of targets for sabotage usually can be predicted with reasonable accuracy. The saboteur generally will look for a target that is crucial, vulnerable, accessible, and at least partially conductive to self-destruction. Saboteurs in general are enemy agents, disgruntled employees who commit sabotage for revenge, or individuals who are mentally ill or have been duped by enemy propaganda.

The methods of sabotage can be classified as follows:

Chemical   The addition or insertion of destructive or pollutant chemicals

Fig. 4-2. Continued.

Electric or Electronic   Interrupting or interfering with electrical or electronic processes or power, and jamming communications

Explosive   Detonating explosive materials, or damaging or destroying by explosives

Incendiary devices   Ignited by chemicals, electrical or electronic or mechanical means, or any ordinary means of arson.

Mechanical   Breaking or omitting parts, using improper or inferior parts, or failing to lubricate or maintain properly

Psychological   Inciting strikes, boycotts, unrest, personal animosities; or causing slowdowns, or work stoppage by excessive spoilage of inferior work.

Preventing sabotage can be accomplished by reducing target accessibility and vulnerability. This can be done by allowing only authorized access to the potential target; screening and placing employees according to security requirements; designing, constructing, and modifying equipment with built-in protection against sabotage; conducting continuing education of employees on prevention of sabotage; and having a plan with organization and procedures for handling potential or actual sabotage.

Bomb threats

Compared with other plant emergencies, the covert and criminal nature of bombing incidents make bomb threats a highly complex problem for management and emergency service personnel. Consequently, prior planning to meet the threat should include contact with the local or neighboring law enforcement agency, particularly if it has a bomb disposal unit. Arrange to obtain the assistance of experienced personnel. In sensitive cases, training programs for plant specialists in handling improvised explosive devices should be utilized when they are available through Military Explosive Ordnance Disposal Control Center (MEODCC) and/or Law Enforcement Assistance Administration (LEAA) programs.

Experience has shown that more than 95 percent of all written or telephoned bomb threats are hoaxes. However, there is always a chance that a threat might be authentic. Appropriate action should be taken in each case to provide for the safety of employees, the public, and property, and to locate the suspected explosive or incendiary device so it can be neutralized.

Although the responsibility for action rests primarily with the police department, this responsibility will be affected to some degree by other people involved. For example, the senior manager must make the decision whether to evacuate the building after a bomb threat has been received, and where to send the people who are evacuated. Also, whether or not people who work in the threatened building, and who know what does or doesn't belong in or near the building, should conduct the search for a suspected bomb.

If the object is located and thought to be a bomb, and the local police cannot dispose of it, the services of a bomb disposal unit previously arranged for should be requested.

Burst pipes

Many data processing people are unaware of the proximity of very high pressure steam and water pipes to their computer room or data input area. Occasionally, such pipes burst or leak severely. If these pipes are close to, or above electronic equipment or paper records storage, the damage can be extensive. Building management or facilities administrators should be consulted about the locations of steam or water pipes, and methods of protection from them. Their location should be considered in the construction of a computer facility. One large data center in an office building was flooded severely by a bombed pipe in a rest room two floors above the data center, placed by a saboteur.

Building collapse

Building collapse usually is related to earthquakes, but might occur for lesser reasons in older buildings that are being reconstructed, or when another building is being built close by, and the ground is being blasted. It is a less-common type of disaster that should be considered for older brick or frame buildings, or in areas where there are occasional high winds.

Political disasters
Riots, strikes, and civil disturbances

Recent years have seen a variety of demonstrations for different purposes in many locations throughout the country. Some demonstrations develop slowly, allowing the authorities to assess the problem, and to conduct negotiations with the organizers and arrange for control measures. On other occasions, violence can flare up with little advance notice. But even these incidents usually are preceded by earlier indications of a buildup of tensions and pressures.

In a situation that is developing slowly and deliberately, management might operate during the preliminary or negotiating phase out of their regular offices, calling staff directors as required, and routinely circulating information to departments concerned.

In a situation where there is a sudden eruption of violence, accompanied perhaps by attempted arson and assaults, plant security personnel usually will be involved initially and will serve as the source for information regarding the characteristics and extent of the disturbance. Their intelligence-gathering capability, coupled with

Fig. 4-2. Continued.

that of local police agencies, generally will provide the information needed to make appropriate decisions.

War and nuclear attack

Measures to meet the threats of war and nuclear attack usually transcend the areas of responsibility of company management. Advice will be given to organizations by appropriate government agencies if immediate actions are to be taken to minimize damage. Most organizations with sensitive or crucial financial information keep backup copies of such information in underground or highly protected commercial storage facilities. Only in extreme cases can anything be done about maintaining the operation of data centers that can come under attack. Any planned backup facilities must be very widespread geographically.

The blast and heat effects of nuclear weapons, while similar in nature to conventional weapons, are enormously greater in power, and pose the added threat of radioactivity. The effects of nuclear weapons differ from those of conventional weapons in the following principal ways:

- Nuclear explosions might be many thousands (or millions) of times more powerful than the largest conventional detonations.

- A fairly large proportion of the energy in a nuclear explosion is emitted as light and heat, generally referred to as thermal radiation. This can cause skin burns and can start fires at considerable distances. The nuclear explosion also releases a burst of highly penetrating and harmful invisible rays called initial nuclear radiation. The initial radiation effect is overshadowed by blast and fire effects that can cause almost total destruction within a radius considerably larger than that affected by initial nuclear radiation.

- A nuclear detonation also produces an electromagnetic pulse (EMP), sometimes called radio-flash, which, under proper conditions, can affect large areas. The bulk of EMP energy lies within the radio frequency spectrum, ranging from power-line frequencies to radar system frequencies.

- If a nuclear explosion occurs at or near the ground, great quantities of radioactive earth and other materials are drawn upward to high altitudes. The radioactive particles can fall back to earth over a period of several hours, over a wide area. This phenomenon is known as radioactive fallout, and particles emit what is called residual nuclear radiation.

In an all-out nuclear attack against U.S. military, industrial, and population centers, severe to moderate damage from the blast and heat effects would occur in about 2 percent of the nation's area. In addition, radioactive fallout could be expected to spread over about 75 percent of the land area of the United States, in varying intensities, contaminating many places for periods ranging from hours to weeks with potentially fatal or disabling effects on the population.

Although the direct effects of a large-scale nuclear attack could cause millions of casualties, other millions of Americans could survive the radiation effects by seeking protection in fallout shelters.

This text is extracted from "Disaster Planning Guide for Business and Industry," now out of print. Similar information is available from the Federal Emergency Management Agency.

---

consideration by I/S alone. The same procedures to back up the I/S facilities will apply, but there will be less I/S concern with maintaining the organization's cash flow immediately. There will be far more concern with the protection of the people in the area and the recovery of overall organization services. Safety of employees always should be the preeminent concern.

The most likely threats to occur should receive the most attention. These more common disasters can be localized in the computer, communications, or data input areas. Preparations to prevent these disasters will be the direct responsibility of I/S management. Consider all possible disasters. Concentrate on the most probable disasters.

The possibility of disaster caused by virus attacks and other software penetrations should not be overlooked. These should be prevented by adequate security measures.

If the organization is widespread, there is considerable incentive to maintain a distant (at least 100 miles) backup site within the organization's control. If an organization operates in a narrow geographic area, the backup site could be much closer, such as within ten miles, or even a few blocks in a large city. If there is a severe storm or earthquake affecting a specific area, it is not reasonable to ask employees to leave the area for a distant site. Their primary concern at the time will be the maintenance and recovery of their own homes and families, and rightly so. Distant backup sites should be operated by employees from other areas during a regional disaster, or by commercial installations.

In all cases, the decision on the backup sites for the vital records and important papers of an organization is independent of the decision on the backup operations sites. Disaster recovery backup sites are needed for the operational backup of the business of the organization. This might, or might not be separate from the storage of important records.

Most probable disaster occurrences

After having reviewed the types of disasters that should be considered for the structure, the area, and the business, the study team and management should come to agreement on the most probable disaster occurrences. This list should be kept to a reasonable length because some problems can be mitigated by adequate security preparations. If there are several different types of possible disasters, and the effects of each type would be different, the possible occurrences should be grouped. A disaster recovery scenario should be written for the most probable disaster occurrence, and plans laid for that scenario. These plans will vary from local alternative actions to a complete move of all operations. Less probable disaster occurrences will be subsets or modifications of the most probable scenario.

The most practical approach is to choose from the list of possible disasters the particular group (i.e., fires and building problems) that would be of greatest concern to the I/S area. Such occurrences then would be considered in developing the key disaster scenario. All other disaster incidents could be considered as either:

- Subsets of the key disaster scenario, in which decisions could be made at the time as to what parts of the key plan to activate, or
- Extensions of the key disaster scenario, in which the full plan would be used, together with other systems and operations actions and other organization activities that are deemed appropriate at the time

Normally, the most probable disaster occurrence will be fire, water damage, or electrical failure involving the computer room or nearby area of the computer facility. The key disaster scenario will focus on occurrences that are localized to I/S. This threat can be of particular concern because it would concentrate in the organization.

If I/S is an integral part of the organization's operations, the effect on financial control, cash flow, and customer service could be disastrous. A sustained shutdown of the computer facility, on which the rest of the operation is depending for normal operations, would be most serious for I/S management. Although I/S should not be held accountable for preparing for a possible localized shutdown, they certainly should be held accountable for preparing for a possible localized shutdown. The key disaster scenario and the planned and tested disaster recovery procedures, therefore, should be designed especially to describe the response to such a threat.

There are five types of disaster to which information services operations generally are vulnerable. This is an arbitrary list that should be modified by the study team. They are listed in the order of their probability.

Damage to individual user areas Fire, water damage, bomb threat, or other destruction in a localized situation in a user area is the most probable type of disaster to occur. This disaster could be from common causes, such as electric wiring faults or waste basket burning. It would require some readjustment of the communications and the establishment of new personal computer facilities, depending upon the priority of the operations involved. Responsibility for response to such damage must be shared with the user department involved.

Localized damage in I/S offices Types of disaster similar to those just described become more crucial when they occur in the systems, programming, input, or support services areas of I/S. It is likely that such a disaster could affect production schedules, systems development work, or general information distraction. Such incidents could also affect a number of different users at the same time, and records could be destroyed that are difficult to replace.

Damage to the data center area Substantial fire, water leak, flood, or bomb threat to the computer room and areas adjacent to it represent the most likely serious problems to affect the continued operation of I/S. The location of the disaster could be more important than the size of the disaster in this case. A relatively small service disruption incident in communications switch areas could cripple the whole I/S facility. Damage of this type is uniquely the problem of I/S management, and normally is selected as the key disaster scenario. Although the most likely problem might be a small electrical fire in a contained area, its effect could extend to all users of the computer services, and the response might have to be complete relocation of the computer operation.

Substantial damage to the organization's offices Major fire, major flood from burst pipes or storms, or major bomb or riot threats affecting a large part of the organization's offices can also affect the I/S facilities. In this case, there might be little salvageable equipment or space throughout the area. Organization operational problems would take precedence, but it would be up to I/S to recover operations. It probably would have a serious effect on the I/S plans, but the key disaster scenario still should be the basis of the activities to be undertaken.

Regional damage in a broad area   Extremely heavy storms, floods, hurricanes, or acts of war could affect a broad part of the operating area of the organization. There could be widespread loss of power and telephone lines, disrupted public transportation, and substantial difficulty for employees to report to work. If this damage covered most of the operating area of the organization, then I/S would simply follow overall priorities and apply its key disaster scenario when it became possible to do so. If this damage was regional and the organization is country wide, then the disaster recovery plan would have to include preparations for a major move of all operations to a distant site. Hopefully, that site, and its alternates, would have been selected and prepared, and detailed plans would have been made in advance for the disaster recovery.

The key disaster scenario for most companies need not be particularly concerned with acts of war, such as nuclear bombing, widespread hurricane damage and flooding, or severe winter storms. These disasters will have such an overriding effect on the company's general operations that I/S recovery will be a minor part of the problems facing management. In such cases, for most companies, I/S management probably will be able to follow their key disaster scenario after the initial stabilization of the overall situation.

Each organization must decide its threats of greatest concern, and how incidents will be handled with at least one key disaster scenario. Particular attention obviously must be paid to the I/S facilities area. The threats of fire or flood to personnel must be of prime concern.

Any I/S disaster plan always must be subordinate to the organization's emergency fire alarm procedures, or bomb threat procedures.

Key disaster scenario

The greatest probability of any disaster (fire, water, explosion, etc.) striking I/S will be that a localized service disruption incident will affect one or more user areas. This would cause a need for a small group to move temporarily, and for terminals to be moved and connected in new locations. In such cases, the initial response management team will meet and decide what pieces of the I/S disaster recovery plan to put into effect. They will not call everyone in to participate, but only the personnel directly affected. No specific preparations need to be made in advance for such a scenario, because it will be a subset of the key disaster scenario, and handled accordingly. There is a great variety of occurrences possible in such a localized disaster, and it would be fruitless to try to prepare scenarios for each of them.

There is a crucial disaster scenario, however, which is called the key disaster scenario. It deals with a disaster that could have a marked effect on the company's operations and profits, and it is necessary that I/S make preparations in advance for it to minimize its impact. The key disaster scenario normally will call for the full implementation of the disaster recovery plan.

The disaster that triggers the key disaster scenario likely will be a fire, flood, or explosion that occurs in the vicinity of the main computer room, particularly near the communications equipment and lines or the power supply. The disaster could be on another floor, with the resulting water and smoke damage impinging on the computer room.

The key disaster scenario does not necessarily start with a large and impressive service disruption incident. A small, localized fire or flood can easily knock out a large computer center. The problem that faces I/S management could be that few other people in the organization might even be aware that such an event has occurred, yet all their computer services have suddenly been cut off.

The I/S disaster recovery planning team should examine the areas involved, discuss with others the types of problems that the organization has experienced or that might occur, then outline their opinion of what the key disaster scenario should be to keep the plans in perspective, and to make management aware of what they are working to alleviate.

A typical key disaster scenario, in brief, might be:

- A service disruption incident, such as a fire, occurs in an area close to the main computer room at midnight on a Friday. When there is an incipient fire, leak, or break-in during working hours, the chances are good that it will be controlled before it becomes disastrous.

- A night operator or a security guard detects the event and rings the alarm. Local fire and police departments arrive on the scene.

- The person who rang the alarm also calls the organization's security or building manager, in accordance with the posted instructions in the guard room.

- A security person who knows of the existence of the I/S disaster recovery plan calls one or more members of the initial response (emergency) management team. They, in turn, call the responsible I/S manager.

- The members of the emergency management team gather at the site as rapidly as possible and determine what has happened, and what has already been done by the fire department and others. They make their preliminary estimates in accordance with the disaster recovery procedures, and discuss the possibilities with I/S management.
- A decision is made on the extent of the operational needs, the phone trees are started, and the disaster recovery plan is put into effect.

The initial service disruption incident might have caused:

- Destruction of the communications controller and an undetermined number of telephone or coax lines
- Undetermined damage to the main computer system, with water on the floor beneath the computer room
- Water and smoke damage to the data input and data control areas, and smoke damage to a large part of the programmers' offices
- Water damage to the power supply in the basement below

The study team should consider what likely damage could readily occur to the whole I/S area if fire equipment and hoses were brought in to get the fire under control anywhere near the computer room.

It will be sufficient for most organizations to have a single key disaster scenario, base all its plans around it, and count on the emergency management team and the I/S senior managers to select and handle the response actions. Larger organizations, and those with different-sized data centers, however, might want to plan on two or more scenarios, and lay out the details for all of them. This approach certainly could be satisfactory, but it must be remembered that it will be much more expensive to create, and more difficult to keep updated in satisfactory detail. The possibility of a telecommunications breakdown is always a central factor. The possibility of major virus attacks should not be overlooked.

Assessing resource requirements
Minimum recovery procedures required

The prompt recovery of a data center from a loss of capability depends on the availability of a number of resources. The particular resources to be planned for will depend on the most probable disaster occurrences to be expected, or the key disaster scenario. Some resources will be essential to reestablish operations. The minimum recovery procedures to be developed must include the continuing availability of those resources. Procedures that rapidly recognize the loss of such crucial resources must be in place. There are two categories of resource dependence to consider. These are:

- Resources under the direct control of I/S management. This will include the preservation of vital records and the means of running mandatory and necessary programs.

- Resources under the control of other groups. When resources are under the control of persons outside the I/S area, firm commitments must be obtained to operate them in the context of the disaster recovery plan. It is important to agree on priorities and recovery procedures to have a comprehensive plan that fits well together. Rehearsals and tests must include these resources with those in I/S. Recovery procedures must be uniform.

The continuation of a large percentage of the I/S operations at an alternate site immediately after a disruption is rarely logistically, technically, or economically feasible. It is seldom essential. The tasks performed by a data operator are not all of equal importance. This must be reflected in the recovery procedures. The relative importance of the various functions must be analyzed, and the procedures designed to step through the various functions in priority order.

In addition, the disaster recovery procedures must be tailored specifically to the organization using them. Few computer operations are so similar in equipment configuration, applications environment, and relative importance of functions, that a general purpose recovery plan can be drawn up and used. Even in large organizations with multiple distributed operation centers that are designed identically, the personnel involved, their home phone numbers, and their specific instructions will vary. Of course, an organization can produce a uniform, fill-in-the-blanks plan for its internal units. In this book, therefore, the approach is to present guidelines for preparing a specific plan that will be suitably adapted to the special needs of each data center.

For any disaster recovery plan, for any size or scope of operation, the following three elements should be addressed, as a minimum, in the recovery procedures:

Emergency response procedures Emergency response procedures to document the appropriate emergency response to a fire, flood, civil disorder, natural disaster, bomb threat, or any other incident or activity to protect lives, limit damage, and minimize the impact on data processing operations must be addressed.

Backup operations procedures   Backup operations procedures to ensure that essential data processing operational tasks can be conducted after disruption to the primary data processing facility must be addressed. Arrangements should be made for a backup capability, including the needed files, programs, paper stocks, and preprinted forms, to operate the essential systems functions in the event of a total failure.

Recovery procedures   Recovery procedures to facilitate the rapid restoration of a data processing facility following physical destruction, major damage, or loss of data must be addressed.

In addition, it is a requirement that disaster recovery procedures be tested on a recurring basis, and modified as changes in the data processing facility workload dictate. Crucial applications should be operated on the backup system to ensure that it can process this workload properly.

Application systems requirements

Application systems requirements must be determined individually and in detail before any priorities are set and assessments are made for the disaster recovery planning. The I/S disaster recovery planning team must discuss the attributes of each application system with that, finding out how it is run and getting their view of its priority. Discussions then must be held with the user contacts, or "owners" of the system, to get their views of the availability requirements and the priorities of the system. Finally, management must review the findings and determine the priorities and requirements that will be planned for and funded.

Even if management calls for creating an initial high-impact, short-term recovery plan, the requirements of all operating application systems should be at least briefly reviewed:

- To be sure that no vital applications are omitted
- To establish a full application systems priority listing that can be reviewed by management

When determining the application systems requirements, the whole project could be handled by a small group of systems analysts, or alternatively, form sheets could be used to generate the information required from those who know the system best, then the information could be analyzed and the systems given priority ranking. Three form sheets are given in this chapter to aid in such analysis. One or more of them could be used to assemble the data about the systems in a uniform manner.

Application systems analysis

An overview of the key technical and business aspects of each system can be assembled using Fig. 4-3, Application System Summary. Attachments can be added to this form sheet to give opinions of the programmers or systems analysts who are most familiar with the actual operation and use of the system, and any special comments regarding peculiarities of the system. The entries on this form sheet are self-explanatory. Obviously, some are subjective, such as "business priority," while some are objective, such as "related or dependent systems."

Fig. 4-3. Application system summary.

System No: **Date:**

System Name: **Reviewer:**

1. Effect of extended system downtime on interruption of business service:

2. Business priority in responding to an emergency situation:

3. Crucial business problems incurred by an outage (backlog, loss of control, etc.):

4. Related or dependent systems:

5. Minimum runs required to operate system in a contingency mode:

6. Tolerable duration of a computer service outage:

**Time Computer Down   Probable Financial Loss or
Business Effect**
Four hours or Less (specify)

Fig. 4-3. Continued.

Twelve Hours

Twenty-Four Hours

One Week

Three Weeks

Five Weeks (recovery probable)

7. Minimum system requirements for processing and handling data in a contingency mode:

8. Minimum staff requirements during a contingency:

9. Alternative processing possibilities for the system:

10. Comments and special considerations (use separate sheet):

11. System owner or contact person:
    Phone

    Notes:

MINIMUM RUNS REQUIRED TO OPERATE SYSTEM IN A
CONTINGENCY MODE

Frequency	Job	Name	Procedures	Purpose

Notes:

This form summarizes what could be review work by systems analysts, with a number of discussions with management for the more important application systems. It should be filled out for all systems that are regularly run, whatever their priority, because a full disaster recovery plan should include information on what to do about all systems.

The time scale for the "Time Computer Down" can be adjusted for different businesses. In some businesses, half an hour is crucial, while in other businesses, a delay of a day might not be considered as crucial. The "Probable Financial Loss or Business Effect," is merely the perception of the system users at this time. If a system is deemed crucial and the value of the recovery plan is being analyzed, these figures will be given far more attention at a later time.

The essence of this form sheet is its use as a vehicle to assemble a number of key facts about all systems so that they can be compared readily and sorted by priority.

Application systems service availability requirements

For purposes of discussion and analysis during this first phase of the disaster recovery plan, the team can use Fig. 4-4, Application Systems Service Availability Requirements, to get an understanding of what the disaster recovery needs will be. For large applications, groups of programs can be used to subdivide the entries. Rough estimates are acceptable on the first review and for setting priorities for the application systems. This form simply emphasizes the availability requirements of the application systems that were analyzed previously. Only those application systems that will receive individual consideration in the disaster recovery plan should be included here. It is the first grouping of the key systems. The next form sheet will rank the systems by priority. The columns of Fig. 4-4 are as follows:

- *Application system:* Name of system, groups of programs, or individual programs, as is reasonable
- *Report frequency:* For batch reports; response time for on-line reports, with some estimate of use
- *On-line or batch:* If both, separate the line entries
- *Areas of exposure:* Legal requirement, financial, customer service, public relations, and so forth
- *Unacceptable period of loss of availability:* Start with the user's statements about acceptability of any disruption; discuss later
- *Potential loss:* Give initial estimates for hour, day, week, and

Fig. 4-4. Application systems service availability requirements.

Application System	Report Frequency	On-Line or Batch	Areas of Exposure	Unacceptable Period of Loss Of Availability	Potential Loss	Other Considerations

month, if applicable; if a risk analysis is made later, these numbers will be refined for specific crucial systems

- *Other considerations:* Mention Foreign Corrupt Practices Act, if applicable, and any senior management directives

It will be useful to develop an application systems service availability requirements form for nearly all application systems, even those of low priority, in the first analysis. Clearly, low priority systems need not have the same level of analysis in detail as the higher priority system.

Applications systems priority

After all application systems have been identified and some information has been gathered about them, the team should discuss the systems' priority with more senior management. All key application systems in each group or division of the organization then should be ranked in priority sequence on Fig. 4-5, Application Systems Priority, according to the desires of the management of that group or division.

It is not reasonable to assign a rank order or priority to all systems, so the effort should be put into ranking groups, such as the "Top Five" (or another number that seems reasonable), and then giving only an approximate priority to the remainder. After the application systems priorities have been agreed upon in each group or division, the team then must discuss with senior management how to assign relative priorities to the different groups so that an overall priority list can be developed. This is usually not difficult because it is fairly obvious which are the top priority systems in an organization. The columns of Fig. 4-5 are:

- *System priority:* Firm listing of the mandatory and necessary applications, as discussed, and approximate listing of the remainder. Some organizations consider their "Top Five" systems, assuming that will be all that can be rapidly handled.
- *Application system:* Name of system or group of programs within a system
- *Systems contact:* Name of lead systems analyst for the system
- *User contact:* Names of working systems contact, plus user manager involved with the system operation
- *Basic processing requirements:* Computer system, and the operating system used
- *Report frequency:* For principal reports; note if on-line for reports, data entry, or both

Fig. 4-5. Application systems priority.

Group or Division _____

System Priority	Application System	Systems Contact	User Contact	Basic Processing Requirements	Report Frequency	Minimum Terminal Requirements	New Development?	Comments
Mandatory and Necessary								
1.								
2.								
3.								
4.								
5.								
Other								
6.								
7.								
8.								

- *Minimum terminal requirements:* The type of terminals and the fewest number of them that would be needed in disaster recovery
- *New development:* Note if any substantial modification or development is presently being undertaken on the system
- *Comments:* Management requirements, special considerations, and so on

This form should be filled out carefully for the mandatory and necessary systems, or any systems with special considerations. Less information is needed for lower priority systems. These lower priority systems could be grouped by the period of time by which they can be delayed.

Audit control requirements

The audit control requirements of crucial application systems at the time of a disaster are more complex and might be more difficult to handle than the basic backup and recovery of the system. The team should consult with internal audit personnel about these requirements and pay particular attention to them. It is not unreasonable to suspect that the cause of a disaster could be the cover-up of a defalcation or the poor operation of a system.

It is important that all run controls and audit controls that possibly can be handled remain in use during a disaster recovery period. It is completely wrong to assume that internal controls and audit controls can be set aside because of the difficulties of the operation. It is better to put off running a system than to lose control of it, unless it is feasible to rerun it totally at a later date, and recover the controls.

A brief summary of the application control objectives is given in Fig. 4-6, Application Control Objectives, to review the reasons for maintenance of the controls during a disaster period.

In reviewing application systems for disaster recovery control, the principal concerns are:

- Loss of audit trail
- Insufficient documentation
- Inadequate update controls
- Inability to restart under control

Normal application program controls are in place for the accurate, secure, and complete processing of data. Communication controls are needed to assure that messages are received, and to keep a record of all messages that have been delivered to the application

Fig. 4-6. Application control objectives.

---

1. Accurate Data

Accurate data means eliminating inaccuracies associated with data preparation, conversion to machine-readable format, processing by the computer, or in the output preparation and delivery processes. It also means retaining data control capabilities during a service disruption incident.

2. Complete Data

Completeness of processed data requires that data is not lost during preparation, in transit to the computer, during processing, between interrelated computer systems, and/or in transit to users of that data. It also means retaining the audit trail for the data through the disaster recovery operations.

3. Timely Data

The timely processing of data ensures that management has the necessary information to take action in time to avoid losses. The discussions on priority should determine the recovery actions required to maintain the necessary timeliness.

4. Authorized Data

Controls should ensure that any unauthorized data is detected prior to and during processing. This can be sensitive during a disaster recovery.

5. Processed According to GAAP

Financial data should be processed in accordance with Generally Accepted Accounting Procedures. Controls should assure these procedures are followed, even through a service disruption incident.

6. Compliance with Organization's Policies and Procedures

Organization policies and procedures for handling transaction data should be reviewed by the team. Controls should ensure these policies are followed.

7. Compliance with Laws and Regulations

The laws and regulations of governmental agencies normally are the driving force behind establishing a disaster recovery plan. Controls should ensure that laws and regulations are followed.

8. Adequate Supporting Evidence

Sufficient evidence to reconstruct transactions and pinpoint accountability for processing should enable the tracing from source documents to control totals, and from the control totals back to the supporting transactions. Keeping a trail of evidence through a disaster could be difficult. Responsible users must be involved in maintaining such ability.

---

program. Such message controls are fundamental to successful disaster recovery.

The more controls in place over the transmission of on-line applications, the greater the probability of recovering accurate and complete processing. Terminal controls, message controls, and application controls must be viewed as a package to be assured that recovery would be possible. Checklist 4-1, Application Controls, is a review of some of the key points that should be studied.

The importance of recovering quickly after a system shutdown obviously depends on the type of application. The more closely the application is interwoven into the day-to-day processing of the organization, the more crucial are the recovery controls used to restart the system. Such recovery controls include those that aid the restart of the system, and those that provide the ability to continue capturing transactions at the terminals while the on-line application is down. Security violations can occur during unexpected down-time with uncontrolled restarts.

Even though alternate processing capabilities (backup) are maintained for an on-line application, they must be viable for any type of sudden shutdown. In an on-line system, a backup alternative

Checklist 4-1. Application controls.

1. Is a logging facility maintained in the application system for an adult trail to assist in the reconstruction of data files?

2. Is it possible to trace all recorded messages back to the terminal, user, or point of origin?

3. Do all messages have date and time stamps for logging purposes?

4. Are messages balanced at least daily to each terminal in the system to account for lost messages?

5. Do initial accesses to update files lock the records so that additional access cannot be made until the current processing is completed?

6. Is it possible to take appropriate follow-up action on all error messages?

7. Are error messages coded according to urgency of action so that the most serious errors are handled first?

8. Are all recent changes to the application system thoroughly tested and documented?

9. Do all intelligent terminals maintain totals on key fields so they can be balanced and verified with the application?

10. Is sufficient application documentation maintained on all updating procedures?

11. Does the application have comprehensive edits and audit trails for incoming messages?

12. Is a log of all system errors maintained?

may have to be put into operation within minutes after the main system is shut down, if security is to be maintained. The complexity of the recovery routines will depend on the completeness of the various audit controls that are in place. The more controls that are available in the application system, and at the terminals, the easier it will be to recover from an unscheduled shutdown.

Checklist 4-2, Recovery Controls, lists items to review relative to the ability to recover under control. These items do not have simple answers, and there must be a good understanding of the characteristics of the particular communications systems to appreciate the problems associated with recovery. The reviewer must adjust the responses to the recovery items depending on the complexity of the on-line applications and the adequacy of control in the application, communication system, and terminal areas.

Data requirements

Databases are subject to a number of vulnerabilities that the team should examine in detail during the risk analysis and when considering how to handle the backup and recovery. The data in the computer operating system, the data residing in miscellaneous files around the facility, and the data that is secured in backup storage all must be considered separately.

Accidentally destroying a database can cause a serious disruption of data processing, if backup data are not promptly available. It is mandatory to define the responsibility of individuals who will analyze the protection and recovery of data resources and recommend actions to protect them. This will include:

- What happens if some of the source data is destroyed?
- What happens if an incident disrupts a computer in the middle of processing?
- What types of backup database must be routinely created?
- How many generations of backup files are needed to be sure there is rapid, accurate recovery?
- How much information should be put in geographically remote vital records storage facilities?

Most of the data consideration will have been adequately analyzed if the organization is operating under a controlled database system, and if there are competent database administration personnel.

There can be serious problems involved with the backup and recovery of on-line operations unless considerable thought has gone

Checklist 4-2. Recovery controls.

1. If a peripheral device (e.g., tape drive) should fail, is the system able to switch the file to another device?

2. If a program should fail, can the message causing the failure be logged first, then deleted, and the program restarted?

3. Does the system contain a history log, including:
   • Hardware failure messages?
   • Terminal failure messages?
   • Terminal startup?
   • Terminal shutdown?
   • All input communication messages?
   • All output communication messages?
   • Unusual occurrences?
   • Error messages?

4. Are changes to the operating and communication software packages adequately tested and documented before being implemented?

5. On restart, are the controls sufficient to verify that no messages were lost during shutdown?

6. Does the system have the ability to shut down parts of the system without bringing the entire system completely down?

7. Is an alternate source of power available for terminals in other rooms?

8. Are all retransmissions logged on the audit file?

9. Is adequate documentation maintained on recovery procedures?

10. Is adequate documentation maintained on restart procedures?

11. Do modems have front panel lights to indicate if the line is working properly?

12. Are backup modems available for crucial applications?

13. Are alternate lines available for crucial operations?

14. Have alternate procedures been developed for short-term shutdowns?

15. Have alternate procedures been developed for long-term shutdowns?

16. Have alternate procedures been tested to determine that they work?

17. Is maintenance readily available when and if needed?

into the logging of data input and the establishment of good audit trails. These problems should have been addressed in the original system analysis but might have to have been reviewed in the disaster recovery study.

The detailed problems of the security and backup of data are inherently basic to system designs and beyond the scope of this discussion. However, all data on which a backup and recovery operation is dependent must be adequately recorded and maintained in current condition and backup copies be adequately secured. Having backup copies is the responsibility of the following:

- Systems personnel, to ensure the security of machine-readable data
- The users, to keep records of their input and sufficient backup information to recover from a disaster

If a database management system or even just a data dictionary, has been fully and properly implemented, and sufficient copies are maintained in a current and physically safe condition, most contingency requirements for data can be met. It will not be necessary to describe the system again in the recovery plan.

For each current operating computer system, the following records should be maintained:

- Current off-site data backup
- Current off-site documentation
- Current methods of handling money received and checks disbursed
- Current dependence of the users on the database and the data input facilities
- Current dependence of the users on the on-line interrogation of database

Lists should be maintained of all tape files kept in off-site storage, including:

- Library backups
- Catalog and security backup file
- Production disk and tape backup

Backup tape files must be maintained at a secure site for the disks needed for each mandatory and necessary program to do the following:

- Perform Initial Program Load (IPL)

- Execute production procedures
- Operate the system utilities
- Access production programs

The National Fire Protection Association (NFPA) has defined four classes of data records, as follows:

Class I—Vital records These are the records of the mandatory systems that are legally required to be maintained. They are essential to the operation, are irreplaceable, and are needed immediately after disaster. Such records cannot readily be reproduced physically, and cannot be reproduced legally without sufficient controls in place. They are discussed further on in this chapter.

Class II—Important records These are the data records associated with the necessary application systems that must be run to sustain the operation of the organization. These records can be reproduced from input clerk or end-user files, but, they must have sufficient controls to assure their integrity.

Class III—Useful records These are the data records associated with the desirable application systems that will be run after a disaster, as soon as feasible. Their loss would be inconvenient, but they could be recovered with a minimal set of controls. The files would not be necessary for the immediate restoration of operations after a disaster.

Class IV—Nonessential records These are the data records that are not necessary to replace if lost. They normally will be the user's responsibility, because they might be convenient to have after a disaster.

This classification of records by the NFPA is not solely for the classification of data, but also can be applied to the classification of programs, systems, and other types of information. It is, however, a particularly helpful classification for data files.

Checklist 4-3, Data File Requirements, is a checklist of the more important points to be reviewed relative to data files stored for disaster backup.

Software requirements

Systems software and application programs are a special case of data handling. In fact, most backup disks group all machine-readable data together. In time of emergency, it is the responsibility of systems programming to strip out the various meaningful groups of information.

Software programs tend to have greater stability than data, but they are sufficiently subject to change. Care must be exercised that

Checklist 4-3. Data file requirements.

1. Have all data file records been classified according to the NFPA class of record, in association with the importance of the application system, including:
   - Source documents?
   - Data input records?
   - Control and audit trail records?
   - Magnetic records, on tape or disk files?
   - Data output records?

2. Have the requirements of vital records been reviewed (as previously discussed)?

3. Have the legal record retention regulations for the data files to maintain a recoverable record of:
   - Data entry errors?
   - Data transmission errors?
   - Operational errors?
   - Data altered by error or purposely?
   - Irregular access to the data files?

5. For each current operating application, are the following records maintained:
   - Current status of off-site file backup?
   - Current status of off-site documentation?
   - Current status of controls on money received or disbursed?

6. For all mandatory or necessary vital files, are updated records maintained of:
   - Library backups?
   - Catalog and security backup files?
   - Production disk and tape backups?

7. Is there data reconstruction capability for all magnetic files, with the necessary number of generations?

8. Are routine file dumps and transaction files maintained in a secure area for reconstruction purposes?

9. Are off-site data files routinely checked for readability and accuracy?

10. Are off-site data files maintained in an adequate, secure environment?

current versions of software, and all documentation, are sufficiently protected.

Application programs can be particularly vulnerable in I/S operations if there is not careful management attention to the use of development disciplines and change control. Formalized program management procedures are necessary to be assured that programs can be rapidly backed up. If an author/programmer is in any way needed to keep normal operations going, it will be difficult to have a workable contingency plan.

One of the most important disaster recovery preparations is to work out formal agreements with the vendors of any licensed program packages that are used. The copying of these usually is forbidden in the contract, so it is up to the vendor to maintain readily available replacement copies. Vendors should be prepared to state from where replacement copies will be shipped, how soon copies could be expected after a service disruption incident, and whether vendors will have personnel available to give support to the recovery process.

Checklist 4-4, Software Requirements, is a checklist of a number of points that should be reviewed relative to the adequacy of the software backup storage.

All old magnetic files are subject to deterioration over time when in storage. It is important that these files be tested periodically and systematically as to their readability should a disaster occur. If the tapes show any signs of deterioration, or difficulty of reading, they should be rewritten on new tapes with adequate controls and tests.

Vital records requirements

Vital records are those records necessary to ensure the survival of a business. Each organization has a legal obligation to protect its assets and its financial records. These records can be recorded in both paper documents and computer media, and they provide information and validation of the following:

- Ownership and assets of the organization
- Responsibility of the organization to its customers, members, or users
- Equity and rights of the employees, including money owed them, their position in pension and savings plans, and records of their status

A vital records program has the dual objectives of protecting the records and reconstructing related records.

Checklist 4-4. Software requirements.

1. Is backup operating system software:
   - Stored off-site?
   - Available rapidly from the vendor?

2. Is the backup operating system software:
   - Identical to your operating version?
   - Identical to your operating system release?

3. Has the backup operating system software been tested on the backup computer with realistic data and programs?

4. Do the mandatory and necessary application program system have:
   - Backup copies of the source code maintained?
   - Backup copies of the objects code maintained at regular intervals?
   - Backup sets of test data maintained?

5. If the backup computer is a different configuration than the regular computer:
   - Are the configurations of both maintained and stored?
   - Has the backup system been checked against the stored data and program files?
   - Are appropriate system modifications made whenever either system configuration changes?
   - Are appropriate system modifications made after every new system release is installed?

6. If the software is contracted from vendor, is there a clause in the contract that permits the licensee to use the software on the backup computer?

7. Have specific responsibilities been assigned for software backup, security, routine updating, and control?

8. For the software maintained at the offsite location:
   - Are occasional tests performed?
   - Are old tapes re-written before they are unreadable?
   - Are all updates systematically applied?
   - Is there occasional audit of the inventory?

The first objective is a legal requirement. The second objective is dependent upon the first, and is to ensure the ability to continue operations after a disaster incident. The amount of delay that is tolerable in reconstructing data will depend completely upon the individual organization.

It is important that vital records be given maximum protection from every possible disaster because the information contained in those records can be the single, most valuable asset of the organization. Some vital records are the processing and trade secrets, drawings, formulas, and so on. Other vital records are in the accounting, operating, and engineering information that is resident on computer media.

Normally, less than two percent of a company's records can be described as vital, unless the organization primarily deals with data, such as banking or insurance. In such cases, a much larger percentage of the data is vital. In many organizations, a records manager, or some other similar responsible person, already has determined which records are vital and has established a vital records protection program. It is helpful to I/S if this program has included establishing a remote, safe storage facility that can be used to store necessary backup tapes and documentation.

In a modern data processing operation, the handling of vital records generally is completely interwoven with the handling of the records that are considered crucial for the operations of the mandatory application systems. The vital records will be classified as mandatory, and the systems handling them will certainly be given high priority. I/S backup information on electronic media is seldom separated into vital and nonvital categories, however, because backup tapes and disks usually have full application systems on them ready to be stripped out as needed. The necessary application systems should be preserved with similar care to the mandatory systems.

Despite this fact, the team should be cognizant of which material is vital and which is not. The team will have to assure the records manager or the corporate secretary that all vital records have been considered and identified and are being adequately protected.

The measures taken to ensure the general efficiency of the computer and its use by the company, and to back up mandatory and necessary systems, are identical to those measures used to protect vital data processing operations. It is sufficient for the team to identify the vital records, then treat them in the mandatory class of backup and recovery handling.

Records retention analysis is related to vital records requirements because its prime legal use is for the vital records. It should be extended to all data processing records, however, because of its usefulness in keeping some control on the volume of retained data. There are three types of retention purposes. These are:

1. Legal retention is the period of time required by agencies such as the IRS and the Interstate Commerce Commission. These required records become vital records.

2. Processing retention is the period of time specified in the Operations Manual as necessary to restart the processing of that data in the event an error is detected subsequent to initial processing.

3. Disaster retention is the storing of necessary data on a computer media that facilitates off-site storage on a cyclical basis sufficient to resume normal data processing activities in the event of a disaster at the computer site.

The I/S disaster recovery project team should be able to collect this retention information from the systems analysis involved with the application systems. This information should not need to be developed at the time of the study, but should be known by those responsible for the systems.

Figure 4-7, Records Retention Periods, shows typical examples of the required retention periods. In practice, each organization must determine from its management and auditors the requirements for retention. Figure 4-7 is divided into two sections:

• Records with retention periods specified by government regulations

• Typical records with retention periods fixed by administrative decision.

Checklist 4-5, Vital Records and Records Retention, is a checklist of the key points to consider in a vital records program, records retention analysis, and off-site storage management. It can be used to review whether the program is meeting all requirements. In summary, the eight key steps in a vital records program are:

1. Obtain management cooperation

2. Define the objectives of the program

3. Analyze what functions are needed to meet the objectives, including the information needed and the records containing that information

4. Analyze the records retention requirements, both governmental and internal

Fig. 4-7. Records retention periods.

A. Records with Retention Periods Specified by Government Regulation

Type of Record	Retention Period (Yrs)	Type of Record	Retention Period (Yrs)
Accounting & Fiscal		**Purchasing & Procurement**	
Accounts Payable Invoices	3	Bids and Awards	3
Checks, Payroll	2	Purchase Orders & Reqs.	3
Checks, Voucher	3	**Security**	
Earnings Register	3	Employee Clearance Records	5
General Ledger Records	Permanent	Visitor Records	2
Labor Cost Records	3	**Taxation**	
Payroll Registers	3	Annuity and Other Plans	Permanent
Manufacturing		Dividend Register	Permanent
Bills and Material	3	Employee Taxes	4
Engineering & Specs. Records	20	Excise Reports	4
Stock Issuing Records	3	Inventory Reports	Permanent
Personnel		Depreciation Schedules	Permanent
Accident Reports & Claims	30	**Transportation**	
Changes and Terminations	5	Bills of Lading	2
Injury Frequency Records	Permanent	Freight Bills	3
Job Ratings	2	Freight Claims	2

Fig. 4-7. Continued.

B. Typical Records with Retention Periods Fixed by Administrative Decision

Type of Record	Retention Period (Yrs)	Type of Record	Retention Period (Yrs)
Accounting & Fiscal		**Manufacturing**	
Accounts Payable Ledger	Permanent	Production Reports	3
Accounts Receivable Ledger	5	Work Orders	3
Bank Statements	3	**Personnel**	
Budgets	3	Attendance Records	7
Expense Reports	3	Employee Activity Files	3
Financial Statements, Cert.	Permanent	**Plant Records**	
P & L Statements	Permanent	Inventory Records	Permanent
Commission Reports	3	Maintenance Records	5
Corporate		**Taxation**	
Capital Stock Ledger	Permanent	Tax Bills & Statements	Permanent
Stock Transfer Records	Permanent	Tax Returns	Permanent

Note: The above Retention Periods are given as typical examples. In practice, an organization must determine its own Records Retention Periods.

Checklist 4-5. Vital records and records retention.

Vital Records Program

1. Does your organization have an existing vital records program?
2. Is the vital records program controlled by:
   • Corporate secretary?
   • Other corporate officer?
   • Records manager?
3. Have the vital data processing records been considered in this program?
4. Do you know the location of all organization record safes or vaults?
5. Are these safes or vaults sufficiently large to store records on magnetic media?
6. Is the present storage of magnetic media containing vital records sufficiently controlled and secure?
7. Has authority been obtained to proceed with:
   • Records retention analysis?
   • Creating a vital records program?

Records Retention Analysis

8. Have all necessary corporate officers and key users agreed to participate in a records retention analysis?
9. Have responsible accounting or audit persons determined:
   • What records retention periods are required by government regulation?
   • What records retention periods are required by administrative decision and perceived legal requirement?
10. For each application system, have the following been determined?
    • What assets of the organization and evidences of stockholder equity must be preserved?
    • What programs will need to be reconstructed?
    • What recorded information will be necessary to preserve?
    • What records contain that information?
    • Whether each record can be recreated?
    • Whether extra copies of such records are dispersed under control in the organization?
11. Have the considerations of retention been divided into:
    • Legal retention, as required by government?
    • Processing retention, as required for fault-free processing?

Checklist 4-5. Continued.

- Disaster retention, as required to reconstruct and resume normal data processing activities?

12. Is there currently satisfactory dispersal and controlled storage of the vital records that have been determined by analysis?

13. Will the retained information be available in the required time period for recovery?

Off-Site Storage Considerations

14. Is there a current directory or inventory of the vital records in off-site storage?

15. Is there a systematic, controlled process for keeping this inventory up-to-date?

16. Is there a record of the configuration, operating system, program library, and data files required for each application?

17. Do these records include:
    - Operating system version and level?
    - System flow diagrams?
    - Program maintenance information?
    - Console operating instructions?
    - Key controls and control checks?
    - Disposition of output files and reports?

18. Is an inventory maintained of supplies needed for immediate recovery processing?

19. Is an inventory of all vital tape and disk files maintained?

20. Does the system protect the master files and program volumes from loss of information?

21. Have the responsible systems analysts made plans for the reconstruction of all important files?

22. Will it be possible to retrieve the media containing the vital records quickly from the storage area selected?

23. Will equipment be available to produce copies from magnetic media, microfilm, or hard copy?

24. Are the records in storage tested periodically for usability and readability?

25. Is there a systematic program for re-recording of stored magnetic media to assure its readability on current equipment?

26. Is all documentation of the vital records, including handling schedules, included as another vital record, and stored under control accordingly?

5. Determine the importance and priorities of the records or plan safeguards.

6. Establish a records retention and vital records program.

7. Schedule the records and operate the program routinely.

8. Test and audit the program periodically.

Hardware and communications requirements

All hardware resources of both the current operational system and the planned backup system must be completely documented, and the documentation must be updated for all changes in configuration and requirements. The documentation must be reviewed by appropriate technical personnel, and with the vendor support person, to determine its adequacy. Copies of the documentation must be kept at the central operational site, the offices of the technical support staff, and at the backup site.

It is preferable to keep together, and in parallel, the documentation for the hardware requirements for the existing operation and the documentation for the hardware requirements for the stripped-down operation at the backup site. In this way, changes in the configuration of the other, and the disaster recovery documentation, will remain updated.

Organizations dealing with disaster recovery services will find that your configuration requirements, and the configuration details of the available equipment, will be documented in detail and routinely checked one against the other. Organizations who are handling their own disaster recovery backup sites can do no less.

Checklist 4-6, Hardware and Communications Requirements, is a checklist to review what necessary analytical tasks have been done, and what documentation is needed. It is nonspecific to particular hardware, because every hardware and communications configurations will be unique, with the priorities of the requirements determined by the users.

Backup hardware resources

Hardware resources usually are readily replaceable, if the equipment is of recent manufacture and is produced in sufficient quantity for the manufacturer to have replacement devices ready to ship on short notice. The policy of most hardware manufacturers is that, in the event of a localized disaster, the customer will be moved to the front of the line for shipment of replacement units that are available. Some CPUs might require a larger, more modern unit shipped

Checklist 4-6. Hardware and communications requirements.

Hardware Requirements

1. Has the disaster recovery workload been defined for your essential (mandatory and necessary) systems?

2. Has this workload been translated into hardware and communications system requirements?

3. Has the minimum backup system configuration been agreed upon by technical analysts and management?

4. Has the usage of such a minimum system been defined in terms of individual application system usage and priority?

5. Is a record routinely kept of the complete inventory and specifications of the hardware configuration currently required, including:
   - Name and level of each equipment item?
   - Number and type of tape drives?
   - Number and type of disk drives?
   - Number and type of printers?
   - Number and type of peripheral equipment and other components?
   - Configuration of all equipment?

6. Has a similar equipment configuration been tested for backup purposes in running the essential systems?

7. Are operating personnel trained in the procedures for:
   - Orderly power-down of current equipment?
   - Controlled power-up of the backup equipment?

8. Are all necessary operational procedures for the backup system written, and at the backup site?

9. Are all necessary operational controls agreed upon and in place at the backup site?

10. Have all necessary controls for maintaining an audit trail been:
    - Determined and put in place?
    - Agreed upon by the auditors?
    - Documented, with instructions, for operators?
    - Tested in a simulated backup operation?

Vendor Assistance

11. Have the vendors been consulted as to their part in disaster recovery operations?

12. Have support statements by the vendor been analyzed and verified with both internal management and vendor management?

13. Can the vendor supply the necessary backup hardware during an emergency:
    - At your backup site?
    - At a vendor office or a vendor-selected site?

14. Can the vendor supply such backup hardware promptly?

15. For hardware items that are difficult to replace, has the vendor agreed to a:
    - Firm commitment for the timing of delivery of the items?
    - Firm commitment as to the adequacy of a replacement item?

16. Is your promised vendor support adequate?

17. Do the vendors have a disaster support team that will:
    - Help locate a backup site?
    - Help review disaster recovery plan?
    - Provide equipment and manpower to run backup operations?
    - Provide on-site maintenance and engineering support to help get the backup computer operational?

18. Will the vendors participate in a disaster recovery test?

19. Have the vendors of all supporting equipment been considered in the disaster recovery planning, including those for:
    - Input equipment, such as OCR and MICR?
    - Input forms handling equipment, such as check handlers?
    - Output forms handling equipment, such as bursters, decollators, folders, and envelope stuffers?
    - Specific printer equipment?

20. Have commitments or support statements been obtained from all such vendors?

Communications Requirements

21. Is information on all necessary communications equipment and facilities documented, and in place at the backup site?

22. Does the backup site have power and communication lines laid in place, and connected to the equipment and utilities?

23. Are the switching and modem facilities at the backup site:
    - Installed?
    - Tested for the backup configuration?

24. Is there a configuration chart for the backup site showing:

Checklist 4-6. Continued.

- Location of terminals?
- Number and types of lines?
- Number and types of modems?
- Security and length of lines?

25. Have specific lines and terminals been designated for security?
26. Are there written procedures for what to do in case of problems with the:
    - Terminals?
    - Modems?
    - Lines?
27. Are contact persons, with phone numbers, documented for all communications vendor and service personnel?
28. Has the operation of all communications facilities been tested under simulated disaster conditions?
29. Are identification codes, passwords, terminal IDs, and operator IDs planned and on file at the backup site?
30. Have all written communications backup procedures been:
    - Documented, and placed at the backup site?
    - Reviewed with technical personnel and vendor personnel?
    - Tested under simulated disaster conditions?

---

because the other is no longer in production. For other units, the vendor might ship one that is being used for demonstration. In any event, most hardware vendors are prepared to give the most rapid replacement service possible. Their engineers will normally work around the clock to bring up the needed system. There are some differences between various vendors, however, and agreements or understandings should be obtained well in advance of problems occurring. Only a few of the vendors will put detailed agreements in writing, but experience has shown that the great majority will put forth a "best effort" and will state in advance that they will do so.

Those data centers that have multiple vendors and mixed equipment, must be aware that each vendor normally will supply only replacements for their own equipment, if the replacements are coming out of their delivery line. Otherwise, the vendors could have legal difficulty with their other customers.

There are a number of hardware devices that might be difficult to replace rapidly in an emergency. These include the following:

- Equipment that has a complex array of optional features and has been effectively customized for the application. Complex communications controllers are an example.

- Equipment manufactured in small quantities or on demand. Large memory arrays are an example.

- Equipment that is application sensitive, such as check sorters.

- Equipment that is approaching, or might have reached, obsolescence.

- Equipment manufactured by companies no longer in existence. You can search the used equipment market for replacements.

The ease of replacement of hardware usually is a secondary consideration in disaster recovery planning because all manufacturers are attuned to giving emergency aid. At a minimum, it still takes 24 to 48 hours to get replacement hardware. The replacement then has to be tested. Frequently, deliveries take several days. Therefore, if there are functions that cannot wait a few days and need immediate backup access, the backup hardware to be used must already be in place and operating at an existing site. This could be your own equipment, agreements with others, or commercial installations. The actual details must be carefully arranged in this stage of the disaster recovery preparations.

The priorities established for the processing of functions on the backup facility must be based on a realistic assessment of hardware availability. The vendor can help in this assessment and should be solicited.

Communication requirements

The size and complexity of the communication network supporting a data center is a major factor in contingency planning. The dependency of time-crucial functions must be understood in detail before steps can be planned to provide backup and recovery. The telephone company normally responds very rapidly in restoring communication lines. The problem lies in restoring a sufficient number of terminals, modems, controllers, and so on, and in adjusting the system software to recognize the new configuration from a new computer and a new location. It might be necessary to change local operation to remote and vice versa. Clearly, the system programming problems are considerable and require careful planning if rapid recovery is a necessity.

Common carriers have available the means to switch leased telephone lines under remote customer control from the initial termination to alternative sites. The switch, the controllers, and the lines have separate tariffs and even might be supplied by separate vendors. The complications are obvious, but the rapid switching of many lines might be economically feasible if the organization's dependency on them is great. This all must be reviewed in the preparatory analysis. If there is careful planning, the greatest problem still will be in the development of the required systems software to exactly meet the previously unused configurations.

Clearly, if the importance is sufficient, the capability must be developed to route all communications to each of two (or more) sites. With this alternative, there can be a rapid changeover from a damaged site to the backup. The economic feasibility and the time dependencies must be analyzed carefully to determine the necessary approach to communications backup.

Other resource requirements
Personnel requirements

Personnel are the most important resources of any I/S organization. Recovery from damaging losses is highly dependent on the availability and participation of knowledgeable, experienced personnel. People provide the flexibility, availability, and versatility needed to meet an unexpected situation and to adapt the previously made plans to the situation as it actually exists. It is, therefore, necessary that all personnel who are to be involved in a recovery plan have studied the plan, have been trained in its execution, and have been given an opportunity to suggest changes and additions.

People can be expected to innovate, perform unfamiliar tasks, work under stress, and work long hours if they feel that they are a part of the plan. For a successful recovery operation, the staff must believe in the inherent importance of the organization's mission to motivate the staff to carry out the work under stress. The planners of a backup and recovery operation must consider whether the I/S facility operates in a way that the staff can be depended on in unusual situations.

Personnel safety

Preparations will be different for the handling of personnel when dealing with a localized fire or minor disaster, as compared to those preparations needed for dealing with a regional disaster, such as extreme weather conditions, floods, hurricanes, tornadoes, and so on. It must be constantly remembered that the safety of personnel is of paramount importance, and this will include the safety of their dependents when there is regional danger.

Personnel should not be expected to move out of a general disaster area immediately to help in data processing recovery. The lives and well-being of their families and friends might be threatened, and their first duty will be to secure their own homes. If there are floods, high winds, or earthquake damage, staff should not be expected to go anywhere until the civil authorities have made it clear that even short-distance travel is safe.

Organizations that operate in a large area might appropriately set up disaster recovery centers far from the original site. They should make preparations for these centers to be operated by personnel who live near the new sites. This will be quite feasible if there is adequate cycling of files and testing of emergency operations.

Planning personnel actions

The planning of personnel actions, moving between sites, possibly crowding into offices, and handling unfamiliar tasks, must be considered carefully in detail. People should be informed in advance where they will be expected to report, how they will get there, and what their additional responsibilities will be. In preparation for such moves, it might be necessary to examine floor plans in detail, to have some extra equipment available, to lay in heavier electric power lines, more standby telephone lines, and so on, to be assured that when the people are moved, they will be able to work effectively.

If two or more sites routinely provide backup to each other during periods of equipment changeover, scheduled maintenance, or minor failure, the personnel will become familiar with the operation. It essentially will be a continued rehearsal of a disaster situation. In such cases, the people involved should understand the problems of emergency recovery in detail and should be able to make worthwhile suggestions for the plan.

Telephone trees

Part of the preparation for disaster recovery is assembling the names, addresses, and telephone numbers of all persons who might be involved. This is not necessarily as simple as it sounds, because many personnel departments do not release the telephone contact information for employees. They consider that home addresses and telephone numbers are confidential information that should not be written down and distributed widely where it could be used for someone else's commercial gain. There is a simple way of circumventing this problem, which must be carefully worked out in advance. Do not publish a single, comprehensive "telephone tree," but merely publish the telephone numbers of the key contacts and their alternates. They, in turn, will have lists of the people they should call, and so on. They will keep these lists on their person or at home.

Figure 4-8, Disaster Telephone Tree, is a form for organizing a tree by application system or organization group. Of course, a few I/S management people must keep the complete telephone lists in case there is a breakdown in any part of the chain.

Training

People must be given sufficient training in the problem being considered, the reason for the plan structure, and their parts in it. This must be training with feedback that is repeated periodically or when there is a change of staff. Staff must rehearse their roles to the extent necessary and be provided with any skills training that might be required.

Each person must be recognized as an important link in the overall plan. Because most people involved will be experienced in their own special areas, they should have their suggestions considered seriously.

One possibility to consider is to offer positive rewards for any outstanding performances during emergencies. This would serve to advise all personnel of the special nature of their activities during and after a service disruption incident.

Supplies and forms requirements

Most supplies are catalog items with reasonable availability. Most facilities have a sufficiently large number and variety of such items to make plans for stockpiling needed supplies are not carefully cataloged and analyzed. The storage people must be told what will be needed in the event of an emergency.

Paper stocks and forms obviously are the crucial area to analyze because many of the forms might be special, and very large quantities of some forms might be used routinely. Adequate buffer supplies of stocks should be kept in two or three locations. Vendor information should be available in an emergency for the important stocks. Many office supplies are available on the open market locally and need not be backed up to any great extent.

A strong forms control program can be invaluable in a disaster situation. All forms will be cataloged adequately, with samples, and the information will be available at more than one site. This is most

Fig. 4-8. Disaster telephone tree.

Date _____
Updated _____

Department or Application System

Key Contact (1)	Extension	Home Phone	Address	Other Personnel To Call (2)	Position	Extension	Home Phone
Key EDP Contact							
Alternate Key EDP Contact							
Key User Contact (3)							
Alternate Key User Contact							

Notes:
1. Each Key Contact will have a more detailed telephone and address list.
2. Normally, the Key Contact or Alternate Key Contact will call the Other Personnel.
3. Notify the Key User Contacts first. Some users may not want to be called on weekends. Note this if management approves it.

important with specially printed forms and internally developed forms.

The provision of supplies is not a minor task and must be integrated into the recovery program. Most supplies are stored in basements or near vulnerable areas, and by the nature of paper, they are particularly susceptible to fire and water damage, either from storm floods or firemen's hoses.

Particular care must be given to the identification and continued availability of important items in stock and of special forms on which there might be dependence. The replacement lead time of such items can be great if adequate backup stocks have not been arranged.

Transportation requirements

There are two transportation problems to be considered in disaster recovery preparation. One is the effect of a regional disaster on public transportation and the ability of employees to get to work and deliveries to be made. The other is the rapid movement of people and supplies to an alternate site and the regular shuttling between sites during the service disruption incident.

Events that disrupt the transportation of people and supplies over a region cannot be overcome readily and present a serious problem to the ability of the I/S facility to operate effectively. Even overnight accommodations nearby will be difficult to obtain because of the competition for them. Such problems as a wide power failure, earthquakes, labor difficulties, riots, and so on, can be met only by locating the backup facility at a considerable distance from the affected facility, and depending upon other personnel to operate it.

If the disaster is localized to the data center, however, and an operating backup site is available within 50 miles, a different set of plans should be prepared. In this case, some personnel will be expected to use their own cars and commute in a different direction. Others will be helped by using public transportation in a different way. Still others, who might normally walk to work or share in ride groups, will need to have shuttle buses arranged from convenient pickup sites. Plans will have to be made for rapidly renting such buses or vans, getting drivers, and making the schedules known. A number of smaller vehicles also might have to be arranged for to move crucial personnel and supplies from site to site routinely. Still other arrangements might have to be made to take vans with snacks and drinks to the new site. All such contacts should be made in advance with lists of vendors, telephone numbers, costs, and so forth prepared.

Facility and office space requirements

There are two possible objectives in the selection of space into which a data center can be moved after the loss of an original site:

- Space that can be used temporarily until the original site is restored

- Space into which the data center can relocate with relative permanence

A move from a damaged site to a partially prepared floor space cannot be done rapidly. Cooling water, air conditioners, raised floors, and the like are time-consuming to install. It might take several weeks if environmental equipment is to be acquired. Site preparation must be done in advance if recovery is needed on the same day as the loss of capability, or very rapidly. Communication lines, power lines, and ancillary environmental equipment to support the crucial functions must be installed well before a problem occurs. Such work is expensive, however, and should not be undertaken unless the need for rapid backup is great or if the site could be used regularly for taking part of the normal data processing load. Plans for the new space should therefore reflect, whenever possible, the future growth plans of the organization.

A major consideration in plans for backup space for the computer complex is the ability to provide simultaneous office space for terminal users and other staff on a local basis. Local operations are considerably less complex than remote operations.

Power and environmental systems requirements

Uninterruptible Power Supply (UPS) systems normally fulfill the useful function of protecting against power line transients and other brief interruptions, and thus keep the system running smoothly with fewer restarts and less potential damage to data integrity. They also provide a short period, during a primary power failure, during which a standby generator can be brought into operation to support the crucial data processing functions.

UPS systems further provide a useful function in the case of many other types of disaster. They provide a short period, usually from fifteen to thirty minutes, during which the system can be brought down gracefully without loss of information.

Power and environmental control systems are the most expensive and time-consuming to bring up at a new site. No reasonable backup can be expected unless the emergency site has been prepared in advance with such equipment.

Documentation requirements

All backup documentation should be analyzed so that needed material is available at the off-site facility in time of need. The best approach for backing up operations documentation and systems programs is to use one of the several word processing or similar library systems available and have all the information in machine readable form. It then can be routinely backed up with other data and taken to the backup site. There it can be stripped out if needed.

The greatest problem comes from user manuals, system manuals, and program manuals. These tend to be given narrow distribution and kept in fire-prone areas, such as paper-cluttered offices. One approach is to put them on a library control system and store backup copies at a remote site. However, these manuals tend not to be updated correctly over time. Another approach is to microfilm all such manuals, at least annually, and store in a secure place. This process can be more expensive. The problem of backing up documentation must be studied carefully in the plan preparation phase, even though it is not generally a popular activity.

Of special consideration is the backup of the I/S disaster recovery plan itself. Because the plan will have details of names, phone numbers, contacts, equipment inventories, alternate site agreements, and so on that cannot be readily memorized, copies of the plan must be available immediately at the time a disaster is recognized. This means that copies of the I/S disaster recovery procedures (the action plan) must not only be distributed to key locations in the data centers and the I/S offices, but they also should be kept at the homes of the key people who will be contacted in time of emergency.

There are two reasons for keeping copies of the I/S disaster recovery plan at the homes of key individuals. The first is that a serious disaster could keep people from entering the facility and offices. The second is that most serious fires start at night or weekends. If a fire starts during the working day, it is normally detected quickly, and handled. The same applies to water and steam leaks, and break-ins.

Comparison of the requirements with the objectives

There usually are far more activities that can be performed, and far more money needed for those activities, than are required to meet the basic disaster recovery objectives of management. During the analysis of the recovery requirements, most technical analysts will work toward a smoother and more complex and complete recovery than will be warranted from a financial point of view. The disaster recovery planning analysts should, rightly, try to save and recover as much data and activity as possible. Management, on the other hand, will have the attitude of recovering only that which is absolutely necessary, at the least cost. Management will be prepared to take substantial losses that can be covered by insurance. This approach might make future total recovery more difficult, but it will have a more attractive cash flow.

To determine the minimum amount of data processing activities that are absolutely necessary for disaster recovery, however, it is necessary to analyze a much broader set of activities, and leave the final selection to management. This will entail the objective statement of as many contributing factors as possible to allow the final decisions to be made intelligently and profitably.

After the principal resource requirements have been analyzed adequately, therefore, the analysts should present the requirements in a way that they can be directly compared to the plan objectives. From the analysts' point of view, and from discussions with many managers, analysts also should assign resource preparation priorities, and establish a time frame for disaster recovery. This analysis of resource requirements against the original objectives then can be presented to management, together with an analysis of the appropriate recovery strategies and costs, so that is a final decision can be made.

Note that, as management reviews such an analysis, they might wish to change or refine the statement of the original objectives. Management will be in a position to decide how much to budget for the preparation of the final disaster recovery plan.

The requirements analysis must thus cover a broader area than the final disaster recovery plan, to allow for selection decisions. All strategy decisions to be required of management should be clearly stated, in context, with time and cost estimates.

5

Cost analysis
for disaster
recovery planning

IN A STUDY OF I/S SECURITY AND DISASTER RECOVERY, A NUMBER OF
good plans and desirable measures likely will be proposed. An analysis should be made to compare the cost of the measures with the
possible costs of disruption to the organization.

First, the possible service disruption incidents must be considered and analyzed as their probability of occurrence. Second, each
specific disaster recovery strategy designed to meet these incidents
should be studied independently, considering its priority level and
need. These disaster costs, and the recovery strategies to reduce
them, can be presented for comparison in either tabular form or
simply as a memo description. All assumptions of probability of
occurrence should be stated. Senior management must decide their
preference, and the order of priorities, based on the recommendations of the study team. The forms that follow will aid in performing
this series of summary steps.

The following is a simple approach to cost analysis, which
probably will be needed at least for budget purposes. Risk management and insurance coverage, discussed later in this chapter,
describes more careful assignment of probabilities of events, and
more complex calculations. Some organizations will want the full
analysis, but they are in the minority. Most organizations will be satisfied with the understanding that:

- There is a definite possibility of a disaster occurring.

- There are legal and operational requirements to protect against great disruption of the I/S operations.
- There are a number of alternative strategies available.

What they want to know is, which are the most appropriate and most effective strategies?

Cost of possible losses

In discussing the probability of disruptions and the probable costs with user management, a serious problem will arise. The probable costs given by different users will not be directly comparable, because they will be based on different assumptions. Some users will plead importance, but will have no wish to pay for security. Other users will underestimate the catastrophe to their operations in the event of a major data processing breakdown. Still other users will ask for high reliability, and will back up their requests with sufficient available funds.

The I/S manager must, therefore, resort to an analytical statement of the problems. He or she should list the probability of occurrence of disruption as it is given, the probable cost, and the costs of security solutions as they are perceived. To help prepare this analysis systematically, and to aid in visualizing the problem, three worksheets are given (Figs. 5-1 through 5-3).

Figure 5-1 provides an opportunity to state the most likely problem areas in a form that can be used either judgmentally or as part of calculations. Assumptions are crystallized. Figure 5-2, Probable Economic Loss, gives an analysis of types of loss under varying considerations. Figure 5-3, Possible Costs of Disaster Recovery Strategies, gives a summary of the possible costs of measures for each disaster recovery strategy considered. It does not aid in developing the detail making up the costs. These costs can be balanced against the economic losses, by groups of applications and related recovery strategies, considering the probability of the occurrence of the losses.

Objectives

Figure 5-1 is a worksheet intended to define, by type of asset, the probability of occurrence of service disruption incidents for each of several threats. Determining the potential cost of disasters for each of the categories of assets is the purpose of Fig. 5-2.

The objective of these two worksheets is to facilitate determining the areas of greatest exposure. In areas where probability of

Fig. 5-1. Probability of occurrence of security event.

	Fire	Flood	DESTRUCTION Earthquake	Accident	Sabotage	Other	Fraud Theft, Etc.	Employee Error
EDP Equipment								
Installation Facilities								
Data								
Programs Operating System								
Documentation								

Probability of Occurrence Codes: (Enter in Boxes)

1. High Probability

2. Medium Probability

3. Low Probability

Assumptions made for Probability of Occurrence:

Fig. 5-2. Probable economic loss.

	Replacement or Reconstruction Cost		Performance Failure Loss								
			Without Backup			Current Backup			Desired Backup		
	Without Backup	With Backup	ETR	EE	BIL	ETR	EE	BIL	ETR	EE	BIL
EDP Equipment											
Installation Facility											
Data											
Programs Operating System											
Documentation											
Total											

Note: ETR: Estimated Time to Recover (Days)　　EE: Extra Expense ($000)　　BIL: Business Interruption Loss ($000)

Desired Backup (In this space identify the Desired Backup capability with one-time cost plus annual continuing cost.

Fig. 5-3. Possible costs of disaster recovery strategies.

Strategy No.	Disaster Recovery Measure	Preparation Cost	Operating Cost		Priority Level
			Disaster Daily	Standby Monthly	

occurrence and economic loss combine to produce great potential business exposure, prime consideration must be given to disaster recovery strategies.

Definition of terms

Destruction The loss from accidental and natural causes (e.g., flood, fire, earthquake), malicious mischief, and sabotage. Such events as riot, explosion, and erasure of magnetic files are included.

Fraud, Theft, and Embezzlement The deliberate alteration of data and programs (e.g., modification of tape, disk pack, card files, etc.) plus the removal of physical objectives (e.g., tape reels, check forms, printouts, etc.) Occasionally, disastrous events are planned by the perpetrator to cover up such actions.

Employee Error   Losses resulting from inadequate procedures or systems design, as well as carelessness or indifference by employees. The items particularly susceptible to this problem are data and programs, which can be completely destroyed.

EDP Equipment   Computer mainframes and peripherals, plus data entry and related equipment.

Installation Facilities   The total computer center other than the EDP equipment. It includes the computer and key entry room and library, lighting, air conditioning, wiring, furniture, fixtures, bursters and related ancillary equipment, supplies, forms tapes, disk packs, punched cards (but not the replacement cost of the data or programs contained in these media) and related support facilities.

Definitions of the other assets is considered to be unnecessary because the terms are self-explanatory.

Probability of occurrences service disruption incident

This section will provide information for filling out Fig. 5-1. For the Destruction, Fraud, Theft, Etc., and Error columns, identify the probability of occurrence by selecting the appropriate code from the following table. (For example, if a high probability for destruction exists for data, enter a "1" in the appropriate box, and so on.)

Probability of occurrence codes

1. High probability
2. Medium probability
3. Low probability

The form has space for stating the assumptions made in determining the probability of occurrences. This will point out the crucial problems for the study group. In one sense, filling out this form is an exercise to crystallize the thinking of the disaster recovery planning group and to get them concerned with the more probable problems. It also is used to get a consistent set of multiplying factors in determining the areas of greatest exposure.

Probable economic loss

Figure 5-2 is a worksheet intended to be used to determine the potential cost of service disruption incidents for each of the categories of assets.

The financial loss for I/S equipment, installation facilities, data, programs, operating system, and documentation, is to be determined both for replacement and for performance failure loss. Estimate the order of magnitude of the financial penalty. It is not necessary to develop a finite calculation when a reasonable estimate can be made. The main purpose is to emphasize the areas of concern, and to put the problems in a financial perspective.

Definition of terms

Without Backup   Of or referring to a backup facility for each of the categories of assets (e.g., I/S Equipment) that either does not exist, does not function, or for any reason fails to provide the recovery capability that it was intended to furnish. For example, assume that the data in the secondary storage facility was totally destroyed along with the data in the regular library. The data must then be reconstructed from source documents because there is no backup file.

Current Backup   The current backup facility provides only the recovery capability that it was designed to furnish. For example, if an agreement with another installation had been made to provide computer time equivalent to 50 percent of your current work load, assume that the agreement will be honored.

Desired Backup   The reasonable, cost-effective level of recovery capability you would like to achieve. For example, if you currently do not have a secondary storage facility for data, programs and operating system, and documentation, assume this facility has been created and that the aforementioned materials are fully protected in this storage facility for backup purposes.

Each of the three levels of backup has three subcolumns:

- **ETR (Estimated Time to Recovery)**   The elapsed time (in days) it is estimated it will take to fully replace the asset (e.g., data) for a given level of backup.

- **EE (Extra Expense)**   The necessary additional cost (expressed in thousands of dollars) required to continue the normal operations of the business immediately following the destruction of an asset.

- **BIL (Business Interruption Loss)** The financial loss (expressed in thousands of dollars) resulting from the inability to conduct the company's normal business operations as the result of the destruction of an asset. For example, if a customer order processing system is inoperative because of loss of the programs, this event would have an impact on the profitability of the company.

Completing Fig. 5-2

All figures are to be reported in thousands of dollars and are to be determined without consideration of potential insurance recovery.

If the replacement cost, extra expense, or the business interruption loss is difficult to calculate, but the sum clearly is of major proportions, the term *catastrophic* can be substituted for a specific amount. The option to use this term should be exercised sparingly.

The intent of the Replacement Cost portion of the form is to state the costs required to replace or restore the destroyed asset. The cost to regain full operational status when recovery is facilitated by backup resources might be different from the cost to replace or restore the asset without the protection provided by a backup facility.

The intent of the Performance Failure Loss portion of the form is to obtain information concerning the consequences of destruction or loss of all or part of the data processing function including: ETR, EE, and BIL, the same information required on Fig. 5-1.

The cost of replacing or reconstructing the several categories of assets (e.g., I/S equipment) should not be included in the Performance Failure Loss section of the form. These calculations have been determined in the preceding two columns, Replacement or Reconstruction cost. This is an attempt to determine only the effect of destruction on the ongoing performance of the business. Calculation of performance failure loss is to be made under three different assumptions:

- Without backup
- Current backup
- Desired backup

Replacement or reconstruction cost without backup

- *EDP Equipment*   Replace all existing hardware.
- *Installation facility*   Completely rebuild or relocate the installation.

- *Data* Reconstruct all data files from source documents.
- *Programs and operating systems* Write, compile, and test all from scratch.
- *Documentation* Create all flow charts, record layouts, etc., anew.

Replacement or reconstruction cost with backup

Identify the costs, expressed in thousands of dollars, to:

- *I/S equipment and installation facility* Replace all existing hardware or rebuild the installation with no particular time pressure, and with the capability operating continuously.
- *Data, programs, operating system, and documentation* Become fully operational in each category if a satisfactory secondary (backup) storage site has been established to house copies of the data, programs, operating system, and documentation.

If there are no clear differences, the figures in the "Without Backup" column can be repeated in the "With Backup" column.

Performance failure loss without backup

For these columns, assume that each of the assets has been destroyed, is not available, or does not function because provisions for backup were not made or failed to provide any recovery capabilities.

ETR Identify the number of days it would take:

- *I/S Equipment* For the vendor to replace all computer equipment
- *Installation facility* To rebuild or relocate the installation at a new site
- *Data* To reconstruct all data files from source documents
- *Programs* To write, compile, and test all programs starting from the point records are not backed up
- *Documentation* To create anew all flow charts, record layouts, etc.

EE

- *I/S Equipment* The overtime costs of clerical personnel, hiring of temporary workers, etc., to perform the entire computer's work load or that portion that could be feasibly accomplished for the time period required to replace the equipment

- *Installation facility* The costs of temporary facilities until such time the original installation facility is restored
- *Data* The overtime costs of clerical personnel, hiring temporary workers, etc., to overcome the problems resulting from the lack of machine-readable data until at least half of the data files can be reconstructed from source documents. Note that the I/S equipment is functioning during this time period so the cost of "duplicating" the computer work does not have to be included.
- *Programs and operating systems* The same type of costs as incurred for I/S equipment destruction for half the period required to complete all programs, plus the costs resulting from having clerical personnel working with simple listings of data files until half of the programs have been completed
- *Documentation*—The additional costs of systems analysis and programming in changing systems and programs as the result of the lack of documentation for half the time period required to complete the re-creation of the documentation

BIL

- *I/S Equipment* The loss suffered from the inability to perform the computer's tasks for the time period required to replace the equipment. Do not consider the reduction in the loss that would occur from the performance of all or part of the computer's jobs by a clerical task force.
- *Data* The loss suffered from the nonavailability of machine-readable data for half the time period required to complete all programs, plus the loss resulting from having clerical personnel working with simple listings of data until half of the program has been completed
- *Documentation* The loss suffered as the result of delay in changing systems and programs for half the time period required to complete the re-creation of the documentation

Performance failure loss with current backup

For these columns, assume that the backup facility provides exactly the recovery capability it was intended to furnish. If backup for a given asset (e.g., data) does not exist, repeat the data from the "Without Backup" column.

ETR

- *I/S equipment*   If an agreement has been made with another I/S installation for equipment backup, indicate the number of days it would take to become operational for half of the normal work load. If an agreement for I/S equipment backup for up to half of the normal work load has not been arranged, repeat the figure from the "Without Backup" column.

- *Installation facility*   Same calculation as the I/S equipment figure above, or repeat the figure from the "Without Backup" column.

- *Data, programs, and documentation*   If a satisfactory secondary (backup) storage site has been established to house these three assets, indicate the number of days required to become fully operational for each of them. If a satisfactory secondary storage facility has not been established, repeat the figure from the "Without Backup" column for each of the items that is not protected.

    EE   Given the existing backup capabilities, calculate the additional cost for each of the categories of assets (e.g., data) that would be incurred until a full, normal operating condition has been achieved. Among the costs that might be incurred are the purchase of computer time, travel to and from other computer installations, cost of overtime of clerical personnel, the hiring of temporary workers, and so on.

    BIL   Given the existing backup capabilities, calculate the financial loss incurred as the result of the inability to conduct normal business operations for the period required to achieve the normal operating level. An example would be the profit reduction resulting from the inability to meet production schedules because of the loss of a portion of the inventory status records.

Performance failure loss with desired backup

For these columns, assume that the best possible backup capabilities are available and will function as intended. If no significant improvements can be seriously contemplated, repeat the data from the "Current Backup" columns.

    For the desired backup capabilities, use the same concepts and techniques in determining the ETR, EE, and BIL as were used for the "Current Backup" calculations. In filling out Fig. 5-2 use the space provided to identify briefly the "Desired Backup" capability with the associated one-time cost and annual continuing cost.

Cost of measures for disaster recovery

The costs of measures planned for disaster recovery are best grouped according to the recovery strategies involved and listed in priority order. Management will not necessarily use the cost/benefit priority applications to pay for disaster recovery measure for the lower priority applications. The worksheet, Fig. 5-3, Possible Costs of Disaster Recovery Strategies, is for a management summary of the various calculations that have been made for the costs of the various strategies investigated. It is essentially a selection list for management.

Figure 5-1, Probability of Occurrence, presents a summary of the possible costs of measures for each disaster recovery strategy and should be summed by strategy. In the disaster recovery study, these costs can be balanced against the possible economic losses, considering the probability of their occurrence. A project budget then can be developed at various levels for approval.

It is important to clearly separate the preparation and development costs from the daily operating costs at the time of a disaster, and the monthly operating costs in standby mode.

This cost analysis approach for disaster recovery study is purposely brief. Some of the numbers can be summaries of considerable analysis, while other numbers are simply estimates. In most organizations, however, this level of analysis will be sufficient, because it will be used more for budget purposes than to make decisions on disaster recovery. In general, disaster recovery decisions are made on a considered need basis by management to determine cut-off points and for budgeting.

Risk management and insurance coverage

Security incidents and emergencies will occur. The following principles should always be kept in mind:

- Plan for a secure operation, but prepare for a disaster.
- Work with insurance managers in disaster recovery planning.
- Never risk more than you can afford to lose.

- Make sure your insurance programs consider catastrophic loss.
- Keep an inventory of what is insured, and be prepared to prove it.

Insurance coverage

There is no way in which absolute protection and recovery from disaster is possible. Realistically, you must minimize possible loss and cover it by insurance. This is called risk management and insurance coverage. It is imperative for I/S staff to consult the insurance manager of their organization about the insurance coverage on the computer and related operations, and the effect of the disaster recovery plan on the insurance coverage. There are several considerations involved:

- A good disaster recovery plan can reduce the cost of insurance.
- The organization might be prepared to concentrate on certain aspects of recovery and simply insure for other aspects.
- The computer insurance problems can be complex.
- There might be extra insurance needed on the backup sites.

The principle of insurance coverage is to transfer risk of major loss to another organization. Each company or organization will have its own standards as to what risk it will hold internally and what risk is to be transferred.

There normally will be an organization insurance manager responsible for deciding the degree of risk to be insured against. It is the responsibility of the study team to discuss the study with the insurance manager, who might not be fully aware of the implications of a computer disaster. Together they should estimate the possible exposure. The team should outline in detail all the property, equipment, records, and media involved, stating their actual cash value and replacement cost. Forms to aid in this effort are supplied later in this chapter.

The problem of loss

There is always a risk of substantial loss despite good management and careful data processing operations. Industrial disasters do occur. Industrial Risk Insurers (IRI), Hartford, CT, a nationwide association of 45 member insurance companies, has reported that in total industrial claims (not just computer related claims), the member companies have paid over one billion dollars in claims over a five-year period. About 40 percent of these losses were from fire, 18 percent from wind, and the remaining losses were in the "all other" category.

The causes of the fires are as would be expected: 20 percent were the result of electrical faults or defects (very possible in computer work), 18 percent were because of overheating, 14 percent were from incendiarism, 7 percent from defective industrial practices (mechanics, installers, etc.), 6 percent from spontaneous ignition (poor housekeeping included), and 6 percent were a result of careless smoking or disposal of smoking materials. IRI points out that nearly all these involve people failures of some kind. Most of these disasters could have been prevented with more careful planning, supervision, and training.

IRI also points out that catastrophic losses frequently occur because of inattention to closed facilities and dramatic weather changes. Many business owners turn down their thermostats to a low setting, and either leave their places unattended or with minimal staff, despite a forecast for abnormally severe weather conditions. The results can be catastrophic, particularly during three-day weekends. Disasters are more likely to occur when the facility is only partially staffed.

Good risk management is an integral part of proper insurance coverage. Effort must be put into loss prevention and control. Insurance coverage is a positive action to transfer the remaining less likely risk to other parties.

Loss prevention and control

A comprehensive management loss prevention and control program is a necessity for obtaining the maximum insurance coverage. This program should be discussed with your insurance manager. It should include:

- Self-inspection program
- Security program
- Assets management considerations
- Written and tested disaster recovery (catastrophe) plan
- Insurance selection

Self-inspection programs are loss prevention surveys that must include a detailed examination of the physical facilities involved. Reject the advice of any consultant who simply tailors a disaster recovery plan on one that has already been created. A contingency plan must address your individual requirements. Certainly there are many common, proven approaches that can be used in disaster recovery planning. They should not be selected, however, until a detailed self-inspection program has been conducted.

The procedures, checklists, and worksheets in this book are an excellent starting point for such a survey. Such a program is not a one-shot activity, however. The most extensive survey should be conducted at the time the disaster recovery plan is being developed. Subsequently, the security coordinator or other person in charge of the plan should make several loss prevention surveys a year in specific areas. Conditions will change, and constant vigilance must be exercised.

Security programs are the fundamental base of all disaster recovery preparations. Detailed security reviews should be undertaken for all phases and areas of the organization's operations, and should be based on information and proven methods for preparation for loss prevention and disaster recovery management.

Assets management has a wider scope than I/S disaster recovery planning, because it is usually the function of senior officers of the organization. Because many of the assets are maintained in the I/S area, however, and because an I/S disaster could cause an appreciable loss of the organization's assets, there are a number of considerations in assets management that should be addressed in disaster recovery planning.

There must be good records kept on the value of the organizations assets. Statements should be maintained on insurable property values, rather than book values or taxable values. Real property will be insured on a replacement value, actual cash value, agreed value, or some other method. This can be quite complex relative to information on electronic media, so it must be addressed.

It also is important that property valuation or inventory records be maintained in a manner consistent with the insurance coverage provided. For I/S, this means that a perpetual inventory must be maintained of all programs, files, and data. This can be done realistically with an automated program that is run regularly and backed up in a safe storage location routinely. Combined with the automated program, there must be indices, location information, and ownership records. A good system will allow complete identification at the time of loss and full recovery in a claim adjustment. It also is one of the fundamental bases of I/S disaster recovery action.

Disaster recovery plans (or catastrophe plans) must be written to meet the existing conditions, and tested by operating personnel to be useful. Your position after a loss will be no better than what you have planned for. Although most I/S disaster recovery planning is technically oriented, it is imperative that any plans be reviewed by insurance personnel (either internal, consultant, or vendor) to determine that the most crucial areas of loss prevention and control have been considered.

Insurance selection usually is the prerogative of the insurance manager or other financial officer appointed by management. It is the function of the disaster recovery study team to understand what is important relative to insurance coverage, however, and to be able to discuss coverage in terms of what is likely to happen from a technical point of view. There are so many uncertainties in the possible occurrence of a disaster that broad coverage is most attractive. There is now considerable experience in the insurance industry in computer-related disasters, so a good property casualty carrier should be used, one that has experience with such planning and is adequately capitalized.

The insurance portfolio

Although the insurance manager will have the final decision on the insurance portfolio, it is important for I/S, and particularly the I/S disaster recovery planning group, to understand what is involved. Insurance is completely complementary to security actions, and the minimum total cost is obtained by considering both together. The study group should, therefore, become familiar with all related insurance policies in order to:

• Know what is covered and what is not covered
• Give an adequate technical review of the coverage
• Understand how the policies would apply
• Understand how to prove loss and aid in collection

Ambiguities and technical language can be clarified by discussion with the insurance manager. The I/S technical language must be clarified for the benefit of the insurance manager to obtain mutual understanding of the best insurance approach.

The principal function of the I/S disaster recovery team will be to outline in detail all the equipment, records, and media, stating their replacement cost and actual cash value, and to give a measure of the degree of risk. Worksheets are provided to aid this process. These worksheets should be filled out by the study team for discussion with the organization's insurance manager. These worksheets are given as Figs. 5-4 through 5-11.

There probably will be several basic types of insurance policies to discuss such as:

• Property and casualty insurance, including fire, property damage, and general liability
• All-risk policies, including earthquake insurance, flood insurance, and valuable papers and records insurance

- Business interruption coverage
- Extra expense insurance

The need for this coverage, or any other special insurance coverage, such as third party liability, business interruption, and so on, should be clearly defined in the discussion. There might be, for example, a considerable business interruption loss that could be insured. However, this is primarily not under the data processing manager's control, and it should be reviewed and requested by the users of the operation, together with the insurance manager.

When data processing equipment is leased or rented, the insurance on it might be borne by the owner. This should be checked in the contract.

The insurance manager also will be concerned that all legal requirements for fire and safety are being met in the facility. Insurance will be valid only if there is full compliance with all fire and safety laws. It is wise to request inspections by both the insurance company and the local fire department. Fire department familiarity with your installation is in itself a useful precaution.

The final decision on the insurance coverage will be determined by the organization policy on such matters. The decision can best be made if the data processing manager first:

- Develops a contingency plan
- Fills out the worksheets carefully
- Considers the probabilities of disaster

The following are brief descriptions of the uses of the attached worksheets:

Figures 5-4 and 5-5, Data Processing and Related Equipment Worksheets   These worksheets are used for listing all computers and peripheral equipment as well as air conditioning and other component parts dedicated to the systems and data processing installation. Include shared facilities, such as air conditioning systems, only if the entire system is dedicated to the data processing installation. If it is shared as part of a central plant unit and insured accordingly, do not include it. Exclude furniture and fixtures, unless they are unique to the I/S function and not apt to be covered under standard property policies. Report gross estimated amounts for the categories. For the purpose of this survey, detailed listings by piece of equipment are not required. However, they might be useful for the data processing manager's records.

Fig. 5-4. Insurance worksheet—Owned equipment.

No.	Description	Date Installed	Replacement Cost	Actual Cash Value
1	CPU			
2	Peripheral Equipment			
3	Terminals			
*4				

*List other directly associated equipment

Insurance Coverage on Owned Equipment

Insurance Company	Date of Policy	Policy Amount	Annual Premium	Amount of Deductible

Briefly describe perils named or excluded in the above policies:

Note the following definitions:

Replacement cost   The cost to replace the property in question with a modern unit in new condition and of equivalent capacity, taking into consideration new materials, technology, and design concepts.

Actual cash value   Replacement cost, less an allowance for physical depreciation (not book depreciation) and functional or economic obsolescence.

Figure 5-6, Records and Media Worksheet   This worksheet is for listing all records and media used or stored in the data processing operation. This includes input records, magnetic media records, paper tape records, documentation, printed forms, and stored output.

Fig. 5-5. Insurance worksheet—Rented or leased equipment.

No.	Contract/Lessor*	Date of Lease	Term of Lease	Annual Lease Cost	Lessor** Liability

* If there are several contracts with a given lessor, these may be combined.
** Indicate the extent to which the lessor assumes liability for equipment damage or loss, installed and in transit.

Insurance Coverage on Leased Equipment

If you are covered separately for the difference in conditions if the rental/lease agreement is on a named peril basis and not on an all-risks peril basis, list the coverage.

Insurance Company	Date of Policy	Policy Amount	Annual Premium	Amount of Deductible

It can be subdivided into the following categories:

Active data processing media   All forms of converted data and programs written on vehicles actively employed in the system. This includes magnetic and perforated tapes, disks, drums, and punch cards.

Source material   All records and data required for the preparation and updating of active processing media. This includes checks, statements, bills, invoices, credit ratings, accounting and service records, and so on.

It is worth listing all types of records or media for insurance purposes. Media vary greatly in importance, however. There should

Fig. 5-6. Insurance worksheet—Records and media.

No.	Number and Type of Records and Media	Need or Priority*	Retention Period	Cost to Reproduce	Replacement Value	Extra Expense

*   1. Vital   2. Important   3. Expendable

Insurance Coverage on Records and Media

Insurance Company	Date of Policy	Policy Amount	Annual Premium	Amount of Deductible

Note: If the above coverage includes the cost of reconstruction and research if either, or both, active media and source material were destroyed.

be insurance to cover all media, but in varying amounts depending on importance or need. Media, with the information on them, can be classified as vital, important, or expendable.

- *Vital*   Crucial organization information that must be replaced with records in event of disaster.

- *Important*   Part of a regular cyclical processing that might need reconstitution to proceed with the next cycle or to complete the audit trail.

- *Expendable* Useful information that might be needed, but is far enough back in the cycle so it probably does not need reconstitution. Only the physical tape, disk, and so forth will need replacing.

Figure 5-7, Extra Emergency Expense Worksheet This worksheet is used for listing the additional cost required to continue

Fig. 5-7. Insurance worksheet—Extra emergency expense.

No.	Expense	Rate of Expense	Total Per Week	Total Per Month
1	Rental of Temporary Facilities			
2	Rental of Backup Equipment			
3	Rental of Other Equipment			
4	Rental of Furniture			
5	Extra Supplies			
6	Moving Costs			
7	Temporary Insurance Costs			
8	Extra Telephone Costs			
9	Extra Traveling Costs			
10	Overtime Payments to Employees			
11	Additional Employees			
12				
13				
14				
15				
	DEDUCT			
	Expenses Reduced at Original Location			
	TOTAL Extra Expense:			

Insurance Coverage on Extra Emergency Expense

Insurance Company	Date of Policy	Policy Amount	Annual Premium	Amount of Deductible

the manual operations of the business immediately following damage to systems equipment, media, and necessary source material. Essentially, this additional cost is the excess of total operating cost during the restoration period over and above the total operating cost that would have been incurred if there had been no loss. Thus, the amount that the expenses will be reduced at the original location must be deducted.

List all emergency expenses that might be incurred in case of a major equipment breakdown, fire, or other disaster. A few of the possible expenses are listed on the sheet.

Figure 5-8, Third Party Liability Worksheet This worksheet is applicable to any service bureau operation, or any systems work, that is provided by your organization for outside customers. Special insurance coverage (errors and omissions) protects the insured against losses experienced by third parties through the

Fig. 5-8. Insurance worksheet—Third-party liability.

Note: This worksheet is used only if any service bureau operations or systems work are provided by your organization for outside customers.

Total Sales of Computer Services to Customers $_____

Total Sales of Systems Work to Customers $_____

Insurance Coverage on Third Party Liability

Insurance Company	Date of Policy	Policy Amount	Annual Premium	Amount of Deductible

If you have reciprocal backup agreements with other organizations having similar equipment configurations, include in this list:

a. Coverage for losses incurred to your property by non-organization personnel.

b. Coverage for losses incurred to non-organization's property by your personnel.

insured's own negligence, error, or omission in providing data processing services.

Figure 5-9, Revenue Bearing Data Worksheet This worksheet is used for listing records such as accounts receivable, fixed assets, and so on, in active data processing media form, which are the basis for future revenue claims. If applicable, it also should be used for identification and location of the organization's assets that are leased to customers or used for other revenue-bearing purposes. Loss or damage to such records generally constitutes exposure to losses greater than that of restoration costs or reconstruction.

Figure 5-10, Business Interruption Insurance Worksheet The consideration of business interruption insurance, or loss of profits insurance, will depend on the individual circumstances of the data processing organization. If the main product is outside service, this insurance should be considered seriously and the calculation of it will have an idea of the effectiveness of emergency backup arrangements.

Fig. 5-9. Insurance worksheet—Revenue bearing data.

Indicate average outstanding balances for a one-year period for revenue bearing data in media form. Specify by type of data.

Average Outstanding
Balance in 19 _____

$_____

$_____

$_____

$_____

Insurance Coverage on Revenue Bearing Data

Insurance Company	Date of Policy	Policy Amount	Annual Premium	Amount of Deductible

Fig. 5-10. Business interruption insurance worksheet.

Is the coverage under:

    a. Standard Fire Policy? _____

    b. Data Processing Insurance Policy? _____

    c. No Coverage? _____

Explain:

Insurance Coverage on Business Interruption

Insurance Company	Date of Policy	Policy Amount	Annual Premium	Amount of Deductible

If the data processing organization is principally a service group within a larger organization, with no formal payments, the loss of profits must be considered for the larger organization in the event of an emergency. Discussions with the users will yield the type of coverage desired. As the users become aware of the problem of a possible emergency, there probably will be funds available to prepare for the contingency operation.

Figure 5-11, Outside Computer Services Worksheet Another insurance problem arises if the organization's data processing requirements are handled predominantly by outside computer services. The data processing media and data are in the control of the third party and there is an exposure to damage or loss that is not covered by the normal organization security measures.

This exposure must be estimated and discussed with the outside computer service. It is important to know if the service bureaus with whom you contract maintain errors and omissions coverage to protect you from loss of profits as a result of their failure, negli-

Fig. 5-11. Insurance worksheet—Outside computer services.

Note: This worksheet is used only if your data processing requirements are handled predominantly by outside computer services.

What is the extent of your exposure to damage or loss of data processing media in the possession of outside computer services? If none, explain.

Do the service bureaus with whom you contract for services maintain errors and omissions coverage to protect you from loss of profits as a result of their failure, negligence, error, or omission in providing services to you?

If this is in writing, attach a copy.

gence, error, or omission in providing services to you. They also should have normal insurance that covers loss or damage to any of your property in their custody.

Actions to be taken after a loss occurs

After a loss occurs, it is imperative to take whatever steps are necessary to mitigate and prevent further damage. This is one of the basic purposes of an I/S disaster recovery plan, and all property insurance policies have this requirement. To understand what is involved, the following proposition is accepted in the insurance business:

"Take whatever steps an individual without insurance would take in similar circumstances."

Your goal is to maximize the recovery of your loss. You must both minimize your loss and have an amicable relationship with your insurance adjuster to do so. All reasonable actions must have been taken to hold loss down. Some of the possible actions follow:

- Document the damage rapidly
- Use experts to evaluate the property loss
- Notify all service companies that can render assistance
- Control information concerning the loss

- Communicate with the insurance adjuster
- Handle salvage professionally

Documentation of the damage caused by the disaster must be handled rapidly. First, memory can be confused at a time of urgency and rapid decision, so all supervisors involved should keep notes of their actions and observations as soon after their occurrence as possible. Such notes can be quite brief, but will be invaluable in later documentation efforts.

Second, photograph the disaster. Appoint one or two staff members to be responsible for taking photos of the damage as soon as is reasonable. No one but fire and police can have access at the time of the disaster, but one of the first people allowed to enter the area afterward should have a camera. This should preferably be of the instant type, so that the usefulness of the pictures can be judged before any cleanup has been accomplished. Such pictures should be guarded carefully and given to the insurance manager. Under no circumstances should any copies be given to the press or other outsiders until these people have been completely cleared by both the insurance and legal departments.

Third, set up a fire loss accounting system. This obviously will be handled by the accounting department, but I/S personnel should be prepared to assist in it and should keep any records that can be helpful. The losses must be accounted for by line-of-coverage in the insurance policies. The framework for such a system is similar to that for a construction-in-process accounting system.

Major losses from fire and disasters fall into accounting for involuntary conversions of nonmonetary assets to monetary assets. Accounting Principles Board (APB Opinion #29) and Financial Accounting Standards Board (FASB Interpretation #30) are the proper references to follow. Because most capital assets are reduced by book depreciation, an insured fire usually results in an extraordinary gain. The recognition of the gain is governed by FASB Interpretation #5.

It is important to identify all losses whether they are insured or uninsured. This is important because it might be possible to impute liability to third parties and receive other compensation for the loss.

Evaluation of the Property Loss should be handled by a team of experts in the area rather than I/S personnel. After a disaster, you are required to prepare a detailed proof of loss, with full documentation, to recover any insurance indemnities. The policies will state how to file such a proof of loss. In addition, all state insurance statutes must be reviewed carefully and followed. Accuracy is important in filing a proof of loss, but frequently estimates or forecasts will be necessary. These can be amended at a later time. The proof of loss will have to be signed by an executive officer of the insured group.

It will be useful to assemble a staff of experts to evaluate the scope of the damage and the property loss. Mechanical and structural damages generally can be handled by professionals using common procedures. The following might be needed in such an analysis:

- Architects
- Engineers
- Building and construction contractors
- Office furniture and supplies companies

Frequently, in computer disasters, the more difficult and less well-defined evaluation is of the damage to storage media, the information contained, and the electronic equipment involved. There are a number of consultants who specialize in such evaluation, and their aid could be valuable.

Another area of evaluation is that of salvage value. This is discussed later on.

Notification of service companies that can render assistance in determining loss, as well as aiding the disaster recovery, should be the appointed function of a staff member. It is easy to forget such notification at the time of urgency unless a particular service is required immediately. Some backup sites have all their utilities already laid in place, so rapid notification of the suppliers might be overlooked.

The service companies to be notified as soon as possible include:

- Vendors of peripheral and minor equipment
- Air-conditioning supply and servicing companies
- Gas, electrical, and plumbing contractors
- Office equipment suppliers, including used equipment suppliers
- Security equipment and services companies
- Building construction and elevator contractors

Control of information concerning the loss is crucial from the insurance and legal viewpoints as well as for public relations. It is obvious that the news of a loss could have a deleterious effect on the stock value of the company, as well as on the manner in which it is viewed by the public and the confidence that people will have in the organization. It is for these reasons that very little information is publicly available on a great many I/S disaster losses, and it is difficult to obtain information from most organizations who have experienced a disaster loss. Even a story of an excellent I/S disaster recovery experience would not allay the many doubts that would be held about the affected company.

There must be proper control over information during the disaster and about insurance claims information after the disaster. They are two sides of the same coin. If either type of information becomes public, your organization will receive a great many requests from the media, other insurance companies, and people who are studying their own problems.

There must be a designated spokesperson in the public relations team. During the disaster, the public relations people will operate from their own control center. After the disaster has subsided, they will operate from their own offices. This is particularly important when supplying information to the media.

The public relations team and the spokesperson can operate where printed information and other hard-copy information is being gathered in a document room. This room must be locked and have tightly controlled access. When there is a large disaster, and the claims will be appreciable, a document librarian should be appointed or hired. This person would index and catalog all the related documents and keep detailed records of who had access to the information, with dates and times, and of what records were reviewed or copied. Every item in the library should be cataloged with a control number.

Communication with the insurance adjuster is of vital importance to maximize your recovery from the loss. The adjuster's role is to settle the loss for only that amount that is required by the policy's terms, and no more. There can be a somewhat adversarial relationship, but it is crucial to handle it in a reasonable and cooperative manner. The goal should be to arrive at an equitable settlement of the loss. There can be no advantage in having a difficult adjustment process.

If it is possible, have a review of the problems that can arise and the actions that will be taken in a disaster with the insurance adjusting group, at the time that the disaster recovery plan is being written. This will, at least, allow an understanding of what information will be required about the disasters, and how the adjustment process will most likely be carried out in the event of an incident.

The insurance adjuster normally will be particularly skilled in the adjustment process because of prior experience and an intimate understanding of the details of the coverage. This will put the insured at a disadvantage in any negotiation. Because of this, it is frequently helpful to use outside consultants, familiar with both I/S and insurance, in the negotiation process. You then will know what facts are most vital.

It is unwise to have lawyers in the adjustment process unless there is arbitration or litigation involved. Their presence immediately establishes an adversarial relationship and facts will be harder to obtain.

Handling salvage professionally is a difficult and little-understood job. A great deal can be done to salvage damaged equipment, media, information, and furniture. The process should be started promptly, before destructive processes have continued and outsiders remove what might be of value. Salvage vendors, or salvors, should be identified in the disaster recovery plan with their 24-hour emergency numbers. This includes vendors who handle buildings, equipment, and documentation, as well as those who specialize in computer work.

A salvage company is essentially a general contractor for handling the contents of a building. The salvage company staff are specialists in protecting and preserving property as might be required by the insurance contract. A salvage company might be called a "contents general contractor" in its own description. The staff can arrange for the following:

- Preparations of a scope of damage to all contents
- Movement of damaged computer equipment and supplies
- Restoration and cleaning of furniture, fixtures, and equipment
- Corrosion control, which must be done rapidly
- Preparation and verification of an inventory of all contents
- Controlled removal of debris
- Deodorizing of the building and contents
- Sale of salvage of contents too badly damaged to be retained
- Complete, routine reporting of all expenses involved

The salvor should be independent of the insurance company to aid in negotiations. It might be helpful to name the preferred contents general contractor, or salvor, in the insurance policy so that it is understood with whom there will be communication, and what types of services will be provided during the adjustment period. Experienced salvors also can be used to provide consultation services during the disaster recovery planning effort.

Salvage vendors are listed in many Yellow Pages sections. Your insurance agent might know of reputable firms.

Your position after a loss will be no better than what you have planned for. A great deal can be done to salvage damaged equipment, supplies, and media. For example, electronic equipment frequently can be washed down with a mixture of deionized water and alcohol, with nearly 100 percent reusability, if the damage has been only water and smoke, and action is taken promptly.

It is important that information be included in a comprehensive plan as to what salvage personnel can have access to the area after a disaster, and what they might salvage, such as equipment, furniture, and documents. Actually, professionals salvage a great deal of information even from paper that is wet, smoky, and charred; particularly if access is quickly available.

Always remember, however, that fireproof vaults that are used to store records must be allowed to cool sufficiently prior to opening them. If they are opened while still hot, the contents can explode when exposed to the air.

Risk analysis

Risk analysis is the process of identifying and estimating expected losses as a consequence of undesired things happening to resources. The cost of the safeguards to be implemented to prevent such losses then can be compared to the risks involved. The cost of the safeguard can be limited by the size of the expected losses that would be prevented by the safeguard. Otherwise, the maximum cost of any safeguard should not exceed the expected losses. There are some safeguards, such as fire protection, protection against loss of life, and protection of vital records, which are legally required of management. These safeguards can be included in the risk evaluation study, but they normally will be installed, whatever the cost.

Full risk analysis calculations of all application systems and facilities against all possible disasters are time-consuming and expensive. Organizations that perform any risk analyses usually limit them to crucial systems and probable disasters. One of the problems of a risk analysis calculation is that there are a number of assumptions to make a number of probabilities to estimate. Frequently, managers consider that their own good judgment and common sense are just as accurate a way to arrive at the same conclusion. In addition, the pressure of the Foreign Corrupt Practices Act of 1977 has virtually made disaster recovery plans a requirement, and the risk analysis step can be skipped.

On the other hand, in a large operation, it is a severe problem to determine, other than analytically, how many of the applications systems will be protected by disaster recovery plans and how rapidly the backup operation need be initiated. Simplified risk analysis calculations can greatly help in these decisions.

In addition to providing a basis for the selection and cost justification of disaster recovery measures, a risk analysis provides data on time as a factor in assessing the possible consequences of losses. Knowledge of the consequences of not being able to perform each system function for specific time intervals is essential to the creation of disaster recovery plans that will be adequately responsive to the needs of the organization.

With few exceptions, a large percentage of a data center's work load is deferrable for periods of time, without causing unacceptable hardship. On the other hand, there is usually a percentage of the work load that must be run, because its delay would cause intolerable disruptions. It has proven very difficult to guess reliably and accurately into which category each data processing activity should fall. It is also difficult to guess accurately the maximum tolerable delay for the processing of each deferred activity. A properly conducted risk analysis yields this data, which then can be used to justify or reject disaster recovery plan elements based on actual, quantitative needs of the organization for I/S services.

Examples of risk analysis procedures are available, if the full analytical approach is worthwhile to your organization. Recommended is the work of Robert H. Courtney, Jr. of IBM, which was described in *Security Risk Assessment in Electronic Data Processing Systems,* IBM Corporation. The complete calculation procedure is given in Federal Information Processing Standard 65 (FIPS PUB 65) *Guideline for Automatic Data Processing Risk Analysis.*

6

Selection of appropriate disaster recovery strategies

A WIDE RANGE OF ALTERNATIVE RECOVERY STRATEGIES IS AVAILABLE for consideration. These include internal, commercial, and cooperative strategies and their variations, plus combinations of selected strategies. The approach to determining acceptable recovery strategies is described in this chapter, noting service availability, operating considerations, and cost factors. Strengths and weaknesses of the strategies are listed.

Some internal recovery strategies are given, with some of the considerations of each. Six broad types of commercial recovery strategies are reviewed, with some of the key advantages of each. Cooperative recovery strategies are briefly discussed. An approach to looking at combinations of strategies is given.

Because of the great importance of the selection of disaster recovery backup sites, for any recovery strategy, some checklists are provided to review the subject in detail, including general commercial considerations and detailed backup site considerations.

The planning for the use of the commercial backup site, and the move to it, are reviewed.

Evaluating alternative recovery strategies

The alternative disaster recovery strategies are considered after the requirements for the crucial applications and resources have been assessed, and a decision has been made on whether to develop a long-term strategy, or a short-term, high-impact plan. The disaster recovery objectives and the key disaster scenario also have been established at this time.

A wide range of alternative disaster recovery strategies are available to consider. These include:

- Service degradation strategies
- Internal recovery strategies
- Commercial recovery strategies, such as:
  ~ Equipped recovery operation centers (ROCs), or "hot sites"
  ~ Ready rooms, or empty shell ROCs, or "cold sites"
  ~ Commercial service bureaus
  ~ Time brokers
  ~ Hardware vendor facilities
- Cooperative recovery strategies
- Combination of strategies

These disaster recovery strategies will be briefly reviewed, because consideration of any disaster recovery strategy must be in context with the other options that are available. All decisions should be related to the specific requirements of individual, high priority applications. Selections should be based on the functional requirements that have been determined, and modified by any specific management directives that have been received.

A good disaster recovery procedures manual has a great many specific details in it, so that some decisions are already made. The recovery strategies selected determine these details. Thus the evaluation and the selection of the recovery strategies is the key to optimizing the design and development phase of preparing the plan. This evaluation and selection of the strategies should include:

- Requirements based on management priorities
- Consideration of a combination of possible strategies
- Cost analysis of alternative strategies
- Selection of acceptable strategies based on the requirements

Figure 6-1, Acceptable Recovery Strategies for Applications, helps to identify the requirements based on management priorities. It is a worksheet that can be used to list the application systems in priority order, with the maximum acceptable recovery time for each. The tentative most probable acceptable strategy for each system then can be entered. Initial cost estimates then can be made for the development and preparation of the strategies, at least for the

Fig. 6-1. Acceptable recovery strategies for applications.

Application	Priority	Maximum acceptable recovery strategy	Most acceptable recovery strategy	Estimated costs in preparation of strategy
Use (daily)				
Mandatory or crucial				
Necessary or noncrucial				

important systems, and the daily cost of the strategy when in use. These costs can start as rough estimates, then be refined as the crucial application systems and their recovery strategies are further understood.

Figure 6-2, Matrix of Recovery Strategy Possibilities, lists a number of alternative recovery strategies, and roughly indicates the types of strategies that are reasonable, depending upon the acceptable recovery times for the application systems. These two figures are the key to the initial screening of recovery strategies. The application systems must be fitted to recovery strategies with acceptable costs and recovery times.

Figure 6-3, Recovery Strategy Options—Service Availability, is another view of Fig. 6-2. It shows that only sites internally managed or controlled generally can be counted on for availability immediately, or up to 4 hours. A number of other possibilities can be made available within 24 hours. Any of the options that require the moving of equipment will naturally take several days. Even if the emergency site simply requires the movement of operating personnel, it

Fig. 6-2. Matrix of recovery strategy possibilities.

Maximum Acceptable Recovery Time	Alternative Recovery Strategies										
	Internal			Commercial					Cooperative		
	Degrade Service	Second Site	Available Space	Service Bureaus	Equipped ROC	Shell ROC	Time Brokers	Hardware Vendors	Mutual Aid	Equipped ROC	Shell ROC
4 Hours	x	x									
8 Hours	x	x		x					x		
24 Hours	x	x		x	x		x	x	x	x	
7 Days	x	x	x	x	x	x	x	x	x	x	x
14 Days or More	x	x	x	x	x	x	x	x	x	x	x

Fig. 6-3. Recovery strategy options service availability.

Alternative recovery strategies	Maximum acceptable recovery time	Usage duration	Availability for use
Internal			
Multiple sites	4 hrs or less	Depends on conditions	Rapid
Available rooms	7 days	Long term	Immediate
Service degradation	4 hrs or less	Negotiable	Immediate
Commercial			
Equipped ROC	24 hrs	Up to 6 wks	Immediate
Shell ROC	7 days	May be long term	Immediate
Service bureau	8 hrs	Negotiable	As agreed
Time broker	24 hrs	Negotiable	As agreed
Hardware vendor	3 days	Short term	Rapid, but no guarantee
Cooperative			
Mutual aid	8 hrs	Short term	As agreed
Equipped ROC	24 hrs	Short term	As agreed
Shell ROC	7 days	Negotiable	Rapid

will take several days to come to full staff for a large operation. Note that these estimates are for medium- to large-scale equipment. A company with similar-sized computers can be moved and brought on-line much more rapidly.

Any cooperative site, or multiple-user hot site, usually will have a time limit on the duration of emergency usage that is allowed. This is reasonable, because if a client moves into a large hot site and uses most of the facilities there, the other clients essentially have no backup during that period.

Figure 6-4, Recovery Strategy Options—Operating Considerations, points out that only internally managed sites usually have the full measure of management control and security guaranteed. Access can be completely limited to internal personnel. This does not mean that commercial sites might not have excellent security and control. In fact, their actual controls might be superior to your internal con-

Fig. 6-4. Recovery strategy options operating considerations.

Alternative recovery strategies	Security	Control by own staff	Ability to modify OS/hardware	Support services available
Internal				
Multiple sites	Very good	Strong	Agree Internally	Yes
Available rooms	Very good	Strong	Yes	Yes
Service degradation	Very good	Strong	No	Yes
Commercial				
Equipped ROC	Good	Adequate	Little	Yes
Shell ROC	Good	Adequate	Yes	Yes
Service bureau	Fair	Weak	No	Yes
Time broker	Fair	Weak	No	No
Hardware vendor	Low	Weak	No	No
Cooperative				
Mutual Aid	Good	Adequate	No	No
Equipped ROC	Good	Adequate	No	Few
Shell ROC	Good	Adequate	Yes	Few

trols. They are not completely under your management's control, however.

The ability to modify the hardware and the operating systems on the equipment and the number of support services available will depend on the agreements that can be used with the owners of the backup sites, internal or external, and the arrangements that can be made with other current or potential users.

Figure 6-5, Recovery Strategy Options—Cost Factors, gives a general indication of the levels of costs that might be expected for the various options. Installing a completely equipped backup site is often too expensive internally, and must be fairly expensive externally, or there would be many clients that would possibly use it. Using outside or mutual services has a low cost, but the availability is less reliable.

Development and maintenance costs refer to the substantial costs of developing a disaster recovery plan, having the software and the specific hardware ready, and keeping the plan and the software updated. This can be low if the plan is for simple transfer of the sys-

Fig. 6-5. Recovery strategy options cost factors.

Alternative recovery strategies Internal	Ongoing cost	Disaster usage cost	Development maintenance cost
Multiple sites	Low	Low	Medium
Available rooms	Medium	High	High
Service degradation	Medium	Low	Low
Commercial			
Equipped ROC	High	High	High
Shell ROC	Medium	Medium	Medium
Service Bureau	Low	High	Low
Time Broker	Low	High	Low
Hardware Vendor	Low	Medium	Low
Cooperative			
Mutual Aid	Low	Medium	Low
Equipped ROC	High	High	High
Shell ROC	Medium	High	Medium

tems to an equivalent computer that someone else is maintaining. It can be high if you also are responsible for the maintenance.

Figure 6-6, Strengths and Weaknesses of Recovery Strategies, expands on the options listed of recovery strategy possibilities and indicates some of the key points that will aid in their selection. Note that many of the strategies have unique strengths. Others have weaknesses that might be important or might be overlooked.

The decision on strategies must be individual to the particular organization and situation. It is important to recognize, however, that very seldom will a single strategy be the optimum route to follow. At the minimum, you might consider a single strategy for certain crucial applications, together with the reduction or withdrawal of services for less important applications. In most cases, some sort of combination strategy will provide the optimum solution for an organization. The strengths of a number of strategies then can be applied where they are most applicable. Of course if all applications are on a single, on-line database that has complete interconnection, it is probable that only one recovery strategy is feasible.

Fig. 6-6. Strengths and weaknesses of recovery strategies.

Recovery strategies	Strengths	Weaknesses
Internal recovery strategies		
1. Service degradation		
• Reduction of service response	• Simple to apply	• Difficult to apply on-line applications
	• Good for low-priority work	
• Revert to manual procedures	• Keeps some customer service	• Impossible for some on-line applications
	• Good for analytical work	
• Withdrawal of services	• Relieves work load	• Produces nothing
	• Good for long-range work	• Unacceptable to customers
2. Multiple internal sites	• Under management control	• Expensive if not fully used
	• Quick cut-over capability	• Need for extra site management
	• Familiarity with work loads	• Redundant facilities usually
	• Company security standards	
	• Hardware configuration control	
	• Test runs at any time	
3. Available room or "empty shells"	• Rapid access	• Communications facilities may be lacking
	• Relatively inexpensive	• Time consuming to install equipment
	• Under management control	
Commercial recovery strategies		
4. Commercial service bureaus	• Computer system operational	• Upfront and storage costs
	• Service Bureau staff support	• May be busy when needed
	• Telecommunications capabilities	• Not primary business
	• Low holding cost	• Operations not under your control

5. Equipped Recovery Operation Center (ROC)

- Ready for operations
- Immediate access
- Telecommunications support
- Pretested compatibility
- DR is primary business

  - Costly on standby
  - Limited short-term occupancy
  - Usually logistical problems
  - Difficult moving people to site

6. Ready rooms or empty shells (ROC)

- Reasonably priced
- Immediate access
- User control of facility
- DR is primary business

  - Computer must be installed
  - Teleprocessing must be installed
  - Effort great for short term
  - Difficult moving people to site
  - Time may not be immediately available
  - Weak control of configurations
  - Relationships vital
  - Larger configurations usually not available

7. Time brokers of regional facilities

- Reasonably priced
- Contractual arrangement
- Sites in same area

  - Prefer short-term occupancy

8. Hardware vendors

- Good for smaller computers
- Good service will be attempted
- Routine contact with vendor

  - May be configuration changes
  - Limited short-term occupancy
  - Depends on relationships
  - Heavy usage of backup computer may prevent cooperation

Cooperative Strategies

9. Reciprocal agreements or mutual aid

- Usually inexpensive
- Logistics are favorable
- Rehearsals and tests possible
- Similar, compatible systems

10. Cooperative Recovery Operation Center (ROC)

- Ready for operations
- Immediate access
- Pretested compatibility
- Lower shared costs

  - May be contention problem
  - Configuration management is difficult
  - Costly on standby
  - Limited short-term occupancy

Fig. 6-6. Continued.

11. Cooperative ready room or shell (ROC)

- Reasonably priced
- Immediate access
- Adequate control of facility

- Computer must be installed
- Teleprocessing must be installed
- Effort great for short term

Combination strategies

12. Any planned combination of the above strategies

- Priority programs may be backed up in hours
- Concentration on necessary systems with no confusion
- Lower overall cost
- Personnel may all be used where needed

- Takes more planning and
- Dependent on many people different functions

In that case, it will have to be another computer of equal size and configuration to the first. Yet, most organizations have a variety of running applications over a full range of priorities. There will be a number of ways of separating applications over a full range of priorities even if it means the writing of a great many job control language programs for specific cases.

Figure 6-6 has abbreviated remarks, but most are expanded in the later text. All of the notes are from a management and control point of view, rather than from an applications programming or system's programming point of view. Most of the solutions represent a great deal of work for technical personnel. The ideal solution, of course, is for an identical backup facility at relatively close proximity to the original facility. This is by far the costliest solution, and most companies would find it impossible to justify.

It can be justified if the entire organization depends upon the immediate information from an on-line network system, and the costs are great if the system fails. This is obviously true in the case of airline reservation networks, a number of national defense systems, and many process control applications. It is simply not practical for most organizations. Each applications being run must be reviewed considering its criticality and handled as is required operationally. This will usually mean considering a combination of several recovery strategies, so none should be rejected until the analysis is complete.

Internal recovery strategies

Internal organizational control over all the backup facilities and the systems to be used in an emergency often can be an effective and efficient I/S disaster recovery strategy because:

- The computer systems can be maintained at the optimum configuration.
- Test runs can be made at the convenience of the organization.
- Security controls can be placed equally on all facilities.
- The systems can be made available whenever management requires.
- Hardware and software upgrades can be coordinated easily between systems.
- There can be routine balancing of the use of the various systems.

Most of these points are important for internal equipped facilities. Some advantages can be realized with internal empty shells.

When an internal site is to be selected and prepared for disaster recovery backup, considerable thought should go into its analysis to get the best returns on the money spent. There are a number of criteria to be considered in the selection process:

- Is the site suitable for future normal expansion of data center operations?
- Could the site be readily used for normal data center operations?
- Is it in a good area for telephone and messenger service communications?
- Is there commuting convenience for the employees, including good roads, protected parking facilities, and bus service?
- Are there reasonable lunch room or fast-food facilities within walking distance, or could an in-house lunch room or a truck canteen service be used?
- Is the area considered safe for night shift workers?

The disaster recovery planning team should go to some effort on site selection. Frequently, the first ideas that are put forward are found to have flaws. All considered sites should be visited by the team, and their merits discussed with engineering or buildings department personnel. During the site visits, Checklist 6-1, Internal Backup Site, can be used to note the adequacy of the site, or the problems associated with it. After several of these checklists are filled out, several sites can be compared rapidly. Each organization will have its own understanding of what site elements are crucial, and what elements are merely desirable. Of course, if two or more large data centers already exist in an organization, there is no problem of site selection.

Commercial recovery strategies are important, but no considered decision about the use of commercial strategies for disaster recovery makes any sense unless it is placed in the context of possible internal or cooperative strategies, and compared to them from the viewpoints of management control, effectiveness, and cost. Some organizations might study the commercial offerings and decide on a completely internal recovery arrangement. Others might look principally at the total costs, and will arrive at some combination of internal, commercial, and cooperative solutions. The commercial recovery strategies never stand alone, but are a key part of most recovery plans.

The following are some of the possibilities that should be studied in combination with commercial strategies:

- Multiple internal sites

- Available rooms or "empty shells"
- Service degradation
  - ~ Reduction of service response
  - ~ Reversion to manual procedures
  - ~ Withdrawal of services

If multiple internal data centers are available or are possible to justify, they can be effective and efficient. The internal organizational control of the backup facilities and the systems to be used in an emergency allow direct control of the hardware configurations, the software systems, and the security controls. It is not always simple, because internally there also will be a number of different users competing for the priority use of the equipment, and those in charge of disaster recovery preparations are seldom at a high enough level to set adequate priorities. Senior management will, of course, give general guidelines and assign responsibilities. The complexity of the programs being run at any specific disaster date or time always will cause some conflict in the reduced backup operation. It is much clearer to argue on a contractual basis with an external provider of services than it is to settle opinion differences of senior managers.

Multiple data centers in an organization usually are developed by dividing the required computer power into at least two geographically separated locations. The smallest computer in the network must be able to off-load sufficient work and to carry the important work load for the time needed to reestablish the inoperative facility. Thus, this strategy does not imply the installation of excess capacity great enough to carry the crucial work of the other center. It simply implies the physical dispersion of their normal capability into two or more locations, and the management mandate to cut some services at the second locations when the first has a disaster. All systems at both locations need to be analyzed.

Available "ready" rooms, or *empty shells* are prepared spaces that can be made available for backup purposes, if necessary. They must be sufficiently large to install a replacement computer, and they are much more useful if they have had utilities and environmental controls laid in. It is of some use to simply identify *unconditioned*, or unprepared, space as available during an emergency. These are called "bare rooms." The problem with them is that the preparations to get them usable are very time-consuming. These rooms are of better use if they have been "conditioned" by the installation of sufficient power and communications lines to the building and into junction boxes, a raised floor, air conditioning and environmental controls, and physical controls and other security controls.

The empty shell provides a planned site to install replacement hardware rapidly when it might be needed. It is only of use if there is some assurance that the vendors of crucially needed equipment can deliver soon enough to restore the operations before unacceptable losses occur.

Service degradation strategies are useful for most systems in any organization, but are seldom of any use for the vital systems. They are generally simply a way of off-loading the bulk of the computer work to allow operation on smaller or less-available equipment. Those groups who are faced with service degradation during a security incident are excellent candidates to use external timesharing services, or to have cooperative arrangements with others. Thus, it is a strategy for running lower-priority jobs without firm schedules. It cannot be applied to transaction-oriented, communications-dependent applications.

Reversion to manual procedures is another possibility for some systems. This might be possible for many engineering or statistical systems, where personal computers in any location might offer nearly as much capability as the central system. There can be problems with access to data, of course. Other classes of systems that can revert to manual on occasion are point-of-sale terminals in many stores, and productions control systems on machine-shop floors.

Withdrawal of services might be possible for another class of applications. There are some application systems, such as long-range analytical and planning work, and some classes of system development work, where the obvious strategy might be simply to not perform the calculations until the computer has recovered from the disaster. Again, this is a management decision.

Commercial recovery strategies

There is a widespread need for disaster recovery backup services, and a variety of commercial offerings are available. The selection approach should always be:

- Determine your own specific backup and recovery requirements
- Develop a written definition of your functional requirements
- Review the literature and obtain advertising material from the vendors
- Have direct discussions on defined topics with selected vendors
- Choose the best approach for your specific requirements

Figure 6-7, Commercial Recovery Strategies, lists the six broad types of available strategies. It is likely that your final selection will be a combination of at least two of these types of service because each can be preferable for certain requirements.

Fig. 6-7. Commercial recovery strategies.

- Commercial Service Bureaus
- Ready rooms or recovery operations centers (ROC)
  ~ Some equipment installed
  ~ Communications lines installed

- Equipped recovery operations centers (ROC)
- Time brokers of regional facilities
- Portable recovery units
- Hardware vendors

Commercial service bureaus

There are more than 3,000 service bureau operations, or processing services companies, in the United States. They vary from two-person operations, with little equipment, to large corporations, with far-flung networks of computers. Some are highly specialized and concentrate on a single industry. Others try to supply any service that their equipment and personnel can handle. The complexity of possibilities is great enough so that there is only one reasonable approach to the selection problem for the prudent manager: the classical systems analysis approach. By systematic analysis and decision, appropriate and effective service can be obtained with a good chance of mutual satisfaction with the arrangement.

Some of the service offered by service bureaus are outlined in Fig. 6-8, Processing Services Offered by Service Bureaus. This is a broad and attractive menu but, of course, the specific service must always fit your particular requirements. For further information about service bureaus, you can contact ADAPSO (The Association of Computer Services Organizations), 1300 North Seventeenth St., Arlington, VA 22209.

Commercial service bureaus offer both batch services, with pickup and delivery, and on-line, or timesharing services. If the service bureau is large enough to handle the work being considered for disaster recovery, the owners will expect to make sales presentations, hold discussions, and have a contract signed. Most service bureau personnel will not contractually obligate themselves to hold

Fig. 6-8. Processing services offered by service bureaus.

Application Processing
- General business data processing
- General purpose systems   (nonindustry specific)
- Special purpose systems   (industry specific)
- Batch computing services   (local and remote batch)
- RCS   (On-Line to Terminals [RJE])

Time-Sharing and Network Services
- Data communications and network access
- Access to specialized languages and software
- Access to proprietary databases
- Use of specialized equipment, such as graphic terminals

Input and Output Services
- Data preparation on machine-readable media
- Distributed and interactive data entry
- Output report transmission and printing
- Computer output microfilm (COM)

Machine Time Sales
- Raw time sales   (space and equipment only)
- Enhanced time sales   (staff and supplies included)

Value-Added Services
- Combination of the above
- Public programs combined with proprietary information and programs
- Specialized reporting and delivery, such as industry statistics

---

reserved time on their computer waiting for your disaster, because they would lose revenue in the meantime. They must, therefore, be large enough to readily absorb the extra load in an emergency. If an agreement for future possible services is signed with a service bureau, the normal steps taken are the following:

- Establish yourself as a customer by signing a contract and obtain access information and codes
- Attend classes in the bureau's particular systems and languages

- Convert the job control language statements of your vital systems to fit their operating system
- Use existing object disks and run tests at the service bureau to determine compatibility
- Store all required source disks, object disks, and data onto one of their disks and begin payment for it
- Make some test runs by simulating a disaster event

Because this is the service bureau's business, it can be handled smoothly but is costly to maintain. There are frequently up-front costs and minimum charges. There also are the charges for the continued storage of your material on the disks, and for the various tests that should be run.

The service bureau approach is applicable for such important systems as payroll, which must be run at specified times, disaster or not. One problem with service bureaus, as with other commercial services, is that there might be configuration or JCL (Job-Control Language) changes from time to time that cause extra effort and cost.

One problem in planning to use service bureaus for disaster recovery is that the personnel must favor their best customers, and must give all of their regular customers continuing service, even when an organization has been faced with a serious I/S service disruption incident. Making substantial monthly payments to the bureau on a continuing basis to guarantee their service when they are needed might be what it takes to ensure being a "better customer," and get the required service. The cost of such an approach is high. If only the modest monthly payments are made simply to hold onto the access codes, maintain files at their location, and be recognized immediately as a customer, the result is proportionately lower priority when you need increased services suddenly. You cannot expect the bureau to bump other regular customers simply to accommodate you on short notice. You can expect, however, that the bureau staff will make every possible effort to find time on one of the shifts when you can get sufficient access to their computer.

It is unreasonable to expect a service bureau to turn over its entire facilities to one client who has experienced a service disruption incident. Most service bureaus will offer contingency services only in a shared environment with other customers. In some cases the staff will limit their offering of contingency services to existing customers only. For crucial applications such as payroll, and for many timesharing applications, service bureaus can provide suitable backup services. Before service bureaus are selected, analyze the following:

- How much capacity really will be available?
- Will the operating system match the requirements?
- Will there be sufficient security, considering the other customers present?
- Are telecommunications available for the load required?
- What would be the duration of service availability?

Service bureaus have unique capabilities to satisfy many processing requirements, and should be given careful consideration as one of the strategies to be used.

Over the past few years, large recovery service vendors, such as Sunguard and Comdisco, should be looked at as a viable alternative. They have many sites and hundreds of subscribers, and provide a wide spectrum of hardware, software, and communications capabilities.

Ready rooms or recovery operations centers (ROCs)

Many vendors have established large empty computer facilities in controlled-access buildings for possible use in an emergency. To date, very few have actually been put to use during a disaster, but they offer an interesting and useful possibility for recovery backup. Called *empty shells*, these buildings stand prepared as alternate computer rooms for companies that have entered into a contractual arrangement for their possible use. In the event of a disaster, the client company is provided the use of the ready rooms and related facilities to assemble a backup computer system that is brought in by a vendor or broker on short notice.

The shell site is a fully conditioned, fully accessorized computer room without the computer. It is constantly in a state of standby readiness and is capable of accepting a client company's hardware at the time of a disaster. Because of the relatively low cost of empty shells, and the availability to rapidly obtain computer equipment, empty shells have proved to be one of the most viable alternatives for long-term disaster recovery. It must be realized, however, that the equipping of a shell site will take a week at minimum. There are many last-minute arrangements to be made to get one operational. The basic elements of the shell site concept are:

- They will accept a variety of hardware systems
- They usually are available for rapid occupancy

- They usually are located in controlled areas, away from the problem location, but close enough to be accessible to employees
- They have 24-hour guards and effective security systems, as well as the required fire detection and suppression systems
- They usually are shared by 60 or fewer member companies, which reduces the cost to any one individual member
- They can be used as a combination backup site, and the storage site for important documents, tapes, and disks so copies of important data would be available rapidly
- They offer a realistic and affordable approach for batch processing and simpler communications systems

When a ready room or empty shell is used it becomes a command center under the control of the occupant in a nonshared environment. It is an excellent alternative that clearly addresses all the usual requirements during a contingency if a brief delay is acceptable in starting up the operation. Other than ready rooms that are available internally to an organization, the empty shell site is the most viable long-term recovery measure to which a company can subscribe. It is a service that enables a customer to return to a relatively normal processing mode for the full time that is necessary for a new internal site to be prepared. The organization's own people can take over the site during occupancy, make it their command center, and install their own specific hardware.

Ready room sites usually can be counted on for immediate availability and long-term occupancy. They can offer high levels of security and control. They are fully prepared for computer operations and are reasonably priced.

Ready rooms will vary in the number of communications lines that have been preinstalled, and the level of communications support that is provided. This will need to be examined. Some have ancillary equipment installed so that most of the support functions of data processing can be easily handled without bringing in more than the computer and the communications controller. High-speed teleprocessing lines will have to be installed when occupancy takes place, because they are expensive to hold on a standby basis.

Ready rooms might not satisfy short-term emergency needs, but they are attractive for long-term usage.

Equipped recovery operations centers

Equipped and dedicated contingency centers offer the concept of the computer facility that is staffed and available for use for both testing and during a contingency event. Such facilities are available to large numbers of subscribers on a membership basis, with usually a one-year minimum contractual relationship.

The equipped ROC is the most expensive commercial contingency service available, but it is a viable alternative for those organizations that require rapid resumption of processing capabilities during a disaster emergency. The equipped ROC is not generally feasible for longer-term backup processing capabilities for two reasons. First, an equipped ROC is expensive to use, although the expense might be warranted for a short period. Second, there are only a few such contingency sites in the country, and it is likely that they will be geographically remote.

The advantages of a fully equipped ROC are:

- Rapid access is possible, usually within four hours.
- The hardware is ready to operate as soon as the staff is in place.
- Telecommunications facilities and lines are in place.
- Software and operational support are available.
- The center can be tested routinely.

The disadvantages of a fully equipped ROC are:

- It is very expensive.
- Occupancy is short term—usually six weeks maximum on the hardware.
- Configuration changes over time might be a problem.
- Logistical problems can be significant if the ROC is not in the immediate area.

The planned use of a fully equipped ROC requires the prior consideration of several factors, such as:

- Compatibility of hardware, in all essential configuration elements
- Restoration of communications, which can be a complex problem if the main node of network must be changed
- The cost of initial occupancy. The cost of "declaring an emergency" can be great, in which case you might have second thoughts about using the service during a minor service disruption incident when the service could be helpful.
- The security problem if other organizations are sharing the same facility
- The probability of more than one client needing the facility at the same time

- The distance for key people to travel from the permanent site. Subsequent recovery at the home site could be difficult if the key staff are too far removed.

The more successful of the equipped ROCs have strong tele-communications facilities installed, and have made network surveys and backup network designs with their clients. These services can include:

- Backup network design
- Backup network optimization
- Communications facilities procurement
- Backup network installation
- Network diagnostics and maintenance

Because of the complexity of such operations, the subscription fees are expensive. Some typical fees that are charged are:

Service	Fee
Regular monthly standby fee	from $2,000 to $8,000
Disaster usage daily fee	from $4,000 to $10,000
Ready space occupancy fee	from $4000 to $800 (per day)
Disaster initiation fee	from $20,000 to $60,000
	(depending on speed of access)
Network design and installation	varies up to $25,000
Communications cost	varied

The fully equipped ROCs offer an excellent service. They generally are based on the assumption, however, that only one or two subscribers out of sixty or more will have simultaneous disasters.

Time brokers of regional facilities

A number of organizations, frequently related to leasing companies, offer the service of brokering time on computers that are not fully loaded, between two or more companies. Most of the time broker-age activity tends to be for the startup or overload needs of clients. Brokerage activity also is used for providing backup in the time of a disaster.

The broker enters into contracts with all parties involved and can guarantee the availability of predetermined computer facilities. Yet the agreements usually specify that the computer will be available only if the work can fit in. Thus, certain peak-load periods might be contractually excluded.

All decisions on the use of the facility and the contractual terms are made with the broker. There is no direct negotiation between the two parties with computers. A typical agreement is shown in Fig. 6-9, Computer Service Backup Agreement.

This is a type of mutual aid agreement in which the computer users do not have to take the time to search for compatible computers and then hammer out agreements. Essentially, two nonaffiliated companies agree to provide backup processing for each other in the event of an emergency or an overload situation, and the contractual arrangements are worked out by a third party. A time broker might serve to arrange with several companies in a geographical area to reserve excess computer time in their data centers to be used by other companies as needed. The broker charges a set monthly fee. The user pays the site owner for the computer resources used in an emergency or overload period.

This backup agreement is an inexpensive approach and has very favorable logistics if several companies in an area are brought into the agreement. It can work if good relationships develop between the companies that are involved. There is often a list of alternative sites, and a convenient site can be arranged. The problem, of course, is systems compatibility, and the correct computer configurations. Maintaining sufficient system compatibility over time and being assured of system availability when there is an emergency are serious problems. These problems can be managed satisfactorily if each party understands the other's needs, and maintains communications about system changes. If the technical personnel are in contact, the proper JCLs can be prepared and ready after any system changes.

Intercompany reciprocal agreements can create legal problems, but having the contracts handled by a third party can get around such problems readily. The ongoing changes in hardware and operating systems obviously creates technical problems, but these problems can be surmounted by routine contracts between the technical personnel of all parties. Usually, such arrangements are only for short-term, limited occupancy because the time being offered is usually for the "windows" during the month when some excess time is available.

Such brokeraged agreements can work well, but cannot be guaranteed for long periods. To make them work, it is necessary that:

- Each party has developed a contingency plan
- Each party must be prepared to support the others, even when inconvenient

- Routine discussions must be held on configurations and operating systems
- Constant communications between the managers must be maintained

The computer time broker has all interested companies fill out a simple questionnaire that is used to make an initial screening of possible compatibility, and to discuss the possibilities with prospective clients.

A number of competitive organizations have found that they can gain the advantages of brokeraged agreements through the medium of their professional associations and other contacts. The association essentially acts as the broker, and helps to maintain sufficient compatibility through the mutual exchange of application programs and operating systems. A prime example is the large group of smaller banks. Many banks have identical equipment and identical programs. Because they are bound by law to maintain the integrity of their systems, they are legally able to enter into mutual aid agreements. A number of disasters have already occurred where such mutual aid agreements have worked satisfactorily.

Fig. 6-9. Computer service backup agreement.

(Typical agreement with time broker)
Computer Service Backup Agreement

Agreement entered into this _____ day of _____,
19_____ by and between Computer Service Company and _____
_____ having an office for the transaction of
business at _____
_____
_____

hereinafter referred to as the Customer.

Witnesseth
Whereas, the Customer desires to have available for its use certain backup data processing capabilities and services compatible with its present facility operations which consist of:

Whereas, _____ represents that it has compati-

Fig. 6-9. Continued.

ble backup data processing equipment available for Customer's use during designated times,

Now, therefore, in consideration of the mutual covenants and promises contained herein, it is agreed as follows:

1. _____ hereby designates _____ having an office for the transaction of business at _____

_____

as the backup installation at which there is data processing equipment compatible to Customer's data processing equipment above described, and which will be available for use by the Customer in accordance with the terms and conditions herein.

2. The data processing facilities and equipment shall be available, to the Customer during the following times:
Days _____ from _____ to _____
Days _____ from _____ to _____
and for a maximum of _____ hours per week.

3. The data processing equipment will be available for Customer's use at the designated times for a maximum of _____ continuous weeks. After such continuous use period, the facilities will not be available for subsequent use until seven calendar days thereafter.

4. Customer agrees to pay _____ a service charge of $_____ per month payable in advance and an hourly rate of $_____ for all use of the equipment at the designated installation. Charges for hourly use of the equipment at the installation shall be paid to _____ within thirty days of invoice.

5. If a designated installation is not available by reason of equipment malfunction, power failure or any other causes beyond the control of _____, including, without limitation, acts of God, acts of public administration, decrees, war, riots, labor disturbances, strikes, civil commotion, and the like, _____ shall use its best efforts to locate an alternative installation compatible with Customer's equipment. If the equipment at such alternate installation is of more advanced design and, therefore, capable of completing Customer's output in less time than the equipment at the designated installation, the charges for use of such alternate installation shall be based upon the normal hourly operating time of the equipment at the designated installation, if such equipment were used to produce the equivalent output.

6. Unless available by reason of an occurrence set forth in Paragraph 5 herein, the data processing facilities at the designated installation shall be available for a minimum of _____ hours per week and for _____ weeks per month at the base hourly rate set forth herein, and if additional time is required and is available, the hourly rate for such time shall be $_____.

7. _____
represents that the equipment at the above designated installation is basically compatible with the Customer's equipment above set forth, however, Customer shall test the equipment at the designated installation for compatibility purposes once each calendar quarter to assure continued compatibility. Charges for the use of the equipment during such test periods will be at the normal hourly rate set forth herein, and such test shall be for a period of 2 hours.

8. Customer agrees to provide all operating personnel and software support at the designated installation and shall notify _____ of its intention to make use of the data processing equipment 4 hours prior to making any use of the facilities at the designated installation.

9. _____ agrees to provide, at the designated installation, security services and reasonable work area and space for Customer's use during such time as the installation is in use by the Customer. Storage space for use by the Customer will be provided if same is available.

10. Within three hours of request by Customer, _____ shall provide transportation services to pick up cards, tapes, disk packs, and other material required for the operation of Customer's program at the installation and shall thereafter deliver same to the installation.

11. _____ shall have the right to change designated installations on thirty days notice to Customer; however, if such change is effected within a calendar quarter in which a compatibility test has been conducted by Customer at the prior installation, a test of equal duration at the new installation will be made available without hourly charge to the Customer.

12. The services under this agreement shall be first available on _____, and the agreement shall continue for a period of one year thereafter; however, either party may cancel the agreement on thirty days written notice to the other by Certified Mail, Return Receipt Requested, at the respective addresses above designated.

13. Upon termination of this agreement, the Customer shall remove all of its materials which may be stored at the installation within fifteen

Fig. 6-9. Continued.

days, and upon failure to do so, _____
may remove and dispose of same at the expense of Customer.

14. It is agreed that in the event that material and data received by
_____ for transportation to the installation and/
or used at the installation are lost or destroyed through equipment failure, or act of _____, the sole liability, if any,
shall be limited to the cost required to regenerate the lost data from Customer's supporting materials on such equipment deemed suitable by
_____ for such regeneration. If the Cus-
tomer has not maintained such supporting material, the liability of
_____, if any, shall be limited to cost
of such regeneration had the supporting material been available. The
supporting material for the purpose of this agreement is defined as exact
copies of the punch cards, magnetic tapes, disks, or other data, excluding records and data not in machine-readable form.

15. In no event shall the liability of _____
arising out of the furnishings of devices hereunder, or the use of the
installation, exceed the price paid in service charges for the month in
which the error from which the liability results occurred.

16. _____ shall have no liability for gen-
eral, special, or consequential damages, or for any loss, damages, or
expenses directly or indirectly arising from the services or installation
time furnished hereunder, or for any inability to use them, or for any
other cause including, but not limited to, failure beyond its control.

17. The Customer agrees that it shall not, for a period of one year from
the date hereof, attempt to purchase or lease computer time, equipment, or services directly from any backup installation assigned by
_____ pursuant to this agreement.

In Witness Whereof, the parties hereto have hereunto set their hands
the day and year first above written.

By _____
Customer _____
By _____

Portable recovery units

Much of the previous discussion has been directed to the users of
medium- to large-scale computer equipment with considerable
complexity. A great many computer users today have their work on

powerful smaller computers that have standard operating systems, simpler configurations, and less-complicated communications connections. There are always many available sites where such equipment can be set up.

Systems of this type are the IBM System 34, IBM System 38, and similar equipment from other manufacturers. These systems frequently handle important applications, yet do not take up much space. The operating systems tend to be standardized. It might take several hours to boot up a new system, but the procedures are standard, and the backup system takes minimal storage space. The standard approach to the backup of such equipment has been the use of equipment at vendor premises, or elsewhere in the same organization. Such an approach usually leaves much to chance.

A new approach to the backup of these smaller computers is rapidly gaining favor. Some companies have regional ready rooms with equipment available that can be moved into place rapidly. Other companies are offering portable recovery units. These recovery units are essentially the computer, such as a System 38, mounted in a trailer and prepared with all the necessary ancillary equipment. The trailer can be pulled to a site wherever the client can set up the business, and simply needs connection to the necessary utilities. The choice of leaving the computer in the trailer and operating it there, or of moving it into a prepared site is open. The quick setup of the operation in the trailer makes it attractive.

As an example, many banks have operated small branches out of trailers for construction sites or emergencies; the concept is easy to sell. Banks have had considerable experience with the security and control aspects of working out of trailers.

Portable recovery units usually are advertised in the professional literature. These units also can be found through user organizations, such as regional groups of System 38 users. These units will be a strong factor in emergency recovery of smaller equipment in the future.

Hardware vendors

Hardware vendors always have a variety of equipment available at the time of a disaster. This equipment might be at their test and demonstration centers, at internal or sales sites, or it might be ready to ship on the vendor's loading docks. Seldom can vendors guarantee the availability of such equipment at any particular point in time; they always have many other clients to be concerned about, and other promises to keep. IBM is now signing contracts assuring their customers that certain equipment will be immediately available.

They, and most other computer manufacturers, simply state that they will make the best possible effort to provide equipment when it is needed. Historically, the efforts of all the computer vendors have been excellent in this regard. When a disaster is reported to computer vendors, they spare no effort in finding replacement equipment or services.

There is one major difficulty with relying on such services. Normally, the systems that are run by hardware vendors at their test and demonstration centers have constantly changing configurations, or special features, that make the assurance of compatibility difficult. This can be balanced, however, by the ready availability of experienced technical help in the systems area. Another problem, however, is that hardware vendor facilities are usually showcases and might have serious security problems.

Hardware vendors of medium to small computers often are an excellent source of backup equipment. In the smaller sizes, computers tend to be much more standardized, with fewer operating system variations. Hardware vendor facilities also are particularly good backup sites for key entry computers, engineering computers, and the like. These generally are standardized.

Hardware vendors are often attractive because of their pretested compatibility and favorable logistics. Even on a temporary basis, however, they are not the best solution. The hardware vendor is simply not equipped to handle this type of situation because it interrupts their regular business. If non-prime-time, short-term processing can help, however, and if it is a logical fit within your organization's disaster recovery plan, this can be a viable alternative.

Some hardware vendors will not agree in advance to participate in your disaster recovery plans. They must be approached as to their attitude, and as to what they will suggest. Vendors are usually very responsive at the time of a disaster.

Vendors are eager to help with reasonable arrangements with their customers, and will work day and night to help them in an emergency to restore their computer operations. Hardware vendors have been known to turn their display offices temporarily into secure facilities to aid a customer in an emergency.

Cooperative recovery strategies

Cooperative disaster recovery strategies are approaches that do not necessarily make use of a third party or commercial company to provide the backup agreements. Some of the possible types of recovery strategy are:

- Informal mutual aid

- Reciprocal agreements
- Co-op ROC
- Co-op ready room or shell

Cooperative disaster recovery strategies take considerable effort to pull together and to get management approval because these strategies have some legal problems. For example, what if a cooperative agreement is signed, but one of the parties is not able to provide help at the time of emergency because he or she is busy or not so inclined? Would this be the cause of a suit? Most managers are happier to sign legal agreements in which a third party comes between the two users and screens them from suits.

Informal mutual aid

It is possible to have agreements on an informal basis. Such agreements usually are valueless if there is any complexity involved, but there are times when informal agreements will work. One example is when the agreement is between several companies in an industry association and there is more than one possibility for backup. Another example is when one of the parties is a customer of the other. The vendor party might not wish to sign a contract, but would certainly like to help during an emergency. This possibility is becoming more feasible as vendors provide computer services to their clients.

Reciprocal agreements

In a number of cases, groups of companies have pooled their planning resources to save everyone money. They have formed legal associations for the protection of all parties involved. Formal contracts or simple reciprocal letter agreements are exchanged. The details depend on the type of industry, or whether trade secrets are involved.

Reciprocal, or formal mutual aid, agreements are conceptually possible when one facility can accept the work of another temporarily inoperative facility. Technically, the transportability of work between two facilities requires that data and programs from one be acceptable to the other with only modest changes. Rehearsals are most helpful, but they usually are costly and generate unwelcome disruptions in the "backup" organization. The rehearsals should include full operations of the crucial functions and should be thoroughly realistic, that is, independent of the use of any resources from the inoperative facility. Such rehearsals are difficult to conduct in a mutual aid environment, because compatibility of the backup system can be assured only if the important functions are run realistically at the backup facility as part of the normal job stream, with test data, files, and so on.. This can be done off-shift, if necessary.

It is difficult to make mutual aid agreements totally reliable. Changes in either system may render the arrangement invalid. Further, management shifts might invalidate the arrangements without prior notice, leaving a previously supported facility without backup.

Although mutual aid agreements are conceptually feasible, they rarely prove workable when needed, except in the case of medium and smaller systems. The high risk of discovering in time of need that the backup is not actually available is too great to warrant confidence in this strategy for larger computer operations.

Reciprocal agreements can be either formal or informal, and either bilateral or with a group. Figure 6-10, Contingency Backup Arrangement for Totally Disabled Computer Equipment, is a sample of a nonlegal and bilateral agreement. It is usually common to simply exchange "letters of understanding" between the organizations, signed by a manager who can stand behind the agreement. Figure 6-11, Sample Letter of Understanding, is an example of such an agreement. Such letters, of course, need to be reaffirmed when managers change in either organization. The security coordinator should keep such agreements up to date.

Fig. 6-10. Contingency backup arrangement for totally disabled computer equipment.

(Sample)

Contingency backup arrangement for totally disabled computer equipment

Purpose: Each of the undersigned parties (each of whom is herein called a "Company" and collectively the "Companies") hereby recognized and acknowledges (i) the possibility of a total disabling of its batch processing computer equipment (herein called its "Equipment") and (ii) its desire to safeguard itself from the consequences of such an occurrence to the extent possible by means of the informal, non-legal Contingency Backup Arrangement evidenced hereby.

Contingency Backup Arrangement: In the event that a total disabling of any Company's Equipment shall occur, the Company whose

Equipment has been totally disabled (such Company being herein called the "User") shall inform each of the other Companies of such occurrence (each such other Company being herein called a "Provider") shall concur in the User's determination that the User's Equipment is totally disabled, then the User shall become entitled to utilize such of the Equipment of the respective Provider's as is specified in the respective Providers' Exhibits (any Equipment specified in any Provider's Exhibit being herein called such Provider's "Offered Equipment").

Any utilization by any User of any Provider's Offered Equipment shall be subject to the terms and conditions set forth in the respective Provider's Exhibit.

Notwithstanding anything to the contrary appearing herein or in any Exhibit, however, each Provider's obligation to allow any User to utilize said Provider's Offered Equipment during the hours and days specified in said Provider's Exhibit shall terminate 60 days after the total disabling of said User's Equipment. If at any time subsequent to said total disabling, however, said User renders its Equipment (whether by repair or replacement) operable to an extent sufficient to enable said Company to serve as a Provider should the occasion arise, then each Provider shall again become obligated to provide said Company with said Provider's Offered Equipment in the event that said Company suffers another total disabling of its Equipment (although each Provider's obligation to do so shall again terminate 60 days after said subsequent total disabling).

Provider's Exhibits: Each Company shall set forth, in a separate Exhibit attached hereto, the following information: (i) the Offered Equipment which it shall make available to any User (specifying the various types and amounts of such Offered Equipment, which Offered Equipment shall constitute a dedicated system owned or leased by the respective Provider); (ii) the approximate geographic location of said Offered Equipment (which Offered Equipment shall be located in an installation owned or leased by the respective Provider); and (iii) the days of the week on which and the hours of such days during which any User may utilize said Offered Equipment.

Multiple Users: In the event that there are two or more Companies which qualify as Users during the same period of time and said Users desire to utilize the Offered Equipment on a pro rata basis (without in any way limiting said Users' respective rights to utilize the Offered Equipment of each of the other Providers). Moreover, the fact that a Provider has made its Offered Equipment available to one or more Users shall in no way affect its obligation to make its Offered Equipment available to any other Users (regardless of whether or not any other Provider has previously done so).

Security Precautions and Liability Provisions: Any User who utilizes the Offered Equipment of any Provider shall adhere to whatever

Fig. 6-10. Continued.

security arrangements are put into effect by said Provider with respect to said User's utilization of such Offered Equipment.

Each User shall reimburse the Provider for any repair or replacement costs incurred by the Provider as a result of any physical damage to or disabling of the respective Offered Equipment caused by such User's negligent utilization thereof. No User shall be liable for any damage or disablement attributable to normal wear and tear, however.

Utilization Costs: In the event of an emergency situation arising which causes the provisions of this agreement to be put into effect, charges for the use of computer equipment may be made if specified in the Provider's exhibit, or if agreed previously between individual user and provider companies. For testing purposes, however, no reimbursement will be made for the use of equipment, except as provider for else where in this agreement.

No provider shall be obligated to provide any personnel (whether technical, security, or otherwise), programs, or such additional resources, except insofar as is necessary to render its Offered Equipment readily available to and operable by the User. To the extent that any Provider does provide any such personnel or additional such resources, said Provider shall be reimbursed by the appropriate User for the costs of providing such personnel and additional resources.

Withdrawals: In the event that any company decides to withdraw from the contingency backup arrangement evidenced hereby, said Company shall notify each of the other Companies of said decision in writing, in which event said Company shall be deemed to have withdrawn from the above-specified arrangement 60 days after written notification is transmitted to the other Companies.

Amendments and Modifications: In the event that any Company desires to amend or otherwise modify this instruction or the above-specified arrangement evidenced hereby, no such amendment or modification shall become effective until transmitted in writing to (and accepted in writing by) each of the other Companies.

Non-Legal Nature of Arrangement: Notwithstanding anything to the contrary appearing herein, it is expressly understood and agreed by each of the parties hereto that this instrument and the contingency backup arrangement evidenced hereby are informal and non-legal in nature and wholly unenforceable at law or in equity. This instrument simply evidences an informal, good faith understanding and arrangement which is wholly non-contractual and not binding in any way on any party hereto, none of which parties shall incur any legally enforceable obligation or liability as a result of its execution and delivery hereof and notwithstanding its or any other Company's subsequent reliance upon or adherence to either this instrument or the contingency backup arrangement evidence hereby.

Now, therefore, the undersigned parties have caused this instrument to be executed (without, as specified above, any legal effect whatsoever) by their respective officers, as of December 31, 19xx.

Revised: January, 19xx

Fig. 6-11. Sample letter of understanding.

(Typical agreement with time broker)
Computer Service Backup Agreement

Agreement entered into this _____ day of _____, 19_____ by and between Computer Service Company and _____ _____ having an office for the transaction of business at _____

_____

_____

hereinafter referred to as the Customer.

Witnesseth
Whereas, the Customer desires to have available for its use certain backup data processing capabilities and services compatible with its present facility operations which consist of:

Whereas, _____ represents that it has compatible backup data processing equipment available for Customer's use during designated times,

Now, therefore, in consideration of the mutual covenants and promises contained herein, it is agreed as follows:

    1. _____ hereby designates _____ having an office for the transaction of business at _____

---

as the backup installation at which there is data processing equipment compatible to Customer's data processing equipment above described,

Fig. 6-11. Continued.

and which will be available for use by the Customer in accordance with the terms and conditions herein.

2. The data processing facilities and equipment shall be available, to the Customer during the following times:
Days _____ from _____ to _____
Days _____ from _____ to _____
and for a maximum of _____ hours per week.

3. The data processing equipment will be available for Customer's use at the designated times for a maximum of _____ continuous weeks. After such continuous use period, the facilities will not be available for subsequent use until seven calendar days thereafter.

4. Customer agrees to pay _____ a service charge of $_____ per month payable in advance and an hourly rate of $_____ for all use of the equipment at the designated installation. Charges for hourly use of the equipment at the installation shall be paid to _____ within thirty days of invoice.

5. If a designated installation is not available by reason of equipment malfunction, power failure or any other causes beyond the control of _____, including, without limitation, acts of God, acts of public administration, decrees, war, riots, labor disturbances, strikes, civil commotion, and the like, _____ shall use its best efforts to locate an alternative installation compatible with Customer's equipment. If the equipment at such alternate installation is of more advanced design and, therefore, capable of completing Customer's output in less time than the equipment at the designated installation, the charges for use of such alternate installation shall be based upon the normal hourly operating time of the equipment at the designated installation, if such equipment were used to produce the equivalent output.

6. Unless available by reason of an occurrence set forth in Paragraph 5 herein, the data processing facilities at the designated installation shall be available for a minimum of _____ hours per week and for _____ weeks per month at the base hourly rate set forth herein, and if additional time is required and is available, the hourly rate for such time shall be $_____.

7. _____ represents that the equipment at the above designated installation is basically compatible with the Customer's equipment above set forth, however, Customer shall test the equipment at the designated installation for

compatibility purposes once each calendar quarter to assure continued compatibility. Charges for the use of the equipment during such test periods will be at the normal hourly rate set forth herein, and such test shall be for a period of 2 hours.

8. Customer agrees to provide all operating personnel and software support at the designated installation and shall notify _____ of its intention to make use of the data processing equipment 4 hours prior to making any use of the facilities at the designated installation.

9. _____ agrees to provide, at the designated installation, security services and reasonable work area and space for Customer's use during such time as the installation is in use by the Customer. Storage space for use by the Customer will be provided if same is available.

10. Within three hours of request by Customer, _____ shall provide transportation services to pick up cards, tapes, disk packs, and other material required for the operation of Customer's program at the installation and shall thereafter deliver same to the installation.

11. _____ shall have the right to change designated installations on thirty days notice to Customer; however, if such change is effected within a calendar quarter in which a compatibility test has been conducted by Customer at the prior installation, a test of equal duration at the new installation will be made available without hourly charge to the Customer.

12. The services under this agreement shall be first available on _____, and the agreement shall continue for a period of one year thereafter; however, either party may cancel the agreement on thirty days written notice to the other by Certified Mail, Return Receipt Requested, at the respective addresses above designated.

13. Upon termination of this agreement, the Customer shall remove all of its materials which may be stored at the installation within fifteen days, and upon failure to do so, _____ may remove and dispose of same at the expense of Customer.

14. It is agreed that in the event that material and data received by _____ for transportation to the installation and/or used at the installation are lost or destroyed through equipment failure, or act of _____, the sole liability, if any, shall be limited to the cost required to regenerate the lost data from Customer's supporting materials on such equipment deemed suitable by _____ for such regeneration. If the Customer has not maintained such supporting material, the liability of _____, if any, shall be limited to cost

Fig. 6-11. Continued.

of such regeneration had the supporting material been available. The supporting material for the purpose of this agreement is defined as exact copies of the punch cards, magnetic tapes, disks, or other data, excluding records and data not in machine-readable form.

15. In no event shall the liability of _____ arising out of the furnishings of devices hereunder, or the use of the installation, exceed the price paid in service charges for the month in which the error from which the liability results occurred.

16. _____ shall have no liability for general, special, or consequential damages, or for any loss, damages, or expenses directly or indirectly arising from the services or installation time furnished hereunder, or for any inability to use them, or for any other cause including, but not limited to, failure beyond its control.

17. The Customer agrees that it shall not, for a period of one year from the date hereof, attempt to purchase or lease computer time, equipment, or services directly from any backup installation assigned by _____ pursuant to this agreement.

In Witness Whereof, the parties hereto have hereunto set their hands the day and year first above written.

By _____
Customer _____
By _____

Cooperative recovery operations centers

In several large cities, the computer-in-place concept has been handled cooperatively. One such organization is Large Scale Computer Users Backup Association (LSCUBA), which was formed in the Philadelphia area by 14 varied, participating users. It was formed to study and provide a viable solution to the problem of computer disaster recovery and to contract for a group backup center. It received a number of facilities management bids to run the projected facility. Within a year, 27 companies had signed up.

Cooperative backup associations need to have sufficient computer power standing by to service the largest participating member. That computer power can be used as an EDP service bureau on an interruptible basis when not required for disaster backup, or for the great deal of systems development and testing that is needed for creating and maintaining the members' backup systems. It also requires that the criteria for a "disaster" are mutually agreed upon. It assumes that there might be problems if more than two participants have a disaster situation simultaneously.

Cooperative ready rooms or empty shell ROC

Some organizations have discussed the idea of cooperative contingency centers, called ready rooms or empty shells. There is less advantage in savings in this concept because the reduced costs from a fully equipped ROC are offset by the added inconvenience of geographic distance in any cooperative venture. It is a cost-effective route, however, and will always be under consideration.

Cooperative ready rooms have similar advantages and disadvantages to in-house or commercial ready rooms. One of the main advantages is that the special, controlled structure and the environmental control equipment is obtained in advance of any problem. It is always more time-consuming to put together the ready room than is the hardware configuration that goes into it.

Combinations of strategies

Very few organizations have the necessity for full, rapid backup of their total application systems portfolio. Most organizations have a vital group of application systems that must be backed up rapidly, a larger group of systems that must be backed up in reasonable time, from two days to two weeks, and a number of systems that do not need backup for one or two months.

These systems do not all need to be handled by the same strategies. The EDP disaster recovery team should discuss the list of applications and their requirements generated in Fig. 6-1, Acceptable Recovery Strategies for Applications, and group different priorities of applications in different strategies that are cost effective for each group's needs. For example, in a particular organization:

- Some accounting programs can be backed up within hours on a computer in place.
- Certain operational programs can be backed up in batch operation at a service bureau the next day.
- A number of engineering programs can be backed up with a timesharing service.
- Some data input and check handling programs can be backed up at a cooperating center on the next evening shift.

- A few analytical programs might not be backed up until extra computer equipment is brought into the ready room and tested, possibly taking several weeks.

It will be the job of the disaster recovery team to pull together a combination of strategies, application by application, analyzing the requirements of each. I/S Disaster Recovery Approaches a visual presentation of this problem.

Selecting disaster recovery backup sites
General backup site considerations

There are many types of backup sites, both internal and commercial, to consider in planning. It might be that more than one site is selected for a combination strategy. The selection of a particular backup site should proceed as analytically as possible, although there might be overriding factors that point to a particular selection. The degree of detail in the analysis of the selection will vary greatly, depending upon whether it is a wide-open decision to be made, or whether certain directions have been already established in the organization.

Fig. 6-12. I/S disaster recovery approaches.

Application System	Priority Group			
A	1			
B	1			
C	1	Strategy 1	Strategy 2	
D	2			
E	2			
F	3			
G	3			
H	3			
I	3			
J	4	Strategy 3	Strategy 4	Strategy 5
K	4			
L	5			
M	5			
N	6			
O	6	Strategy 6		

Time →

The impact of microcomputers and telecommunications networks in recent years has started creating environments that are complex to recover in the event of a disaster. This does not mean that only certain recovery options are now indicated. It simply means that these new developments require careful considerations in any selection of a commercial strategy for contingency planning. These influences include:

- The increasing complexity of systems and applications, as more on-line systems and networks are required, causes more extensive backup site preparations to be necessary.

- As more systems are developed, and many are put on-line, the group's disaster recovery planning must be reviewed routinely for adequacy. A backup site that is adequate one year might be inadequate another year.

- As information processing becomes more integrated into the operations of the organization, the greater dependencies will make more complex backup arrangements difficult to handle externally.

- Decisions on commercial backup sites should take into account the future needs of greater communications requirements and more on-line operation. Simple solutions will be useless.

- Most disasters are localized fires or communications or equipment breakdowns. Most recovery operations will be for a limited set of applications, and smaller commercial sites can be variable.

- The investment required for contingency planning and the contracting for alternative processing methods already is substantial and will continue to grow.

It should be emphasized that commercial backup sites do not need to be remote and far from the original site. There are good reasons for many organizations to select sites that are widely scattered geographically, or in highly secure locations, or both. Corporations with sensitive requirements have a number of excellent commercial backup sites from which to select.

Backup sites generally are not helpful within the same building, however, because security incidents such as fires, bombs, or demonstrations will likely close down both sites simultaneously. It might be useful to have a backup site in a complex of buildings, or in a nearby building, but only if the site is separately controlled from the security aspect. There are a number of questions that must be asked individually for each selection of a backup site. Some of these are listed in Checklist 6-2, Selection of a Commercial Backup Site.

Checklist 6-1. Internal backup site checklist.

Site   **Date**

Item	Superior	Adequate	Inadequate

1. Vicinity:

Nearby buildings

Employee parking

Nearby food and motel

2. Premises:

Facilities and maintenance

Signs and access control

Power and telephone lines

Other company operators

3. Computer Room:

Access control

Air conditioning

Environmental control

Electric panels

Telephone panels

Hazards

4. Tape Library:

Access control

Sufficient space

Housekeeping problems

5. Terminals:

Facilities

Space for desks and PCs

Control

6. Data Preparation:

Staff space

Facilities

Equipment space

7. Other Equipment:

Electrical

Environmental

Checklist 6-1. Continued.

Burster/decollector/mailing

File

Other

8. Administrative:

Fire hazards

Fire equipment

Waste disposal

Dock control

9. User groups:

Desk space

Source data handling

Checklist 6-2. Selection of a commercial backup site.

1. Have all fees been considered in the use of the site, including:
   - Annual subscription fee?
   - Disaster initiation fee?
   - Daily usage fees?
   - Communications fees?
   - Support services fees? (Includes consultation, design, etc.)
   - Special equipment or services fee?
2. Can conflicting requirements between two organizations be resolved satisfactorily?
3. Is the organization financially solvent and well backed?

4. Will requirements for special equipment or services be met?

5. Can personnel be housed readily near the site?

6. Are the physical security and control features at least as strong as those at your site?

7. Can backup tapes and disks be transported easily to the site?

8. Is there a satisfactory backup site for the storage of magnetic media?

9. Is the necessary support equipment quickly available?

10. Is the distance to the site great enough to reduce sufficiently the risk of a possible disaster affecting both sites?

11. Can the site be put under internal control by the organization?

12. Can the backup site be guaranteed to be available in the event of a disaster at the main site?

13. Can the workers at the main site easily commute to the commercial backup site?

14. If the backup site is distant, is there a pool of trained workers available near it?

15. Can the available workers be assigned readily, on short notice, to backup activities?

16. Is the backup storage facility equally accessible from the main site and the commercial backup site?

17. Is the backup storage facility separate from commercial backup site, so that it can be used for backup storage during a contingency situation?

18. Is the power supply at the commercial backup site from a different source than the power supply at the main site to avoid the adverse affects of a power failure?

19. Is there a uninterruptible power supply installed at the backup site?

20. Is there adequate power available at the backup site?

21. Are there adequate telephone lines available at the backup site?

22. Will the telephone company install sufficient drop line there?

23. Can the communication network be connected readily to that site?

24. Is there sufficient space for those terminal operators who must be near the computer installation?

25. Is the backup site adequately fire resistant, with sufficient fire alarm and suppression equipment?

26. Is there adequate regional police and fire protection at the backup site?

Checklist 6-2 cannot be used appropriately until there has been an initial analysis of the requirements, a definition of the functional requirements approved by management, and a survey of the existing situation and possible sites to consider. The use of the questions will depend entirely upon the organization's own situation. A national organization, for example, might use major data centers that are located far apart, and have a routine distribution of media between them and a safe commercial storage point. An organization that operates in a regional area might want to use a second site within twenty miles of the first and use a common, shared data storage location. Also, an organization that relies heavily on its people using on-line terminals might need to develop a backup site that is reached easily by the commuting staff, and with most of a communication network installed in advance of possible use.

Checklist 6-2 covers the main points regarding recovery operation centers, whether they are hot sites or ready rooms, from the viewpoint of backup planning. It does not touch on the use of commercial service bureaus, time brokers, or hardware vendor facilities, although similar considerations must be taken into account with them.

Commercial backup sites are preconditioned facilities that will have communications lines and power laid in, but might or might not be equipped with hardware. Subscribers pay fees on a standby basis, then additional fees if the sites are used. The sites vary widely in services, functions offered, and costs. There is no way of making an adequate comparison of various sites without basing it on specific functional requirements and the specific response that will be expected in the event of an emergency.

Consideration must be given to the number of subscriber clients to each commercial site and to the effect that can have on the availability of the services in the event of a disaster. This is a relatively minor consideration, however, because the great majority of disaster incidents will be localized to a single organization. If there was a widespread disaster, few organizations would require rapid response.

Remember that one of the principal effects of a widespread disaster is always that most of your key personnel will need to stay near their homes for the safety of themselves and their families. There are only a few extreme situations in which the maintenance of computer operations would be immediately required after a major storm, earthquake, or act of war.

Specific features to consider

The routine backup requirements of the operation, plus the disaster recovery systems, hardware, and communications requirements planning will be handled by the technical support staff, rather than the disaster recovery team. It is the responsibility of the disaster recovery analysts to know exactly what is required, and to see that the facility is adequately prepared to be able to operate smoothly. Each hardware, software, and communications combination will be unique, but it will have to be installed and managed in similar facilities.

The decisions on the backup site facilities will center on the physical facilities, and the manner in which they will be managed. Checklist 6-3, Backup Site Considerations, lists the various details that must be planned and contractually agreed upon. It includes checklists of items that must be arranged for, including:

- Management considerations
- Building considerations
- Environmental controls
- Management resources
- Building controls and services
- Community fire and safety
- User contact and support
- Backup site resources
- Computer backup information
- Ancillary equipment availability
- Data handling and control support
- Administration responsibilities

The decisions on the backup site facilities will depend uniquely on the interim processing requirements and strategies that are decided on. They will be driven by the backup computer configuration and the backup communications network configuration that have been determined by the technical support group and approved by management. The disaster recovery team then will be responsible for the physical facility planning, the emergency personnel responsibility planning and office space assignments, the emergency move plan, and the testing of the backup site.

Checklist 6-3. Backup site considerations.

Management Considerations

1. Have all aspects of the use of the vendor site been agreed on?
2. Is the disaster notification procedure keyed to the use of the site?
3. Is there a vendor coordinator named who is responsible for managing control at the backup site?
4. Are there adequate communications between the Emergency Control Center and the backup site?
5. Are all the people on the notification list familiar with the backup site?
6. If necessary, can the vendor backup site be used as a backup Emergency Control Center?
7. In the event of a widespread disaster, has a second-level backup site been agreed on?
8. Have arrangements been made for the backup of data entry equipment and special equipment, such as OCR and MICR?
9. Do all recovery personnel know the location, address, and phone numbers of the Emergency Control Center and the vendor backup site?
10. Has the vendor agreed to a test plan for the backup site?

Building Considerations

11. Are floor plans of the site available?
12. Are there detailed computer room floor layout plans, with templates, floor markings, and cutouts?
13. Has the square footage of the facility been checked in detail?
14. Is there adequate office space, operator space, work areas, and meeting rooms?
15. Is the building suitably fire resistant?
16. Can the building and the rooms be secured and controlled at the same level as the internal site?

Environmental Controls

17. Have electrical control and telephone panels been installed?
18. Are there fire detection, alarm, and suppression equipment installed?
19. Are there smoke and thermal detection devices?
20. Are there sprinkler and Halon systems, as appropriate?
21. Is there full security, with an alarm system?

22. Is there adequate air conditioning, both under the equipment and the racks, and in the rooms?
23. Have all necessary computer cooling systems been installed?

Management Resources

24. Have contacts been made, with names and telephone numbers listed, for installation and repair services for:
    • Electrical?
    • Plumbing?
    • Building construction?
25. Have telephones been installed for management use?
26. Are disaster recovery plan manuals available at the vendor site?
27. Have lists of nearby housing and restaurants been prepared?
28. Have arrangements been made for food and water at the site?
29. Are there sufficient toilet and washroom facilities for the backup staff?
30. Are personal care items, such as soap, available?
31. Have arrangements been made for cash and credit cards for the supervisory staff?
32. Are there organization, emergency, and local telephone directories at each phone?
33. Is at least one automobile available for the supervisor?
34. Are portable and CB radios and battery clocks available?
35. Are battery tape recorders and cassettes available?
36. Is there a dispensary nearby, or first aid equipment?
37. Is there adequate emergency medical equipment?
38. Are there vendor machines, or a ready source of food?

Building Controls and Services

39. Are there sufficient security services and equipment?
40. Is the security manager familiar with those who will supervise the backup operations?
41. Have identification lists of all backup personnel been prepared and distributed to the vendor site?
42. Have extra keys and instructions about the site been prepared and stored safely in place?
43. Is the manager of the building completely familiar with the possible disaster recovery operations?
44. Have cleaning services been approved and arranged for?

Checklist 6-3. Continued.
Community Fire and Safety

45. Have contacts been made with the local fire and police departments?

46. Have contacts been informed of the possible emergency use of the site?

47. Have contacts been requested to review and comment on the preparations?

48. Have all applicable local codes and ordinances been reviewed and met?

49. Are phone numbers of contacts listed in the disaster recovery plan?

User Contact and Support

50. Is a user telephone number list stored at the backup site?

51. Are the notification procedures documented?

52. Have user contacts and their alternates been identified?

53. Do all user contacts have the vendor backup site phone number?

54. Have user travel considerations been made, including:
    • Travel procedures and checklist?
    • Airline ticket availability?
    • Cash and credit card arrangements?
    • Hotel accommodation arrangements?
    • Rental car arrangements?

55. Has the microcomputer disaster recovery plan been distributed and explained?

56. Do the users have documentation on:
    • Application specialists in an emergency situation?
    • Probable schedules and priorities?
    • Data reconstruction procedures available?
    • Applications software documentation available?
    • Assembly procedures available?
    • Data entry instructions at the backup site?

57. Are copies of crucial user operations documentation stored at the backup site?

58. Is a reconstruction plan and worksheet available?

59. Have key user personnel been identified for disaster recovery activities?

60. Have those key user personnel been identified for disaster recovery activities?

Backup Site Resources

61. Are vendor building control and security arrangements complete, including:
    - Security services and equipment?
    - Backup site security identification cards or bandages?
    - Identification lists?
    - Extra keys and instruction?
    - Arrangements with cleaning, food, and other services?

62. Are stocks maintained, or arrangements made at the vendor site, for:
    - All necessary computer supplies?
    - Necessary forms, and forms replacement capability?
    - Cash credit arrangements for supplies?
    - Access to off-site supply storage areas?

63. Are all off-site storage areas documented at the vendor backup site?

64. Are all pertinent hardware and software vendors listed, with contacts and phone numbers?

65. Are updated copies maintained in a secure vault at the site of:
    - Disaster recovery plan?
    - Run documentation?
    - Communications network documentation?
    - Computer vendor manuals?
    - Personnel and telephone lists?

66. Has emergency office space been arranged?

67. Are telephone books and phone lists readily available?

68. Will food and water be available when needed?

69. Have the backup site manager's home and work phone numbers been distributed?

70. Have directions to the vendor backup site been distributed?

Computer Backup Information

71. Has Technical Support documented the following:
    - Computer configuration?
    - Memory availability?

Checklist 6-3. Continued.

- Disks—types, compatibility, space availability?
- Tape drives—number, density, and tracks?
- Disk and tape storage procedures?
- Tape library system and tape controls?
- Scratch tape availability?
- Projected days and hours computer is available?
- All required systems control programs and procedures?

72. Has the technical support staff designated a disaster recovery consultant?
73. Have computer operators been planned and instructed in the procedures?
74. Will tape librarians be available for 24 hours, 7 days per week?
75. Has a disaster hot line been planned, with operators designated?
76. Have media racks, modem racks, and storage cabinets been installed?
77. Has the communications coordinator documented the following:
    - Backup communications network?
    - Availability of lines ports and line sets?
    - Modems and baud rates?
    - On-site terminals?
    - Phone numbers to be used?

78. Has the telephone company been given details of the requirements should there be a disaster recovery situation?
79. Has the computer vendor agreed to the sufficiency of the plan?
80. If computer equipment must be brought in, have all agreements been documented and signed?

Ancillary Equipment Availability

81. Have the following pieces of equipment been installed or arranged for in case of emergency?
    - Extra printer?
    - Decollator and burster?
    - Copiers?
    - COM and microform equipment?

82. Will sufficient terminals and typewriters be obtainable?
83. Have desks, chairs, and tables been acquired or planned?
84. Are racks for disks, tapes, modems, and forms in place?

85. Are vending machines and coffee machines available?

Data Handling and Control Support

86. Have procedures for the input/output group been agreed upon and distributed, including:
    - Responsibilities and assignments?
    - Notification and supervision procedures?
    - Travel arrangements, such as scheduled bus pickups?
    - Procedures for activating the backup site?
    - Messenger and data transport schedules and controls?
    - Data entry instructions and priorities?
    - Balancing and error handling procedures?

87. Have input/output group manpower levels and schedules been documented?
88. Have procedures for reconstructing the data for crucial applications been documented?
89. Have data entry procedures, setup procedures and JCL's been documented?
90. Have arrangements been made for special equipment?

Administration Responsibilities

91. Have all administration support functions been identified?
92. Have personnel assignments been documented, distributed, and explained?
93. Have master lists been developed and distributed of supervisory names, addresses, and telephone numbers?
94. Have responsibilities been defined for:
    - Public relations and statements to the press?
    - Management and control of the backup site building?
    - Security arrangements?
    - Transportation arrangements?
    - Clerical support arrangement?
95. Have liaison positions been established for:
    - Finance department?
    - Insurance department?
    - Personnel department?
    - Legal department?
    - Medical services?

Checklist 6-3. Continued.

96. Does the vendor backup site manager have documentation on:
    - Hardware and communications configuration?
    - Crucial applications and persons responsible?
    - Supplies and forms examples and sources?
    - Travel information on airlines and vehicle rentals?
    - All organization locations and possible secondary backup site?
    - All procedures that have been distributed?

97. Is a disaster recovery telephone and address list, and telephone tree, at all sites?

98. Has an updated list been prepared, and sent to all locations, of the contact persons and telephone numbers of:
    - Local police, sheriff, and highway patrol?
    - Local fire department?
    - Hospital, medical, and paramedical services?
    - Organization and building security?
    - Equipment and service vendors?
    - Telephone company contacts?
    - Electric, gas, and water company contacts?
    - Disaster recovery consultant?
    - Special equipment vendors?
    - Data captor and entry vendors?
    - Alarm system vendors?
    - Truck, car, and equipment rental vendors?
    - Travel and airline companies?
    - Forms vendors and distribution companies?
    - Off-site storage sites and contacts?
    - Other cooperating companies?

99. Is documentation available on all security precautions?

100. Is documentation available on possible second level recovery sites if the first site also suffers loss?

There are several other areas that must be planned by the team:

- Security controls and management at the site
- Facility and equipment maintenance
- Power monitoring and protection

- Off-site data storage for the backup site
- All support services
- Local government and press liaison
- Food and lodging services

Most of these decisions will be made as the planning process proceeds, and as tests are conducted on the plan at the vendor site. Because disaster recovery preparations usually are not a high priority in an organization, decision making is slow and decisions are sometimes altered; multiple plans are required for different scenarios, and many of the decisions that have been discussed might not be made for months. Most organizations find that the decisions on the backup site and the preparations for its use take more than a year. Many of the decisions can be speeded up by hiring a disaster recovery consultant to crystallize the requirements and possibilities. There is still time-consuming work to be done by the technical support group, however, with a conflict of priorities for the systems programming capabilities that are available.

Although the decisions and preparations to be made are listed together here, many of them are agreed upon at widely different times.

Most vendors will give substantial help in planning the use of their backup facilities. All of the points that were discussed previously in the selection of the vendor must be reviewed in detail to determine whether there is a complete fit with the required plans.

In addition to the normal physical facility planning that will be necessary for any use of the commercial backup site, plans should be made in the event of an emergency for the following:

- Electronic equipment installation
- Communications network connections
- The move to the site
- Personnel and space assignments
- Off-site data storage
- Testing the use of the site

The electronic equipment installation, including the computer, peripheral equipment, modems, and so on, and the communications network connections will be planned by the technical support group, or other group that has the responsibility for computer and communications planning and layout. This might or might not be handled by the vendor of the services. The technical support group should be responsible for all related details, down to cable lengths and floor cutouts. Elements of the preparations, such as installing racks, electrical panels, and so on, must be included in the facility preparation plan, however, because they will need to be in place before proceeding in the installation of the backup computer. Thus, there will be many details that are not under the control of the disaster recovery preparation team, but must be monitored by them to be assured that the planning has been done.

Elements of the move plan

The plan for the move to the site in the event of a disaster should be prepared in the same manner, and in the same detail, as any other data center move. This does not mean that it will be possible to carry out in a normal manner, because there can be great disruption. The plan should be prepared as if it were possible to handle all details, however, to be able to check on whether it is possible to operate the new site both expeditiously and under proper control. Such a plan will be different if it is prepared for a hot site with the computer and communications in place, or for a ready room in which most facilities and services are in place, but the computer is not installed. It must, therefore, be individualized for each installation. Checklist 6-4, Elements of a Move Plan, notes some, but not all, of the details that should be included. Each of these elements will need to be discussed with the person who will be responsible for them, and a realistic time frame assigned to their completion during an emergency. It is obvious that if the total time necessary to handle all these items is greater than would be acceptable to the organization, then more preparations must be made in advance at the backup site.

Emergencies can generate confusion, but many of the problems can be dissipated by assigning responsibility to oversee the physical move of equipment and documents. With control, no items should be dropped, damaged, improperly packed, mishandled, or left on elevators, trucks, or loading docks. The flow of movement to the backup site must be monitored.

One of the more important problems in an emergency move is to make sure that everyone knows exactly where they are to go at the backup site. Some personnel will be assigned there who are not on important work, and are not needed for bringing up the system. These people can waste a lot of effort on the part of those supervising the move if they have to ask questions about their tasks or assigned area. If Fig. 6-13, Emergency Space Assignments, is filled out carefully during the planning stages, there will be many decisions that do not have to be made during an actual emergency.

Checklist 6-4.   Elements of a move plan.

Time	Item	Responsible Group/Individual

Necessary Electronic Equipment Installation

- Confirm emergency delivery of computer

- Confirm delivery of communications equipment

- Check on racks, lines, and coax

- Check on electric power installation

- Check on floor cutouts, power plugs, and racks

- Lay and label cables

- Check on safety and fire detection equipment

Communications Network Connections

- Install telephone company Demarc

- Install communications processor

- Gen and test communications processor

- Run telephone cables and coax, and install modems

- Install terminals

The Move to Site

- Document preferred schedule of an emergency move

Checklist 6-4. Continued.

- Ensure that listings, tapes, and output logs are moved

- Confirm movement of incidental equipment

- Clean area and assure continued cleaning services

- Ensure security for the computer and office area

- Install all available equipment and furniture

Personnel and Space Assignments

Assign job responsibilities from the disaster recovery plan

- Assign coordinators to each involved vendors

- Assign spaces and desks according to the plan

- Ensure security for both the computer and office areas

- Arrange security for the loading dock and deliveries

- Arrange schedules for all personnel involved

- Document and distribute the security plan

- Document and distribute the fire protection plan

- Review maintenance agreements and check with vendors

- Determine insurance situations

Fig. 6-13. Emergency space assignments.

A. Primary Response - Recovery operation of mandatory systems
B. Secondary Response - Recovery operation of necessary systems
C. Alternate Response - Recovery operation in event of widespread disaster

Personnel	Space Assignment	Equipment Required

Assignments can be documented similarly but there usually will be many changes to planned assignments because of the effects of specific security incidents.

User responsibilities for disaster recovery planning

THIS CHAPTER DISCUSSES SOME PRACTICAL USER MEASURES FOR disaster recovery planning. Fundamental for such planning is data protection, or security, and data and software backup. Sample policies are furnished for user responsibilities for data protection, data and software backup, and security measures required for data. Also included in this chapter are brief reviews concerning the security of user data and legal considerations about data. Some exemplary procedures for managing personal computer systems for disaster recovery and backup also are provided.

Practical user measures for disaster recovery planning

The disaster recovery planning for the data centers in the organization will handle most of the key financial applications, large operational applications, and personnel applications. In the user areas, however, there can be many vital applications for such plans on PCs and minicomputers. At the very least, the smaller user computers will contain a great body of valuable computing work and should be protected by disaster recovery planning.

Disaster recovery planning for user areas need not be as extensive as for data centers, but it should cover all the elements of preparation and recovery that are discussed in this book. A disaster recovery plan should be specific to the organization involved, and tailored to its needs. An off-the-shelf plan is of no use whatsoever at the time of a security event when individuals need to know exactly what their role is, and the steps they must take. The presence of a central "paper plan" provides little disaster recovery capability to the users unless they have become involved for their own applications and computers. All user departments should go through an exercise of disaster plan preparation, training, and testing, before an emergency occurs.

The full disaster recovery planning process that has been described involves a great deal of activity and cost, and need not be followed step by step by the users for their smaller computers. Such an approach could be self-defeating, because user groups would soon lose interest. Attention should be directed to the installation of mandatory and necessary security measures that are most crucial to the specific operations.

The best approach for microcomputer systems is for a small, highly visible team under the direction of a supervisor to design a short-term, high-impact plan to implement a course of action to handle the most pressing needs in the event of a disaster. The steps that should be taken by the team are:

- Assemble all readily available applications and computer systems documentation, including the vendor materials.
- Assemble the reports of any audits or security studies that might be related to the particular user functions.
- Create lists of the operating application systems in their first estimation of the order of priority.
- Consult lists of the operating management to get their opinions as to the mandatory and necessary applications in an agreed order of priority.
- Determine the minimum configuration, or number of PCs, on which these priority systems can run, and arrange for tests on backup microcomputers.
- Determine if these crucial systems are being adequately backed up, and if they can be run off-site, in an emergency, in the time required. In one case, a bank simply told the users to take their portable PCs and important disks home with them every night.
- Give disaster recovery training to all the users, and discuss with them how they can control personally and back up their less important systems for their own convenience.

Users generally develop programs for their PCs and handle their data in a relatively unstructured way, and it is unlikely that many will change their habits because of a possible disaster. It is possible, however, to make them aware of the problems involved with such practices. It is also possible to establish a set of operational policies and procedures that include the importance of controlling the ownership of useful data, and establishing reasonable security regarding it. Policies and procedures might not be enforceable by I/S, but they are a good way of clearly stating what some of the user responsibilities are, and what they should do about it.

Operational user policies

The policies that are approved regarding disaster recovery must be completely interwoven with the policies regarding microcomputer operation, data ownership, security, backup, privacy, legal considerations, and so on. It is all part of the same fabric, and disaster recovery is one thread that runs through the whole and is dependent upon all other policies for support.

Of course, there are a variety of levels of user programs, and disaster recovery might not be an important consideration in many instances. There must be awareness, however, about when disaster recovery is important. In developing programs intended for ongoing use, users should be required to follow the corporate standards for microcomputer programming and data handling, when such standards or procedures have been established. Clearly, if it is a one-time or temporary program, users cannot be expected to adhere to standards that are not pertinent to one-time or temporary programs, yet adherence to the spirit of the standards should be encouraged even then.

When microcomputers are used in ongoing production applications, conformance to the tested and proven corporate standards and procedures definitely should be expected. If the many years of experience in data processing of the corporation are disregarded, the result clearly could be harmful, and possibly cause significant loss.

Operational policies that outline user responsibilities, including those regarding disaster recovery, therefore should be accepted at all levels of the corporation. It would even be useful to have the users periodically, possibly quarterly, review their programs and use of data, and turn in their program listings and data control actions to a central repository, such as a corporate microcomputer inventory. This action of regularly bringing program and data documentation up to date would have the effect of reminding all the users of their responsibilities regarding data control and disaster recovery.

The following list is a representative set of standards that covers the principal operational policies of concern. Users must be aware of, and take action on, all of these responsibilities if there is to be any maintenance of the obligations of disaster recovery preparations.

- Users shall maintain a high level of responsibility in adhering to the corporate standards of control because microcomputers and downloaded data are placed in the hands of authorized users.

- Users shall protect data in microcomputer files from disclosure to or modification by unauthorized individuals. Magnetic storage devices containing sensitive data should be securely locked when not in use.

- Users shall recognize the particular ownership of any crucial data, and shall take steps to maintain the integrity and ownership records of that data.

- Users shall protect data and programs from accidental erasure or other loss. Proper use of the equipment and proper procedures for data backup are essential. It is strongly urged that important data and programs be copied and stored off-site for emergency backup.

- Users shall provide adequate documentation of both the data and program for continuity of the application when the current developer and user are not present.

- Users who develop programs and data files shall see that a second user is trained, and that the program and data are documented with adequate user manuals.

- User-developed programs shall be logical, structured, well explained, and adhere to corporate standards of data control.

- User documentation shall be protected to survive a physical disaster.

- Users shall ensure that microcomputers and software purchased by the company are restricted to company use.

- Users shall ensure that data files generated within the company also shall be restricted to company use.

Security of user data

Disaster recovery preparations will not be effective unless adequate security safeguards are applied to the operations, systems, and data files. Users must become familiar with the normal security precautions that are taken regarding data processing, and be aided in deciding which of the procedures and methods are applicable to their work.

The subject of security is a broad one that has been described at length in other documents, and no attempt will be made here to cover many of its aspects. It is sufficient to point out that most professional data processing personnel understand the ramifications of security, and those who work with end users should be ready to interpret the time-proven security rules to the users. I/S staff must be prepared to give aid and instruction to the users in determining which security measures should be applied to their work.

There can be no reasonable approach to disaster recovery preparations unless all affected data files are held securely, and control is passed automatically from one holder of the data to the next. To give security to data that is considered owned by any particular group, the controls must be applied to that data. Without such controls, any records of data ownership and ability to control the data will be irretrievably lost.

The following list includes some of the broad aspects of security, including a number of rules that have been used in actual practice in some corporations. This list offers a shopping list of policies that might be applicable in specific situations.

- Users with the appropriate security clearance will be able to access only copies of company production data stored on the mainframe computer for which access has been approved and arranged.

- Downloaded information is to be kept on diskettes that are locked up when not in use, or on a hard disk that has a security package that restricts access.

- The hardcopy reports resulting from the use of secure information should be locked up when not in use.

- All data residing on a mainframe or a microcomputer will have the same standards of security. Those without authorization to production data on the mainframe will not have access to that data, or derived information, on a microcomputer.

- All microcomputers and their peripherals will be identified by the reference number by using a security tag or engraving. Microcomputers handling protected information also will have software ID codes and passwords that are assigned by the I/S security officer.

- The only microcomputers that can be removed from the premises are the recommended portable microcomputers available from the Information Center. In particular, hard disks and physical storage devices other than floppy disks will remain on the premises.

It is impractical to restrict the movement of floppy disks, so the users who have such disks containing secure information will be held responsible to exercise reasonable precautions regarding these disks.

- Department managers should make all their employees who use corporate data files aware of their responsibility in securing that information from misuse. The misuse of corporate data will be viewed as a serious infraction of corporate policy, and can result in termination and possible legal action.

- All computer programs and data developed by employees using company-owned computer equipment are company property. Individuals leaving the company must return all copies of their programs, data, and documentation to the company.

The extract microcomputer files that are created from corporate data files each will have special security situations, some of which will be concerns about data ownership. By nature, these files are highly transportable, and provide good summary "snapshots" of financial and corporate operations information. This information could be of interest and value to competitors, particularly those files that contain customer-oriented information. In addition, the privacy of both employees and customers potentially could be violated if information about them was made available outside the organization.

User data and software backup

One facet of security frequently overlooked is data and software backup in the event of a disaster or other physical loss. Users who handle information that is important enough to maintain a record of its ownership, should be instructed by I/S in the methods and procedures that are available to handle routine backup and storage of the information. The user's files might not be vital to the corporation, but are certainly worth protecting from loss by disaster because of the amount of effort expended by the user in developing them. It is useful to develop and publish a brief corporate policy for all to use. Data and software backup is not difficult when handled routinely, and has considerable payoff if a contingency arises.

The following list gives some idea as to the level of the policy that might be promulgated.

- The corporate standards and procedures for backup and disaster recovery shall be applicable to any microcomputer system that handles important or valuable data, or contains necessary records of data ownership.

- All important data and programs shall have extra copies stored in a secure, remote location. The storage shall be handled routinely at agreed periods.

- Users shall provide for continuity of an application when the current developer and user are not present. There shall be preparation and maintenance of useful user manuals and other documentation. Normally, a second user will be trained in the requirements and controls of the system. If there are special considerations about data ownership, these will be documented and passed to other users.

Some people question whether any program residing on a microcomputer, which is so vital that it must be backed up using the sophisticated backup technology of the central computer operation, should be on a micro. If it is crucial to the operation of the company, then the program should be evaluated for migration to the central system. On the other hand, one must be careful not to assume that a program and data that is worth backing up needs to meet certain standards of importance to the company as a whole. The program might be of great importance to only the particular user group, and it might represent considerable development effort by them. Almost any program on a microcomputer that has cost an appreciable amount to develop is worth backing up. Also, if that program contains variations of data that are considered to be owned by others, then a permanent record should be kept of how that data was handled, and what form it is now in.

Most data and software backup on microcomputers is handled on floppy disks, which are readily taken to another location and locked, or by transmission from a hard disk to the central computer operations where it is readily handled in the normal backup stream. True hard-file backup technology is relatively new, and only a few standalone systems are available which allow backup to removable tapes. The alternative of transmission to the central system might not always be available. Thus, each system must be reviewed on its own merits.

Legal considerations

There might be legal considerations in the protection and backup of data by company users. These will need to be considered by each organization, and clarified by its own legal staff. Some of the considerations center on privacy issues, while others center on data ownership by third parties. Some areas that should be reviewed are:

- Privacy legislation that imposes restrictions on processing some data about personnel on microcomputers unless adequate controls are in effect. Tighter controls are required on data that is stored and processed in computers than for data that is handled manually.

- When users develop software and data files on company equipment, and on company time, steps must be taken to ensure that it is protected from unauthorized copying and distribution outside the company.

- When company software or data banks are purchased, the license agreements with the vendor usually expressly forbid its copying and use on more than the specifically designated microcomputers. In this case, the data is owned by a third party. These restrictions frequently are ignored, either deliberately or through ignorance. If such an abuse surfaces, it is quite possible that the company could become the target of litigation by the vendor, particularly to seek publicity and to discourage further abuse.

- Most purchased computer software and data have copyright protection, but many users treat the copyrights with the same laxity in which they allow the photocopying of copyrighted material. Copyrighted material is seldom treated as carefully as patented items. Education is needed in this area to keep the company free from lawsuits.

- Ownership of software or data files developed by employees at home or off company hours can be a complex issue. Legal opinion is needed as to potential conflicts of interest. If data that is clearly owned by the company is involved, the rules should be made clear to employees.

- Frequently, employees work away from the premises on portable microcomputers. A policy needs to be set for particular types of programs and data.

- If support and training are provided by a vendor for a particular software package, the course material should be reviewed to determine whether the information given about program and data ownership is consistent with company policy.

- When external vendors are working with employees on programs and data files, the security of important data, and the ownership of the files used in instruction or testing should be reviewed and discussed with the vendor.

- When specific license terms have been agreed upon for programs and data, all users should be given the necessary information to abide by the terms.

Disaster recovery and backup procedures

Figure 7-1, Disaster Recovery and Backup, gives a minimal set of procedures that should be promulgated by I/S and adapted by each user department in the organization.

Fig. 7-1. Disaster recovery and backup.

Disaster recovery and backup

Definition   Disaster recovery and backup plans constitute preparations and contingency plans for the reasonable continuation, within a determined time period, of all key personal computer activities following a serious disruption.

Objectives   To plan and implement a sufficient set of procedures to minimize the effect of a disaster on the operation of the personal computer.

To estimate the possible exposure to financial legal responsibility and business service interruption, and to prepare to minimize such losses that might occur.

Procedures   A realistic evaluation will be made of the possible exposures and of the problems of disaster recovery and backup, preferably in coordination with I/S and internal audit.

- Existing organizational policies and procedures relative to disaster recovery will be considered and coordinated with any plans that are made.

- Disaster recovery measures that are mandatory, necessary, and desirable will be analyzed separately.

- Existing I/S disaster recovery practices will be considered and coordinated with the plans.

- Disaster recovery and backup plans for all application programs will be documented and discussed with responsible management when there are related operations.

- Occasional audits of such plans will be made, and tests of their effectiveness performed.

8

Preparing the disaster recovery plan

THIS CHAPTER COVERS THE PROCEDURES NEEDED TO PLAN THE management of resources in time of disaster to get management agreement and vendor and external support agreements.

The preparation of detailed recovery procedures and the production of the recovery plan are described in this chapter. This includes the production of Volume II, "EDP Disaster Recovery Procedures," as a usable, working manual for times of emergency.

Also reviewed in this chapter is staff security awareness and the process for the restoration of the permanent facility.

Planning the management of resources

In the functional requirements phase of the disaster recovery planning process one of the first activities of the planning team is to assemble all documentation relative to the inventory of resources, including hardware, communications, software, forms, facility descriptions, etc. (See chapter 3.) This information is used as the basis for the requirements for the important resources. Applications are reviewed and alternative recovery strategies are considered. After the key management decisions have been made regarding the general disaster recovery approach, the planning team must use this same information to define in detail:

- Requirements for routine backup of resources
- Requirements for disaster recovery of resources

Disaster recovery can be successful only if there is a routine backup. When possible, backup of the system software, proprietary packages, programs and data should be done on a daily basis. If this is not possible, it should be done once a week. It should be noted that roll forward recovery might mean that it is seldom necessary to do backup. There should be a program in place for a regular testing of hardware and communications backup facilities.

Routine backup requirements

Figure 8-1, Routine Backup Requirements, outlines some of the general areas that the team have to consider. Specific, detailed plans must be made in all areas. Most of the routine backup will be daily, but it will be more frequent for on-line systems and databases. It is difficult to generalize on routine system backup because of the great amounts of possible variations. A few of the key points are:

- A library management program is almost a necessity. Software packages such as Panvalet and Librarian, are excellent for backup purposes.
- Production programs and data files must be protected against change or deletion for audit control and backup.
- Retrieval and access to confidential data files must be restricted.
- The ability to re-create the entire library and to protect programs and job control streams against loss is crucial to successful recovery.

A history of all prior versions of programs, job control streams, and data files might be necessary for adequate recovery. The extent of the disaster will determine what protection files are needed.

An index of all documentation and backup material stored off-site should be kept up to date for audit purposes. Any additions or deletions should be recorded.

Disaster recovery systems requirements

The main requirements for the disaster recovery of systems are the capabilities of the personnel and equipment to use the routine

Fig. 8-1. Routine backup requirements.

Secure operating system and all proprietary software:
1. Maintain a central library file of all program products.
2. Dump routinely all necessary software to tape, and store at a secure site.
3. Use a comprehensive library management program.

Maintain adequate file backup for application systems:
1. Review all operational systems for adequate backup and documentation.
2. Establish a routine backup schedule for all operational systems.
3. Review system file security for all new applications and all modifications.
4. Enforce file security specifications and procedures.
5. Ensure that backup files represent the latest data.

Enforce controlled library procedures:
1. Confirm procedures and responsibility for all tape and disk handling.
2. Maintain separation of functions in handling data files.
3. Ensure that necessary library files are routinely rotated to a secure site.
4. Duplicate and keep off-site all run books, operational JCL, and procedural JCL.
5. Establish procedures for copying tapes, duplicating microfilm, reading cards to tape, or performing other operations necessary to maintain backup files with the latest available data.

Review backup and recovery procedures with the user departments:
1. Determine which files must be backed up.
2. Establish backup responsibility and schedules for each user area.

---

backup materials to reconstruct the data, programs, and conditions of the last successful run before the service disruption. The systems programming staff will be the key to a successful recovery because they are in the best position to do the following:

- Determine where the systems were at the time of disaster
- Reconstruct the data, programs, and conditions

- Modify the job control language and streams as necessary
- Produce a repeated run on the new equipment for audit review

On-line transaction systems and database systems offer many specific recovery problems that often are unique to the particular systems. Most on-line systems will have built-in "reconstruct processes." They will use such methods as periodic dumps, delayed updates with the transactions put on a transaction tape, before and after read records, and so on.

In most large operations, the database systems will be the simplest key to controlled recovery, if adequate controls on their use are in place. The systems programmers and database analysts will proceed to the backup site and do the following:

- Systems programmers will load the files down from the backup tapes, as they exist from the last good run.
- Analysts will test the procedures on the files by running the files exactly as they did the previous day.
- Each analyst will be responsible for testing certain requirements of the system.
- Analysts will have to analyze discrepancies individually, and might have to redo some of the previous day's work.

For economic reasons, most disaster recovery sites will be equipped with computers that are smaller than the original computer but compatible with it. The initial strategy at the backup site probably will be to run only the most important programs at first. It is clear that the greatest problems will be in setting up the job control stream and in operating a different computer. It is, therefore, important to consider these two concepts:

- The systems programmers consider the various possible configurations of the backup system and prepare as much of the job control language in advance as possible. This is difficult when it is not known before a disaster how many terminals will still be operable.
- The computer operations personnel should try a number of test runs on the backup computer, using only backup files that would be available in a disaster.

In planning the management of resources, these are the types of considerations that the I/S disaster recovery team must study and decide on. For planning the management of the application systems, the information on the Application System Service Availability Requirements Worksheet (Fig. 8-2) and the I/S Disaster Recovery Plan (Fig. 8-3) will be used.

Disaster recovery hardware and communications requirements

In addition to the preparation of the disaster recovery operations procedures, and the training of the personnel in those procedures, a principal requirement of computer operations is to have full and detailed documentation stored in a secure site for:

- Hardware configurations at the original site and the backup site
- Communications configurations at the original site and estimated for the backup site
- Descriptions of all networks and terminals, with locations and responsibilities
- All operating procedures and standards
- All environmental systems at both sites
- All fire alarm and emergency systems at both sites
- Floor plans of both sites
- Descriptions of all ancillary equipment
- All PCs, data entry, and other special equipment (OCR, etc.)

There is always a problem of keeping such documentation updated. The best solution is to have as much of it as possible, even the equipment configurations, on a programmed documentation system. It then is updated readily at a terminal and is always backed up with the routine system library program.

The team must be assured that all relevant documentation is backed up and secure, and is routinely updated.

Disaster recovery personnel requirements

The most crucial and complex part of the management of resources is in the planning, organizing, and training of the required personnel. Experienced, well-trained personnel will scarcely need detailed procedures, but they must be at the right place at the right time, and sure of their assignments. There need to be personnel plans for:

The time of disaster

- Fire suppression teams
- Evacuation plans
- Alternate work sites

Disaster recovery

- Recovery teams and team leaders
- User department coordinators
- Vendor contacts
- Key person lists with phones
- Briefing on responsibilities
- Security personnel

Handling personnel

- Desk arrangements and telephone assignments
- Parking assignments
- Bus and shuttle service
- Motel arrangements

The team can use Fig. 8-2, Personnel Requirements at the Backup Site, as a worksheet for estimating and planning the assignments of personnel, and planning for space for them at the backup site.

Fig. 8-2. Personnel requirements at the backup site.

1st Shift
    Current/project

    Essential

2nd Shift
    Current/project

    Essential

3rd Shift
    Current/project

    Essential

Personnel

Managers/supervisors

Systems analysts

Software technical support

User personnel

Programmers

Computer operators

Tape library area

Scheduling area

I/O control area

Data entry

Secretaries/receptionists

General clerical

Forms handling

Terminal operators

Communications area

Fig. 8-2. Continued.
Vendor customer engineer (CE)

Other:

Total

Comments: Any pertinent information, such as special procedures for handicapped, etc.

Backup site planning requirements

The backup site is a resource that should be planned carefully. It should be reviewed in as much detail as normally given to any data center design. Some of the considerations are:

Floor layout plans

- Templates, floor markings, and cutouts

Environmental controls

- Control panel
- Air conditioning test
- Repair contact

Service and repair contacts

- Electrician
- Telephone installation
- Plumber

Ancillary equipment

- Decollator/deleaver
- Burster
- COM and microform equipment
- Printer
- Copier
- Forms binder
- Tape cleaner

Furniture and equipment

- Desks, tables, chairs
- Typewriters/terminals
- Racks for disks, tapes, modems
- Vending machines/coffee

Supplies

- Backup supply storage
- Forms replacement capability

Building control

- Security services and equipment
- Identification lists
- Extra keys and instructions
- Cleaning services

Fire and safety

- Contacts with local fire and police departments
- Fire detection, alarm, and suppression equipment
- Sprinkler system
- Halon system
- Burglar alarms
- Protected electric/phone closets

Management and user agreement on actions

When the detailed recovery procedures are in rough draft, they will require approval of both management and users, and they should be reviewed in detail with the personnel who will be expected to carry out the plans. There must be agreements reached in four areas:

1. In the descriptions of the responsibilities and functions of the I/S disaster recovery teams, some of the actions will be highly specific to the people involved. In addition, the preplanning that must be done will refer to many technical areas. The team leaders and the people involved must be given an opportunity to review these responsibilities and actions, confirm if they make good sense, and modify them as appropriate, as long as they do not change the structure of the plan. This might require more than one discussion.

2. The plan must be confirmed with the operational management of the organization as reasonable and appropriate, and conforming to other existing organizational emergency plans, such as fire alarm procedures, bomb threat procedures, and so forth, that apply to a much wider organizational area.

3. There should be specific agreement among all I/S departments or groups that the division of responsibilities among the various disaster recovery is reasonable and equitable, and does not interfere with regular management of the area.

4. There must be cooperation and agreement among the users on establishing the priorities of operation and the minimum system requirements for the emergency computer systems and networks. The final decision will come from senior management, but it must be discussed with all participants in advance.

After such agreements or decisions have been obtained, the plan can be finalized, and presented formally to all concerned. After hearing the presentation of the objectives, arrangements, and planned actions in context with all other aspects of the plan, management and users will be able to give their final approval or request that modification be made.

Management of vendor agreements

Most equipment vendors have a policy that if a disaster hits one of their rental systems, they will take the next one off the line or from the shipping dock to replace their equipment, and they will transport it to the site by the fastest available means. Most vendors will send along a team of systems engineers and installers who will work around the clock to help the user recover from the disaster. If the facility has mixed-vendor equipment, they will have to bring in all the vendors. Few vendors will break their sequence of delivery for equipment that is not already installed. Most vendors will work diligently and cooperatively to bring up a mixed-vendor installation rapidly.

The larger vendors normally will give verbal statements to the above effect, and refer to general company policies. Smaller vendors might supply written letters of intent as to their policy in time of disaster.

It is worthwhile for the team to contact all vendors, despite their published policies, and discuss the ramifications of a disaster with their local salesman and sales manager. Frequently individual salespeople have not considered the problems of a disaster in a center, and are not aware of who the best contacts in their company are. In these discussions, the vendor should be expected to supply emergency phone numbers to call 24 hours per day, 7 days per week. Salespeoples' home phone numbers are of little use, because most disaster calls will be at irregular hours when salespeople may not be at home.

A serious problem to discuss with the vendor is what to do if your company has older equipment that is no longer on the production line, or is obsolete. Vendors can legally replace such equipment in emergencies with the closest available upgrade of the equipment, involving extra cost and extra systems programming.

Most vendors will divert equipment from a production line, that is scheduled for other customers, and ship it to the customer with a disaster situation. Some vendors are careful to add, however, that they cannot promise such delivery if there is a general disaster.

The telephone company should be included in the vendor discussions. The telephone company's normal policy falls under the liability section of their General Regulations. It might state something similar to the following:

> The subscriber is liable for and shall reimburse the telephone company for the cost of replacement, installation and/or repair of any telephone instrument, facility, or equipment subscribed to by him which is lost or damaged due to theft, vandalism, willful injury or negligence or any other cause whatsoever except flood, fire other than fire intentionally caused by the subscriber or his agent, or other natural disasters.

Preparing detailed disaster recovery procedures: The action plan

When there has been sufficient analysis of the problem, and the management of the resources has been planned for the key scenarios, the I/S disaster recovery procedures can be assembled. These constitute the action plan. This plan tells specific individuals, or positions, what their responsibilities are and what actions to take. It tells the who, what, when, and where, with little discussion of the why. When an emergency strikes, people should be able to take the disaster recovery procedures and follow their own sections, confident that they are working in concert with the rest of the team.

An example of an outline of an I/S disaster recovery plan is given in Fig. 8-3. It has been arbitrarily divided into four phases:

- Phase 1: Initial response
- Phase 2: Disaster recovery at backup site
- Phase 3: Full disaster recovery at sufficient sites
- Phase 4: Recovery at original or alternate site

This cannot be a detailed, fill-in-the-blanks, plan because each organization will have unique requirements, and will have developed their own strategies. In addition, the majority of activities will take place in parallel by the different recovery teams, coordinated by management. Also, the recovery times after the disaster event will vary depending on the need of the organization and the preparations that have been made. The major steps, and the principles illustrated, will be valid for all companies.

The action plan procedures must be simple listings with little explanation. The use of "playscript procedure" writing can be helpful for the overlapping activities. Key actions must be in the front of each section and highlighted.

A separate list of actions can be developed and maintained for each of the major problem scenarios considered possible. For example, different responses might be required for bomb threats, fires, serious power outages, and so forth. The list of people, of course, will remain the same, and many of the actions will be the same. For most organizations, a single list of actions will be sufficient with management selecting and giving appropriate orders.

Copies of the instructions must be readily available when a disaster occurs (as is discussed in the next section).

Phase 1: Initial response

The emergency response procedures are started as soon as a disaster is recognized. This might be after a fire alarm has been pulled, and the organization's emergency departments have been alerted. As soon as a disaster to the I/S area has been recognized, the emergency management team is notified, and they notify others and assess the damage. These procedures, therefore, should list key personnel to be called, the immediate actions they must take, and the telephone trees they must start in response to the emergency. These procedures must emphasize the immediate actions that must be taken to protect life and property and to minimize the impact of the emergency before recovery procedures start.

The emergency response procedures should be coordinated with any fire alarm procedures, bomb threat procedures, storm

Fig. 8-3. I/S disaster recovery plan.

PHASE I
Initial response

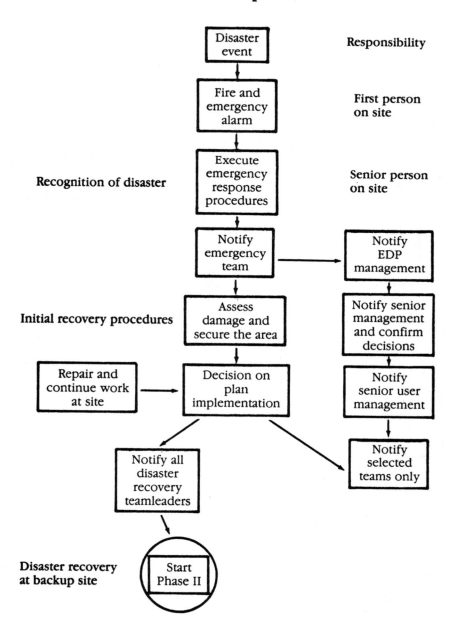

Fig. 8-3. Continued.

Phase II
Disaster recovery at backup site

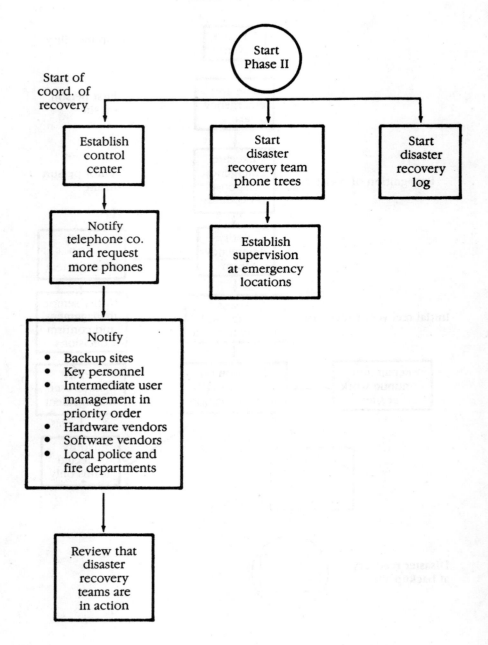

PHASE II
Disaster Recovery at backup site (continued)

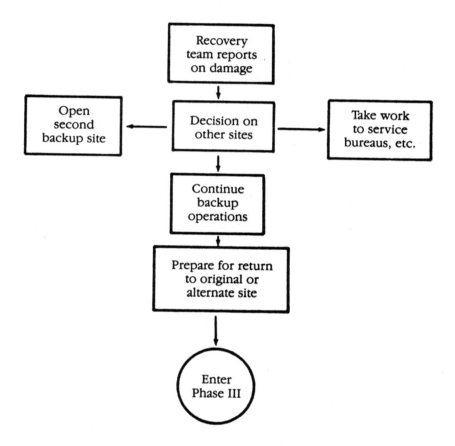

Recovery activities in parallel

Within 6 hours of disaster event
- Give vendors preliminary hardware requirements
- Assemble at backup site and off-site storage site
- Initiate transportation system
- Start movement of supplies
- Establish administrative support

Within 12 hours of disaster event
- Assemble backup media and listings at backup site
- Confirm future hardware requirements with vendors
- Order necessary equipment, supplies, and furniture
- Assemble sufficient supplies and equipment at back-up site

Fig. 8-3. Continued.

PHASE II
Disaster Recovery at backup site (continued)

Recovery activities in parallel (cont.)
Within 24 hours of disaster event
- Restore system pack and test system
- Start operation of critical systems
- Have backup site stocked and operating
- Have transportation system working for people and supplies
- Bring up full operating system
- Bring up and test database
- Test and debug systems
- Have all critical application systems operational
- Establish processing schedule
- Inventory application systems availability at site
- Notify all concerned users
- Inventory salvageable material
- Reassess damage

PHASE III
Full disaster recovery at sufficient sites

Recovery activities in parallel
- Have all resources in place at backup sites
- Bring up and test systems at all sites
- Establish off-site storage locations
- Resume backup and off-site storage procedures
- Install communications network and equipment
- Test all new equipment
- Complete salvage effort
- Debriefing of staff and report to management

PHASE IV

Recovery at original or alternate site
- Decisions on recovery timing and equipment
- Site preparation
- Development of recovery procedures in reverse direction
- Repeat of recovery procedures
- Bring up all systems
- Report to management

emergency procedures, and so on, so they might be standard practice in the organization. I/S operations are important but are subservient to the overall operations. I/S personnel should have made sufficient previous preparation so that they do not interfere with fire, police, or senior management activities.

The initial recovery procedures are started as soon as damage has been assessed and management has been notified. Management will depend on a rapid decision made as to the extent of the disaster regarding the following:

- Whether to repair the damage and continue the work at the site
- Whether to close only portions of the site and notify selected teams which will be affected
- Whether to declare a disaster and notify all disaster recovery team leaders

The first people on the site will be intent on minimizing the effects of the disaster and securing the area. The I/S management involved will be in contact with their senior management and other interested officers of the organization and will be careful not to declare a disaster without the knowledge and approval of responsible persons.

Phase 2: Disaster recovery at backup site

As soon as a disaster has been declared, key people will be called to start disaster recovery teams telephone trees to get them all in action. The emergency management team will establish a control center and start the coordination of the recovery. Disaster recovery logs will be started by the management team and each of the other teams so that there is a record of the actions taken.

A great many activities will then be started in parallel. These will depend upon the particular organization. Some examples are noted in Figure 8-4. There will be many routine and special tasks to accomplish, such as the following:

- Notifying management at the backup facility
- Setting up operations at the backup facility
- Notifying users of the disruption of service
- Ensuring that all employees know their new tasks

- Arranging transportation and setting up schedules
- Retrieving backup supplies
- Assembling copies of all documentation, etc.

The backup operation instructions should be very specific as to room locations, personnel functions, application priorities, and tasks to be accomplished. The organization and responsibilities of the disaster recovery teams was discussed in chapter 3. A planning form sheet (Fig. 3-4) and nineteen examples are provided.

The instructions in this section of the plan will be more general because they will depend on the actual effects of the disaster and the effort that will be involved in bringing up possible additional sites, taking some work to service bureaus, and so on. As Phase 2 progresses to handle more and more of the original work load, there are many possible, different scenarios, which will depend upon conditions at the time.

Some of the actions will be:

- Survey the facility to determine the specific damage.
- Submit equipment orders to vendors for the replacement of damaged equipment.
- Salvage all usable material and documentation.
- Arrange with the telephone company and other communications vendors for temporary installations, then more complete network installations.
- Retrieve backup files and documentation from remote storage if they will be helpful in the restart.
- Work closely with the building management and maintenance groups.

There will be no room in the plan for full details of the necessary operating instructions. Such material should have been prepared in advance, tested, and backed up at the alternate site or other location.

Phase 2 ends when all initial backup operations have been set up and are operating.

Phase 3: Full disaster recovery at sufficient sites

If preparations have been made in advance, it is reasonable to plan for all resources to be in place at the backup sites within four weeks.

If sufficient preparations have not been made, it could be closer to four months to obtain the site, prepare it, and bring in environmental control equipment. Planning is crucial to speed.

The types of parallel activities listed in Fig. 8-3, Phase 3, are typical of what will be developed in the plan. This phase finishes when all planned systems and communications networks are operating and well tested and the salvage effort has been completed.

It is time to debrief the staff as to the activities that have taken place and the operability of the plan. The disaster recovery logs should be collected and analyzed. Individual meetings and group meetings should be held with the teams. EDP management then can report to senior management about the accomplishments and the efficiency and effectiveness of the planning effort. Preparations then begin for the return to the original site or a selected alternate.

Phase 4: Recovery at original or alternate site

While operations are running at the backup sites, plans must be made for full recovery at the original site. If it has been a major disaster, or if it fits the organization's plans, the full recovery can be accomplished at an alternate, improved site. In essence, this phase is simply the development of the same recovery procedures in a reverse direction. The same recovery teams probably will be in action if they proved themselves originally.

It probably would be expedient to have the same planning team assemble a detailed, phased plan for the transfer of the operations back to a permanent site. Very little information should have to be developed. It should be a rehash of originally discussed procedures.

The greatest effort in planning phase 4 will be on the decisions for, and the assembly of, the new hardware as well as the site preparation. Again, the construction and preparation of a site and the purchase and assembly of all the special equipment involved will be the most time-consuming process.

Clearly, there will be frequent reports to senior management as the disaster recovery work proceeds. When it has all been accomplished, however, and the permanent facility is smoothly operating again, there should be another debriefing and discussion with all participants. The final results, costs, and findings then should be presented to management as a formal report. This should justify the money already expended and the estimated costs of future preparations.

I/S disaster recovery procedures

This book has described the planning required for the preparation of an I/S disaster recovery plan. The work should culminate in a final report described in the next section. Also, a working document, giving the "who, what, when, and where," that is a portion of the final report, should be:

- Inactively bound for ready access
- Limited to the responsibilities and actions that must be taken
- Distributed to all key personnel in the recovery plan
- Kept in available locations, rather than where a disaster might strike
- Used for training personnel in the procedures
- Updated whenever assignments change, and at regular intervals to keep the phone numbers correct

It is advisable that the I/S disaster recovery procedures be kept in a loose-leaf manual for regular updating. The manual should be bound in a bright, readily recognized color, such as bright red (which is frequently used for fire manuals) or bright gold.

The working manual should be succinctly written, so that information can be found rapidly. It essentially should be listings of procedures, people's names, equipment names, locations, phone numbers, and so forth. No one should have to search through their own files for such information at the time of a disaster.

The manual should be under controlled distribution, but a copy should be available to every concerned manager and recovery team leader. The team leaders should keep their copies of the manual at their homes, so that they are available at odd hours, and are not destroyed in the disaster event.

The suggested sections for the I/S disaster recovery procedures are:

1. I/S disaster recovery procedures
   ~ Recognition of a disaster
   ~ Initiation of the recovery procedures
   ~ The phases of the recovery procedures
2. Initial disaster response
   ~ Emergency management team
   ~ Emergency telephone tree
   ~ Initial disaster procedures
3. Computer room emergency procedures
   ~ Powering down the computer

~ Obtaining backup files
~ Evacuation procedures

4. I/S disaster recovery teams
    ~ Team leaders and responsibilities
    ~ Management liaison
    ~ Disaster recovery functions

5. Emergency assignments and locations
    ~ Assignments at the backup site
    ~ New office assignments
    ~ Assignment of terminals

6. Emergency vendor contacts
    ~ Vendors and key contact personnel
    ~ Phone numbers for nights and weekends
    ~ Vendor policies

7. Disaster recovery log
    ~ Record of actions taken, time, and authority

8. Organization charts and facilities plans
    ~ Organization charts of I/S departments
    ~ Organization charts of key user departments
    ~ Plans of data centers
    ~ Plans of office spaces and assignments

Production of the final report for management
I/S disaster recovery plan

The final report will be the full I/S disaster recovery plan. This will include:

- The decisions and assumptions that were made
- The reasoning for the key disaster scenario
- The selection of the preferred strategies
- The management approvals received
- The I/S disaster recovery procedures (probably as an appendix)

Recommendations for action

Figure 8-4, Outline of Final Report—Disaster Recovery Plan, lists typical topics that should be addressed in the plan report. Particular care should be paid to the overview and the recommendations, because they are likely to be all that is thoroughly read by senior management. Much of the rest will be detailed and technical.

Fig. 8-4. Outline of final report—disaster recovery plan.

Management overview
- Purposes and objectives

- Scope and applicability

- Assumptions and definitions

- Responsibilities and approvals

- Strategies considered

- Strategies selected

Required disaster recovery preparations
- People (assignments, responsibilities, training)

- Sites (selection, environmental preparation)

- Software systems (inventory, backup, responsibility)

- Application systems (inventory, backup, responsibility)

- Data and databases (inventory, backup, handling)

- Hardware (inventory, emergency, agreements, documentation)

- Communications (current, backup, planned requirements)

- Transportation (emergency requirements)

- Supplies (lists of crucial items—vendors, stocks)

- Documentation (inventory, off-site backup)

- Other equipments (data, input, COM, copiers, etc.)

- Vendor contracts or letters of understanding

- Test plans

EDP disaster recovery procedures: the action plan
- Emergency response and initial recovery procedures

- Disaster recovery at backup site

- Full disaster recovery at sufficient sites

- Recovery at original or alternate site

Recommendations
- Summary of cost of plan

- Summary of time schedule of plan

- Recommendation for staged development of the plan

- Immediate actions to be taken

- Expenditures to be made in priority order

The management overview section will discuss and describe the key disaster scenario, and any other problem scenarios that might not be subsets of it. The procedures then will be precise actions in response to selected problem scenarios. Some scenarios, such as bomb threats, will require quite different actions than major power outages, but response will be required for each by everyone involved. Some typical scenarios, very briefly, might include:

- Fire or structural damage in the building, but not directly in the data center, might deny access to all I/S areas for several days. After the clean-up and repair, return to the data center would be expected.

- Destruction of appreciable parts of the data center, requiring long-term backup operations while a replacement is prepared. There would be need to bring up all operations, including the lower priority programs, at the backup site.

- A hurricane, tornado, or earthquake that cripples local transportation and causes total power and communications failure in the area, but does little physical damage to the data center. This might call for distant backup operations, and preparations for operating at a reduced level as the center is slowly brought up again.

If any part of the organization is heavily dependent upon the data center for its ongoing operation, it should be emphasized in this section. The overview also should document what applications have been considered as mandatory, necessary, and desirable, so that senior management can have a final say about that selection.

The document should clearly give the basis for the selection of strategies and, equally clearly, develop the cost implications.

The plan should be presented as representing a dynamic, ongoing activity that will need routine funding. It should be subject to testing, reviews, and updates. It should be modified as certain recommended actions are accomplished, or as new problems are anticipated.

Senior and mid-level management have a need to understand the manner in which the priorities are determined. The data sources, the extent of user agreement on the selected priorities, the risk analysis methodology used, and other related matters should be described in the detail necessary to a full understanding of the plan. This includes the rationale used to establish the priorities, and an understanding of the speed of recovery to be expected for various application areas.

If the relative importance of the supported functions varies with time of day, day of week, and month, it should be explained in the description of the priorities.

The general nature and range of service disruptions, against which the plan is directed, presents a difficult concept to grasp, but it must be explained.

Some service disruptions will not be addressed by the plan because of their extremely low profitability, even though they occasionally occur (e.g., a tornado in Connecticut).

Some service disruptions are so extensive in scope as to negate the need for early recovery of I/S operations (e.g., large hurricane, atomic war).

Some service disruptions are too minor in scope to warrant special note in the plan. These generally can be accommodated by slight changes in normal operations. They are essentially subsets of the plan.

These concepts are best discussed in the assumptions section of Fig. 8-4. It should be clearly explained that the key disaster scenario is the most probable, serious disaster that will call for full implementation of the plan. All other scenarios are then variations of it.

Recommendations for action

The recommendations for action are of great importance to I/S management and, therefore, must be emphasized. They can vary greatly, and can include:

- Recommendation that the overall plan be accepted
- The purchase or rental of expensive items of hardware
- The preparation of sites for standby purposes
- The appointment of a disaster recovery coordinator
- The funding of a lengthy, expensive study
- The laying in of special power lines
- The installation of many standby telephone lines at $1.50 each per month
- The purchase of several bullhorns
- The training of large numbers of staff in the procedures

Thus, the recommendations for action should be grouped carefully for timing and importance. If they are accepted, the funding might be all at once, or it can be phased. I/S management must be sure of their priorities for the recommendations.

Preparing and safekeeping documents

One of the most time-consuming and difficult tasks in disaster-recovery preparation is the preparing, safekeeping, and routine updating of the voluminous documentation in the I/S area. Unfortunately, this task usually is given low priority and little concern. It can be handled well only if there is a specific person or group directly responsible to senior I/S management for getting the task accomplished. This staff should be able to establish procedures that remain firm, and are followed. There are currently three common areas of documentation preparation and safekeeping:

Hardcopies

This is the most common way that vendor manuals, applications documentation, printouts, and variations of programs are stored. This can be quite satisfactory, as long as reasonably updated copies are maintained at the backup site and in remote storage. In practice, the updating is irregular, and the completeness of the material usually is poor.

Microfilm

The hand microfilming of hardcopy documents, and the computer output microfilming (COM) of programs and printouts is an acceptable way of backing up materials for ready access. If the procedures are manual, however, they must be managed and routine, or they can get out of date rapidly. Be sure that the microfilming and reading capabilities are included in the disaster recovery plans.

Magnetic media

A number of library, document, and editing programs are available that make it relatively simple to store programs, outputs, standards, procedures, memoranda, reports, manuals, and other documentation on magnetic media. This has two great advantages for disaster safekeeping. First, the material can be readily brought up on a screen and edited, modified, or updated. It is more likely to be kept current than hard copy. Second, the record of the material will be handled like any other computer output, and will be routinely backed up at the disaster recovery site or other secure storage.

Be sure that the overall disaster recovery plan itself, and the I/S disaster recovery procedures are protected with as much security as the programs they intend to secure. The material should be given high priority for regular, controlled backup.

A disaster recovery plan essentially is a volatile document. It will need changes whenever there are any hardware or personnel changes in the organization. The plan will constantly need checking, and updating. The copies also must be controlled so that all are at the same level. For this reason, the I/S disaster recovery procedures should be maintained on a magnetic media document system if at all possible. It offers the best route to handle frequent detailed changes.

There should be a controlled method for preparing, posting, and recording changes to this document. Entries in the record of changes section should include change number, data, pages changed, deletions, insertions, person posting change, when posted, plan distribution, and other information, as required.

Security awareness training of the staff

The I/S disaster recovery plan and the I/S disaster recovery procedures are useful documents. All key individuals, and the bulk of the concerned staff, have had them thoroughly described and explained, and have participated in some part of their testing. Sessions on the plan can be arranged readily by management or training personnel. Methods of testing are discussed in the next chapter.

In this training and practice, the disaster recovery plan must never be considered a standalone document, however. This plan is only one piece of the overall organization's security program. It has been pointed out that fire alarm procedures, and other organized emergency procedures, will normally take priority over any I/S disaster plan. The first priority will always remain the protection of personnel and the safeguarding of the organization's assets. Therefore, training in the I/S disaster recovery procedures should always be accompanied by training in the general emergency procedures to keep the actions in context.

In another scene, the I/S disaster recovery plan actually is a subset of the group's I/S security procedures. The best disaster recovery comes when the security facilities and methods have stopped the disaster at an incipient stage. The less to recover from, the better.

Therefore, even though the I/S disaster recovery plan is a self-contained document, it should mesh with the security plan, and be referred to in context by that plan.

These relationships should be made clear to the staff. They should be trained to understand that the security procedures and equipments have a close relationship to the disaster recovery procedures, and that the I/S organization is not independent from the overall organization.

Training of the staff in disaster recovery should begin as soon as the procedures have been tentatively approved, and should include an awareness of security of the original site, the transfer between sites, and the backup site. When disasters occur, it is not uncommon that their cause be from someone hiding a discrepancy or defalcation with the organization, or from someone with a grudge against the organization. It is, therefore, imperative that disaster recovery operations be kept under tighter security control than normal operations, and that personnel be constantly reminded of their security responsibilities.

In addition, training of staff in security awareness and procedures, and in disaster recovery procedures, should never be given once and then forgotten. There should be periodic refresher classes, and periodic realistic tests of the capabilities of the staff.

Planning for the restoration of the permanent facility

Restoration of the permanent facility is a substantive part of the I/S disaster recovery plan, but it can seldom be planned and rehearsed in detail in advance. The actions to be taken will depend on the following:

- The intention to remain at the same permanent site or to take the opportunity to move
- The degree of damage to the permanent site, and the time it will take to make it usable
- The system changes that occur during the time at the backup site
- The experiences in system transfer during the disaster event

Restoration of the permanent facility should be discussed and considered in generality. The details should be left to the time of need, however, unless decisions have been made in advance about moving to a new permanent site. Such action is not avoiding the issue, because the detailed procedures for the recovery teams that have been carefully thought through will normally be usable in reverse for the final recovery action.

As soon as the move to the temporary backup site has been successfully completed following the disaster, management should set up a site restoration team to plan for and direct the return move to the permanent site. Prominent on this team should be a senior person from the computer operations department, because this department will be fully responsible for operating the site after the restoration. It also will be helpful to include persons from the communications, systems, data control, and data input departments. Frequently, the original site will have had troublesome conditions that were low in priority to be corrected. If there has to be extensive rebuilding and fresh preparation of the site, however, it is a good time to consider all types of input as to how the physical site should be structured.

The organization's chief security officer and the I/S security manager should clearly be represented on the site restoration team. Their input must be carefully considered, especially after the problems that led to the original disaster have been thoroughly analyzed and measures to prevent their reoccurrence have been agreed upon.

The return to the original site finally should be accomplished with all the teams, and team personnel, that directed the move to the temporary site. Their experience will be invaluable. The same management checklists should be used that were used previously and the same cooperation obtained from all the user groups. If the operations at the backup site are running reasonably well, there should be no rush to move back to the permanent site until:

- All needed facilities are in place
- There is user agreement that the move will not be excessively disruptive
- All financial and operational controls are firmly established and checked
- The detailed plan has been reviewed by all affected management

Checklist 8-1, Site Restoration Considerations, is a checklist of some of the crucial points that should be handled in the planning for the restoration of the permanent facility. In essence, the return to the reconditioned or new permanent site is simply a reversal of the move following the disaster, except that more time should be available for the move, and there should be more assurance determining that all managers involved are satisfied with the new situation.

Checklist 8-1. Site restoration considerations.

1. Have the proper site facilities been installed and checked by buildings management, including:
   - Power and lighting?
   - Air conditioning?
   - Humidity control?
   - Telephone service?
   - Alarm systems?
   - Door locks and entrance controls?

2. Has there been a discussion with local police and fire officials about any necessary features to help prevent a recurrence of a similar disaster?

3. Is the insurance department satisfied about the following:
   - That moving into the old site will not adversely affect indemnity negotiations?
   - That an adequate self-inspection had been made of the recovered site?
   - That adequate insurance is in place for the recovered site?
   - That the loss prevention program has been reviewed adequately?

4. Has the insurance company been asked if it wishes to review the security preparations at the recovered site?

5. Have photographs been taken of all rooms and features of the site for insurance discussion and future disaster recovery plans?

6. Have the hardware vendors installed and fully tested all aspects of the new hardware?

7. Have the communications services and communications equipment vendors:
   - Tested their equipment and lines?
   - Been fully informed of the start-up plans?

8. Has the operating system software been fully installed, tested, documented and checked against the current version operating at the backup site?

9. Has a duplicate copy of the new operating system and its documentation been stored in a safe location?

10. Has each analyst or programmer in charge of an application system:
    - Prepared a version of the application system for operation at the site?
    - Tested its operation against the current operating version?

- Worked with Internal Audit to assure that controls are in place?
- Duplicated the new version for storage in a safe location?

11. Has the job control language been fully prepared and also duplicated?

12. Has Internal Audit been involved to assure that the move will be under all necessary financial and operational controls?

13. Are all users/owners of the applications systems fully involved in the move preparations and the maintenance of controls?

14. Has a detailed "critical path" plan been drawn up to help manage the move?

15. Has this "critical path" plan been distributed to all involved with the move with management statements about its timing and supervision?

16. Is there a sufficient supply of forms and supplies available at both sites with backup supplies stored at a third site?

17. Has a library been set up for smooth operation:
    - With the necessary files and records?
    - With the necessary peripheral equipment?
    - With agreement on the operation between the librarian and the operations supervisor?

18. Have all critical files, library programs, library documentation, and library records been backed up at both sites?

19. Are copies of all operator run books and documentation checked against the present material and available at the new site?

20. Have sufficient preparations been made for:
    - Security control at the site?
    - Housekeeping at the site?
    - Specialized support service, such as mail, couriers, office supplies, etc.?
    - Engineering or building maintenance?

21. Is the Real Estate Department satisfied that the occupation of the site is in order?

22. Is the Legal Department satisfied that there are no legal problems remaining?

23. Has the Accounting Department made all necessary plans to adjust the lines of account?

24. Has the Public Relations Department been notified of the move and its effect on personnel involved?

25. Have all management approvals been obtained?

9

Maintaining the disaster recovery plan

MUCH OF THIS BOOK IS DEVOTED TO THE DEVELOPMENT OF AN I/S disaster recovery plan. The development is not completed, however, until the plan is installed and tested, and ready to be used in the event of an emergency. Key points of completing the development of a plan and implementing it are discussed in this chapter.

After the plan has been installed, and appears to be reasonably sufficient, there are three principle activities that must be planned and accomplished. These are monitoring of the plan to see that it is kept up to date, in place and understood; maintaining the systems to keep the programs synchronous with hardware, software, and applications changes over time; and testing of the plan to determine whether it is effective, efficient, and under control. These activities are described in this chapter, and appropriate checklists are provided.

Implementing the disaster recovery plan

The work of the plan development group will not be completed until the plan is implemented and documented. There is a widespread and pervasive problem with I/S disaster recovery plans. Many of them are created and documented in outline, because they have never been truly accepted by all levels of I/S and the users, and sufficient details have never been put into them. A plan cannot be said to be implemented until it has been trained, and there has been some testing of its key elements. There is certainly some use for arbitrarily stored systems and documentation, and outlines of what probably should be done in an emergency, but its cost-effectiveness is low. A disaster recovery plan is similar to any other application system. The rerun on the effort is realized after it is installed, tested, and made operational.

Recovery team assignments

After the first I/S draft of the disaster recovery plan has been approved, the next step is to appoint the I/S disaster recovery plan team leaders for each of the teams that will be assembled. Many of these people essentially will have been appointed already, because they will have participated in the development of the plan. The group should be assembled, and a presentation made to all the staff on the objectives and many details of the plan. The plan will include a list of tasks to be accomplished. Most of these tasks will be documented in the "Preplanning Required" portions of the forms that are described in Figs. 3-5 through 3-23. The attempts by the planning team to describe these required tasks should not limit the specialist who will lead the teams, however. They will know what other tasks also must be accomplished to create an operable plan.

The recovery teams should be formed and briefed by their leaders. Each leader should review his or her own responsibilities and procedures from the point of view of his or her own technical understanding of the problems involved. If team leaders believe that there should be modifications in their responsibilities and procedures, this is the best time for them to discuss their ideas with the disaster planning group and I/S management. All details of the plan must make practical sense for it to be successful.

Top management support is crucial at this time, because people from many different groups will be asked to break away from their normal activities and spend time on the staff installation of a disaster recovery plan. If management expresses a strong interest in the activity, supervisors will support it, and the participating staff will feel free to become involved.

Completing the plan details

After general agreement and understanding about the plan has been reached throughout the organization, a number of tasks must be handled to implement it. These will include the following:

- Acquisition of any hardware, software, communications equipment and lines, and other items that are needed in advance
- Negotiation with the vendors, and the signing of contracts for services and facilities
- Agreement on the final, detailed procedures, which must be reflected in all copies of the plan
- Creation, approval, and addition of any further standards and guidelines that might have been found helpful, and have been approved by management
- Training of personnel in the detailed requirements of their functions
- Preparation of backup sites and off-site storage areas and arrangements with local management at the sites
- Initial tests of the plan

Discussions should proceed routinely with management throughout the implementation of the plan. There will come a point, which should have been planned in advance, when the plan is in sufficiently good order to receive final approval. It is then time to undergo more complete testing. All components should be in place before the plan is submitted for review as a completed package. This will include all the necessary products that have been discussed in this book, in addition to plans for the next actions to be taken, which are:

- Development of monitoring plans
- Development of maintenance plans
- Development of test plans

Monitoring and maintaining the disaster recovery plan

After the I/S disaster recovery plan has been installed, and appears to be reasonably sufficient, there are three principal activities that must be planned and accomplished:

- Monitoring of the plan to see that it is kept up to date, in place, and understood
- Maintenance of the systems to keep the programs synchronous with hardware, software, and applications changes over time

- Testing of the plan to determine whether it is effective, efficient, and under control

Monitoring of the disaster recovery plan

The responsibility of monitoring the I/S disaster recovery plan usually is assigned to an individual, such as the I/S disaster recovery coordinator. The plan must be considered as an ongoing project, even if only part-time effort can be applied to it. Someone must be given the responsibility of coordinating the plan and reporting on it at least quarterly to I/S management. If it is not done, there will be a steady obsolescence of the plan, and in time the details will become meaningless.

For future smooth operation of the plan, there must be a continuing, regular concern that:

- The backup tapes are being properly cycled to secure storage
- The backup site is maintained in operable condition
- The systems programmers are modifying the backup systems when they modify the operational systems
- New applications are considered as to their importance
- Names of participants are updated as they change responsibilities and personnel are reminded of them
- Telephone tree phone numbers are kept up to date in the plan

The time of a disaster is not the time to try to figure out what personnel changes have taken place in the last three years, and what the new telephone numbers are. Despite this, experience has shown that many I/S disaster recovery plans are two or three years old, and have never been updated. A monitoring system should be developed, as part of the responsibility of one individual, to see that such details are routinely updated in the plan, and in all copies of it. In fact, there should be a control list of the copies, and they should be reviewed as to ownership, location, and version more than once a year.

The maintenance of the technical aspects of the plan will be the job of the systems programming and telecommunications staffs. It is up to the I/S disaster recovery coordinator, however, to give assurance to management that such maintenance is being carried out and that the updated versions of the programs are in place, in the event of a disaster. It is also that person's responsibility to assure that the systems for routine handling of backup libraries continues to work smoothly, year after year. The work normally will be done by the operations group, but the review of the work should be done by the coordinator.

The internal audit staff will be checking on the accuracy of these routine procedures occasionally, but the I/S disaster recovery coordinator should be familiar enough with the procedures to be constantly aware of whether they continue to work well, or are slowly slipping. Backup operations tend to become very routine in the view of the operators. Because of this, they might get less and less attention paid to them.

The weakest area in backup in most organizations, after they have developed an I/S disaster recovery plan, tends to remain with the documentation of the systems and procedures. This is because such documentation is never considered as high priority by the analysts and programmers, and much of it tends to be on hard copy that is time-consuming and difficult to update. The best solution is to get as much of the crucial documentation as possible on automatic documentation and library systems. If people are trained into the habit of making all documentation updates on a PC as they have been approved:

- The material will be kept up to date
- The accuracy of the material will be reviewed regularly
- The documentation will be routinely backed up up with the rest of the data files, and will be resident at the backup site when it is needed

The standardization of documentation and procedures for all I/S areas, operations, systems, programming, management, and forms, is imperative for long-term, smooth operation of the plan, and automated systems are the only ones that offer real chance of success.

It is senior management's responsibility to monitor the I/S disaster recovery plan, and to be assured that an effective plan is in place, and can be activated readily if required. Management will get occasional assurance on this point from internal audit studies. The full-time or part-time job of the I/S disaster recovery coordinator is to give management ongoing assurance that all necessary parts of the plan remain in place, and that there is continuous refreshing of the information. Checklist 9-1, I/S Disaster Recovery Plan Monitoring Considerations, is a checklist for the occasional review of the tasks that should have been accomplished, and the features that should be in place. It could be used by the coordinator before the periodic reports to management, to be sure of the status of the plan.

Checklist 9-1. I/S disaster recover plan monitoring considerations.

1. Are there updated contingency plans in place that will cover three levels of response to trouble:
   - Delay and correct situation?
   - Readjust scheduling and use some off-premise equipment?
   - Shift to backup computer site?

2. Is the working tape library located in a separately locked room within the secured control area?

3. Are crucial tapes identified and backed up to protect specific systems considered vital to the business?

4. Are these backup tapes routinely updated?

5. Is the use of data files routinely logged?

6. Are the run manuals kept in fireproof storage each shift they are not used?

7. Is a control copy of each run manual stored outside the data processing area?

8. Have the run manuals been updated to the most recent versions?

9. Is a supply of important forms kept in a separate building or with the vendor?

10. Are all the forms the most recent revisions?

11. Is documentation stored on a magnetic tape for printout as needed?

12. Is the documentation updated routinely?

13. Is there a listing of all administrative and technical manuals maintained to assure their identification if lost?

14. Are input data records sent to the user for storage in another area?

15. Are all users aware of the audit and disaster recovery importance of these records?

16. Are formal reciprocal agreements for backup current with other organizations?

17. Are the signers of these agreements still in charge of their operations?

18. Do the agreements include specifications as to:
    - Machine type and mode?
    - Tape units: number, tape density and tracks?
    - Disk units: type and number?
    - Core size?
    - Release of operating system used?

- Compilers?
- Utilities?
- Input procedures?
- Available hours for backup processing?

19. Does the backup facility management keep you aware of any changes made to either hardware or software?
20. If the memory units or other resources of the backup facility are fewer (less) than the prime facility, have the job control language changes been taken into account?
21. Does the backup facility itself offer satisfactory security?
22. Is the backup facility at a reasonable distance for moving operations?
23. Are the available hours for use of the backup system known, and still agreed upon?
24. Have the crucial jobs to be operated at the backup site, together with their datasets on tape or disk, been identified and kept up to date?
25. Has the use of the backup facility been tested within the past six months?
26. Has the disaster recovery plan been completely developed?
27. Have all recovery team assignments been accepted?
28. Is each step of the plan assigned to an employee?
29. Are all necessary employees still in position to participate?
30. Has the plan been received by the organization's safety department or engineering group?
31. Does the plan fit well with other organizational emergency plans?
32. Has it been approved by all current managers involved?
33. Has the cost of the contingency plan been developed and approved?
34. Has a disaster been tested within the last six months, where the backup facilities were used and tapes were brought from storage?
35. Is the plan periodically revised, as a consequence of information derived from tests?
36. Are the details of the plan (names, addresses, phone numbers, etc.) routinely updated by an assigned individual?
37. Has there been concurrence on the plan by the current managers of all affected departments?
38. Is senior management aware of the completed plan and the dependence on them for supportive action?

Checklist 9-1. Continued.

39. Has the legal department reviewed the legal requirements that show the need for the plan?
40. Has a risk analysis been prepared and received by management?
41. Does the completed plan make good, common sense?
42. Are updated copies of the plan currently in the hands of all key people?

One aspect of the continuing monitoring of the plan is the keeping of records as to which personnel have been trained in the use of the plan, and which personnel have been given new assignments that would indicate that they should receive training in disaster recovery. I/S disaster recovery coordinator probably is in the best position to provide the necessary training. That person will know the subject, and will know the experts in particular areas of interest. The coordinator might not be in a good position to arrange for training sessions, obtain management permission, schedule classes, and so on, however. If there is a training group established in the organization, it usually will be preferable to arrange for them to handle all the scheduling and mechanical details of the training. It then will be possible to fit the disaster recovery training in with all the other types of training that the staff requires, and consistent records will be kept of those training sessions that have been attended.

The training group ordinarily will work with the I/S disaster recovery coordinator in developing the training curriculum, gathering the necessary materials, and arranging for tests of the training. It will be hepful to any employee to have consistent, coordinated training records. Disaster recovery tests would appear to be different from other types of training. As long as they are not "surprise" tests, however, they should start with discussions and presentations, and be handled as training exercises.

Routine maintenance of the systems

Routine maintenance of the crucial systems that are involved in an I/S disaster recovery plan must be assigned to the appropriate technical personnel as tasks that are to be performed together with their other activities. The groups that are involved can include:

- Systems programming
- User departments

- Technical support
- Systems analysis and programming
- Computer operations
- Telecommunications
- Quality assurance
- Documentation

Such groups can readily fit into their schedules the updating of the systems and program tapes and the documentation that are required for recovery. The tasks must be specifically requested and agreed upon, however. Because these groups usually are relatively independent, it is then the responsibility of the I/S disaster recovery coordinator, or other assigned person, to see that the tasks are being carried out regularly.

There should be no independent class of programs and tapes for disaster recovery. They should be directly related to, and in phase with, the operational systems that are in use. There might be differences involved because the backup computer has a different configuration than the main computer, and fewer terminals will be involved during a disaster event. Changes in one system should point directly to changes in the other system, however. They should be directly mappable from one to another. Standard procedures should be in place where, after any new system is generated, for any size of modification, a related disaster recovery backup system is generated, and filed to replace the previous system.

Such modified system backup generation should take place at least within a one-day cycle of the changes in the operational system. For most on-line systems, the backup change should be generated as soon as the operational change is tested, accepted, and put on line. If this is not done promptly, it could be most difficult to recover the interim transactions that might have been handled by two different systems, if necessary.

Note that the modified backup system should be generated and put in place only after the new development has been completed, tests have been performed, the system has been accepted by both the user and quality assurance, and it is to replace the current operational system. Disaster recovery procedures can be concerned only with the set of systems that are running under the control of the operations department, and have had an acceptance sign-off by responsible management. There are too many versions, with minor differences, of any system under development. Normally, if a system under development is deemed worthwhile to be backed up in the case of a disaster, the responsibility for handling, maintaining, and controlling that backup system will rest entirely with the system development group who are involved.

Checklist 9-2, Control of Program Modifications, is a checklist for the disaster recovery coordinator (DRC) to be assured that the lines of communication with the involved technical staff groups include the necessary controls and products that are needed to keep the disaster recovery system updated. The DRC is usually a single person or a small staff. There is a problem identical to that faced by quality assurance. There is absolutely no way that the DRC can become involved in the technical details of any of the systems development or maintenance that is going on. The DRC must rely entirely on being a "mailing list" recipient of the various program change notices, and the modified programs and documentation. In fact, even those programs normally will be taken to the disaster backup site and installed and tested by operations personnel. The DRC simply receives information on what has happened, although there is

Checklist 9-2. Control of program modifications.

1. Does the I/S disaster recovery coordinator (DRC) have access to the program change and modification records?
2. Are all program changes and modifications reviewed by quality assurance?
3. Does the DRC have access to the quality assurance reports?
4. Is there a systematic documentation of all emergency changes?
5. Are the records of emergency changes copied to quality assurance and the DRC?
6. After an emergency change, is there a document that states the problem encountered and the fix made?
7. Is there a regular procedure for seeing that all program changes become entered in the backup files, such as copying the updated program files after the change has been made?
8. If a modification is partially implemented and the full modification is spread over a period of time, are the interim backup systems up?
9. Have provisions been made to save original input documents in the user areas, so that they can be reentered into the system if required?
10. Is each production version of a program documented and copied, with both the documentation and the copy being taken to backup storage?
11. If changes have an effect on operating instructions, are those instructions updated?

usually some involvement with modification tests at the backup site. Thus, the system and controls must be in place and work for there to be assurance that the most recent program versions are ready for backup purposes.

Routine testing of the disaster recovery plan

Installation and maintenance of a disaster recovery, or contingency, plan is not sufficient to be assured that an operable plan is in place, and ready to be used. It is important to have continual testing and evaluation of the plan. A plan that has not been tested within the past six months cannot be assumed to be useful. A plan that is implemented, documented, tested once, then set aside might prove to be unusable when a disaster strikes. Computer operations are in a continual state of flux.

New systems and equipment are added, new people are employed, and operating systems are modified. Documentation frequently does not keep pace with the changes. It is absolutely necessary to keep the plan up to date with the changing conditions of the computer operations. Any serious attempt at having a disaster recovery plan in place will require at least one full-time employee in charge of maintaining the plan and directing routine tests and monitoring reviews.

Figure 9-1, Monitoring and Testing Activities, summarizes the planning responsibility for the ongoing review of the disaster recovery plan. The monitoring and maintenance of the disaster recovery plan has been discussed in chapter 6. Monitoring and maintenance are completely interwoven. Most of the maintenance will be routine plan changes that are called for by the plan itself, such as changed systems, programs, and equipment. Some of the maintenance will be required because of plan problems that have been revealed by the monitoring, however. The monitoring of disaster recovery preparations is the particular responsibility of the DRC, but all levels of management, including the audit staff, will have a responsibility to observe and report conditions that might give problems to the plan, and to recommend modifications or extensions of it. These should be handled as maintenance.

The simulated disaster recovery tests are primarily the responsibility of the DRC and senior management. If the tests are planned, rather than surprise, however, the I/S operational staff should be involved completely in planning and conducting the test. Note that, in most organizations, the audit staff will not have the time to partic-

Fig. 9-1. Monitoring and testing activities.

Reviews and Tests of the Disaster Recovery Plan	Planning Responsibility			
	Disaster Recovery Coordinator	Operational Staff	Audit Staff	Senior Management
Monitoring and maintenance of the disaster recovery plan	X	X	X	X
Simulated disaster recovery test:				
Planned tests	X	X		X
Surprise tests	X			X
Audit review of the disaster recovery plan			X	X
Audit test of the disaster recovery plan			X	X

ipate in routine testing of the plan. The tests must be a frequent, planned part of the operational activities. It is easy, however, to reach a point where such tests become familiar, with little attempt by the participants at being crucial. It is then useful for the auditors to come in from outside the group and direct a comprehensive, discriminating test that looks at the activities from a new angle, and reviews all aspects of the plan.

The audit review and audit test of the disaster recovery plan is the responsibility of either the internal audit staff or of external auditors. The DRC has no responsibility for planning it, and is simply another participant when the test is called.

Test plans

Test plans should include the goals and the scope of the test, including the recovery teams involved and the particular applications systems or equipment on which the test will be centered. Most test plans will be for modular testing, that is, they will center on a particular area of operations to minimize cost and disruption of the normal operations. The devising of adequate test plans will thus require considerable analysis and skill, to meet the testing goals realistically and economically.

It will be important in planning tests to see that the highest priority systems and the most vital operations are involved. This does not mean that they should be the first areas tested, however. The tests must cover as many possible participants and procedures as possible. The initial tests undoubtedly will be less than completely successful. They are training exercises, and they should be carried out on less sensitive applications. After all involved have been developed some facility in the testing, it will be time to try the most important applications.

Part of the test plan must include a critique of the test experience. The recovery teams involved should be required to write down their observations and recommendations. It will be up to the DRC to monitor the whole process, and to pull together the conclusions and perceptions of the results. Recommendations then can be made on possible strengthening of the plan.

It will take a number of tests, over time, to be assured that the disaster recovery plan is in place and is adequate to meet any likely emergency. Therefore, the plans should quickly cover the testing of the start-up and use of the backup site, which will be key to any disaster recovery operation.

The initial disaster recovery tests can be set up by I/S management mainly to shake down the procedures and to determine if, in fact, the recovery plan will work as it has been visualized. Participants must be careful to follow the detailed recovery procedures as closely as possible to determine if everything is covered in the plan, or if there are needed modifications. This type of testing is best done in a modular way, or a piece at a time, handling merely the start-up of the backup computer, and the running of one or two applications, for example. Other tests could be to see if the correct backup material is in storage, to see if the phone trees work, and whether people will report in time, and so on.

Initial tests are best scheduled for small sections of the plan at a time, to avoid too much disruption of normal operations. Seldom will a test run completely smoothly on the first try.

Crucial tests are those for backup plans that use facilities that are external to the organization. In these cases, there either will be considerable expense involved, or there will be some disruption at the facility of the cooperating organization. Careful planning will be needed.

Disaster recovery vendors, such as Sungard and Comdisco, provide test time to subscribers. This is a very valuable service because it often can be difficult to test without a major disruption of normal processing if done at an operating center. Even where there are multiple data centers providing backup for each other, the feasibility of using outside services, rather than disrupting service and not meeting service level agreements, should be ascertained.

After the plan is in place, surprise tests and drills should be conducted at appropriate intervals. Results should be analyzed, and the plan updated to correct the weaknesses involved. The tests should involve actual computer processing of real data, and not just test data exercises. The runs might be parallel runs to the main center, or they might be the only runs made of the important programs in that period. If it is an on-line network, it will be shifted for operation to the backup site.

Tests should involve varying scenarios, such as type and time of disaster, degree of loss, and unavailability of key personnel. Test reports should be submitted to the top I/S management. Some tests of the emergency plan should be made in cooperation with the security, buildings, administration, and other functions of the parent organization. It even might be helpful to have local fire and police departments participate in a test exercise. These people probably would be pleased to be involved in a test situation when it represents the type of disaster in which they might be key elements if the disaster situation being tested became a reality. Their input to the process could be invaluable.

Test plan goals

Tests should not be attempted without the goals and scope of the tests stated objectively. It is insufficient to merely "test the plan." Because most testing will be partial tests, in which only certain elements of the plan are tested at the time, it is even more important to specify why the test is being carried out. Planning is the process of determining in advance the optimum direction that the recovery efforts should take by establishing goals, defining the steps to take to reach the goals, and later analyzing the actions taken. The questions that are being asked by management are:

- Can the test of the disaster recovery plan be measured in terms that are objective, and clearly demonstrable?
- Can the disaster recovery plan be operated using the resources that have been assigned for emergency action?
- Can the strategies that are planned be shown to be clear to all participants, and effective in operation?
- Will the results of the test, if satisfactory, prove that an operable disaster recovery plan exists for the area tested?

The objective of the disaster recovery plan was pointed out in as making "sufficient agreed-upon preparations, and to design and implement a sufficient set of agreed-upon procedures, for responding to a disaster of any size in the I/S area of responsibility." The goals of test plans are to ensure that this objective is being met in specific areas for specific types of disaster. Clearly, it will be important to include goals that cover the most likely disaster occurrences and the most crucial applications. Goals are measurable results of specific planned actions.

The overall goals of I/S disaster recovery test plans are sometimes stated as:

- To ensure that the crucial applications can be recovered whenever necessary
- To ensure that all personnel understand their roles in an emergency situation
- To ensure that the disaster recovery plan is complete and covers all required actions

Such statements are closer to objectives than to goals, however. It is important to define goals more narrowly, and to make them fit particular actions that must be accomplished. Some typical test plan goals might be:

- Determine if stored data can be read at the backup site, and if the software library can be loaded and can communicate with specific terminals.

- Determine if a particular application can be brought up on short notice at the backup site, handling a specified reduced number of terminals, and if the audit trail can be maintained across the disruption.

- Determine if the backup site has the current version of the operating system in place, together with the supporting and utility systems required, and a new configuration of the telecommunications network can be brought up between the backup site, the central office, and all field installations.

- Determine if cut-over operation of a priority application, with both on-line and batch operations from an arbitrary cutoff at the central site, with only selected "father" tapes available to be carried to the backup site is possible.

- Recover a set of applications to start-of-week status, and process for one full operational cycle. Balance all controls at the start and the end of the batch processing cycle for one day.

- Determine if an on-line system can be started up with a reduced number of terminals and reduced data volume, and operate for a day with fully balanced and controlled data.

- Measure the response time of all members of selected disaster recovery teams from the time that a "telephone tree" message is started to the time that they are at their designated recovery mode positions.

- Measure the delivery time to the backup site of specific supplies from vendors and specific records and tapes from a third off-site storage area.

- Test the backup data at the backup installation to see that it is secured, available, and complete, and can be read by the backup computer system.

- Test the backup data at the backup installation to see that it is secured, available, and complete, and can be read by the backup computer system.

- Test the capability and capacity of the backup computer to support a recovery operation including a specified number of important systems.

- Determine if all the computer operation supplies, materials, manuals, and documentation are available, easily identified, and secured at the backup site.

- Observe the actions of one disaster recovery team, such as the data input team in a simulated disaster, and ascertain the time taken to recover their operation at another site, and the economic impact of the disruption.

All test plan goals should be stated in a way that they can be measured. The plan might call for:

- A certain number of people to be at specific locations
- A certain level of operation of specific applications
- A certain cycle of data to be available at the backup site
- A certain time to bring up a specified number of terminals in a new location

None of these goals are merely a "race" by a few individuals, but they require a cooperative effort of several people and ongoing recovery backup procedures. They should be tested as realistically as possible, with little forewarning, and relying completely on the planned procedures.

Test plan procedures

Most regular disaster recovery tests will be handled by the DRC. They should be modular tests, not affecting the main operation of the central site unless that is specifically called for, and planned in advance. The tests should be in a sequence that builds up to include every recovery team that has been assigned responsibilities.

There should be some full-scale attempts to run at the backup site(s), but not until several partial operations have been tested, and operated satisfactorily.

Before a test is attempted, every affected disaster recovery team should have taken the outline of their responsibilities and functions, as described in chapter 3, and should have:

- Clarified their responsibilities to their own satisfaction
- Assigned all required team members, with records of their telephone numbers
- Made contact with the listed management liaison personnel, and reached an understanding of actions with them
- Reviewed their functions
- Made preparations for carrying out their functions
- Developed a step-by-step procedure, possibly a playscript procedure, to carry out their emergency functions

The stage would then be set for carrying out a test. Figure 9-2,

Fig. 9-2. Disaster recovery test plan procedures.

1. Assign responsibility for the test plan.
2. Establish test goals:
   - Fit the test into the overall testing plan
   - Consult with management on the value of the test
   - Make several partial tests before any major tests
   - Develop specific goals for each test
   - State explicitly the way that the test will be measured
3. Prepare the test scenario.
4. Review the scenario with the team leaders involved, and agree on specific steps that will be taken in the test.
5. Establish a date and time for the test, or agree on calling a surprise test.
6. Schedule personnel to be on call to:
   - Check the telephone tree lists
   - Check for operations that might be affected by the test
7. Notify other affected groups of the test, including:
   - User management
   - Backup recovery site management
   - Backup data storage site management
   - Organizational security personnel
   - Building operations and maintenance personnel
   - Local police and fire departments, if applicable
8. Run the test, observe actions, and measure the results.
9. Have a debriefing session with all project leaders and managers involved, discussing:
   - Observed activities during the test
   - Whether the test met the establishment goals
   - Whether required computer reports were produced and distributed
   - Specific changes that should be made in the disaster recovery plan
10. The disaster recovery coordinator should then:
    - Incorporate into the plan any agreed changes that should be made
    - Distribute information about the test, and the changes in the plan
    - Plan for any extra training that was indicated by the test
    - Plan for the next disaster recovery test, based on the findings of this test

Disaster Recovery Test Plan Procedures, outlines the principal steps that should be followed in sequence. The assignment of responsibility and the establishment of test goals have already been discussed.

The preparation and the review of the test scenario are the most crucial and time-consuming steps. This can be handled either:

- Organized in columnar form, including steps, times, activities, responsibilities, procedures, and resources
- Written in playscript form with times and individuals as the first entries, followed by the actions they are to take

In either form, the purpose is to assign detailed responsibility with specific expectations. These must be documented clearly in a way that all participants understand, and have agreed upon. The observation of the actions and the discussions of results should center completely upon the test scenario. It should be planned, then the actual results should be compared to the plan.

It should be obvious that most of the work and the detailed documentation will be handled by the technical support or systems programming staff who maintain the operating systems and utilities, and a few other systems analysts. They are the ones who must prepare for the system backup procedures, create the data and program backup tapes, and prepare the operating system for the backup site and the laying in of communications lines and related equipment.

The major effort will still be the systems programming work. Much of this work will be done in advance, in preparation for emergency operation, but some of the operating system, database, and telecommunications work will need to be carried out during each test. This is important work and must be done, but it should be recognized as a considerable burden to place on a usually overworked staff. Activity entries made in the plan procedures for the technical support work will represent more effort than most other activity entries. (These comments were simply made to put the "degree of difficulty" of the work into perspective. The systems work must be done and tested with the rest of the plan.)

Running the test, which is Step 8 in Fig. 9-2, might be at a planned time, announced time, or at a surprise time, known only to the senior manager involved and the DRC. Before it is run, however, the test scenario should be documented completely with one copy of the document in the hands of the DRC. As the test is run, the actual actions and their timing can then be checked against the planned actions and timing. Finally, the results of meeting the test plan goals should be measured.

The debriefing session following the test either can be a gathering of all participants or, better, meetings with each recovery team. The experiences and results of the tests are discussed, and specific changes in the disaster recovery plan are considered. A number of detailed meetings can pyramid into a meeting with the team leaders and responsible management, and final decisions can be made about specific changes that should be made in the operational disaster recovery plan.

It is the responsibility of the DRC to incorporate any agreed changes into the plan, and to distribute information about the test, and about the changes in the plan. Extra training can be planned for as indicated by the test, and plans can be laid for the next disaster recovery test. They should be based on the findings of the current test, and the weaknesses that were observed.

Refereeing the tests

The I/S DRC should be the principal referee of the routine recovery tests, but should remain open to any suggestions made by the participants, particularly those who are technical specialists. The routine tests and the initial tests should be essentially training and technical tests, to refine the plan as much as possible.

After a few tests have appeared to be satisfactory, internal audit personnel can be informed that a disaster recovery plan is considered to be in place. They can then direct any level of test they deem appropriate, at any time they decide, to give the benefit of a third-party review of the preparations that have been made. Their optimum procedure is described in detail in Review and Testing of I/S Disaster Recovery Plan, this chapter.

Normally, the internal audit staff or external auditors will call for reviews or tests at irregular times with fairly long periods between reviews. These tests should in no way affect the routine, regular training of assigned participants and the testing of specific areas, which must be an ongoing activity to keep a realistic recovery plan in place.

There should be full-scale attempts to run the backup sites. As the tests proceed, conditions can be imposed that would make for some technical difficulty, and portions of the backup material can be removed to see if obvious problems can be circumvented. Informed decisions then can be made to the validity of the plan.

Both the DRC and the internal audit staff should be given a free hand to call a test at a time that is not expected, as long as it is not too disruptive to sensitive applications. They should keep the results confidential until the full test has been completed, then they should announce their opinions.

The internal audit workers will not necessarily be the sole arbiters of the technical efficiency of the test, but they will determine whether the plan is effective or should be modified. They will review the analysis of all the backup output compared to normal operations, and will be sensitive as to whether the programs were backed up under strict audit control. They could chair the discussions as to which errors in the plan require correction, after their reviews.

Plans can be worked out with senior management to direct a variety of tests of different magnitude, the first year and occasionally thereafter, to be able to assure management that there truly is an effective EDP disaster recovery plan in place. Management, after all, is the final referee.

Feedback from the tests

The information from the tests of the I/S disaster recovery plan is first used to assure management that a plan is in place that is sufficiently effective to protect the organization's assets and to prevent unnecessary loss. It is also used to correct minor errors in the plan details, and to hone the plan to a smoothly working, usable document. It is most important that the information from tests is not help for the use of internal audit workers and management, but that details are fed back to those who are technically responsible so that real advances can be made.

The greatest problems in disaster recovery planning is in the areas of the systems programs and their handling by operations. Changed hardware and network configurations cause considerable effort by the systems programming people. They are the only ones who can assure that the data and program files having been transferred accurately and under control. They should be allowed as much testing and feedback as is necessary for them to ensure the accuracy of the backup operation.

This means that in the first few months after implementation of a backup plan there will be a great deal of testing to get the necessary assurance of the backup procedures. In subsequent years, similar tests will be performed periodically, but they will be mainly for training and audit control purposes. This later routine monitoring of the recovery plan is required to prevent complacency and a slow drift away from the plan, and it should be scheduled irregularly as is any other audit review.

Another aspect of the feedback from the monitoring tests is that it might show where the regular training programs should be modified or strengthened. Continued training is imperative, and the monitoring program can assure that the training approach does not slowly shift to obsolescence. This will be the responsibility of the I/S DRC.

Index

OTHER BESTSELLERS OF RELATED INTEREST

MICROCOMPUTER LANs—2nd Edition
—Michael Hordeski

Pull together a multi-user system from your stand-alone micros. With this book, you gain an understanding of how networking actually happens. This clear, comprehensive source helps you make the right decisions and cut through the confusion surrounding LAN technology and performance. You'll evaluate your alternatives intelligently, set up networks that allow for future growth, restructure or upgrade LAN configurations, and effectively manage and maintain network systems.

Book No. 3424, $39.95 hardcover only.

HANDBOOK OF DATABASE MANAGE-MENT AND DISTRIBUTED RELATIONAL DATABASES—Dimitris N. Chorafas

This book provides database users and designers with the tools necessary to make informed decisions and to keep pace with the advancement of database technology. Now you can identify your needs, define the requirements, evaluate your priorities, choose supports, and determine solutions that are effective both in terms of cost and performance.

Book No. 3253, $49.95 hardcover only.

HANDBOOK OF MANAGEMENT: For Scientific and Technical Personnel
—Dimitris N. Chorafas

Chorafas explains essential techniques in forecasting, planning, marketing, product development, finance, and office automation. Key areas covered include mathematical forecasting; long-term planning; developing new products; administering finances, budgets, and product pricing; controlling a marketing and sales network; and preparing for the challenges of the automated factory and advanced computer and network communications systems.

Book No. 3263 $42.95 hardcover only.

HANDBOOK OF DATA COMMUNICA-TIONS AND COMPUTER NETWORKS —2nd Edition—Dimitris N. Chorafas

Completely revised and updated, this results-oriented reference—with over 125 illustrations—progresses smoothly from concept to concept as theory is combined with concrete examples to show you how to successfully manage a dynamic information system. You'll find applications-oriented material on: networks, technological advances, telecommunications technology, protocols, network design, messages and transactions, software's role, and network maintenance.

Book No. 3690, $44.95 hardcover only.

STRATEGY, SYSTEMS, AND INTEGRATION: A Handbook for Information Managers—George M. Hall

Now you can successfully plan new data processings systems and integrate existing systems. Hall shows you how you can get beyond basic strategic problems and concentrate on mastering the techniques that will meet the increasing demands of your system. From an in-depth analysis of database requirements to key management issues, you'll follow the logical order in which systems should be designed and developed.

Book No. 3614, $39.95 hardcover only.

KNOWLEDGE-BASED SYSTEMS: A Manager's Perspective
—G. Steven Tuthill, Ed.D., and Susan T. Levy

This practical guide explores the high-level concepts and issues facing management professionals who oversee artificial intelligence and information processing networks. You'll apply the five basic functions of management—planning, organizing, staffing, directing, and controlling—to knowledge-based system projects as you progress from theory to project model. You'll also focus on functional areas within each project phase.

Book No. 3479, $34.95 hardcover only.